THE WADSWORTH CONTEMPORARY ISSUES IN CRIME AND JUSTICE SERIES

9766

D0730711

00

Renegade Kids, Suburban Outlaws:

From Youth Culture to Delinquency

WAYNE S. WOODEN

California State Polytechnic University, Pomona

Wadsworth Publishing Company

I(T)P™ An International Thomson Publishing Company

Belmont • Albany • Bonn • Boston • Cincinnati • Detroit
London • Madrid • Melbourne • Mexico City • New York • Paris
San Francisco • Singapore • Tokyo • Toronto • Washington

Editorial Assistant: Jennifer Dunning
Production Services Coordinator: Angela Mann
Production: Ruth Cottrell
Print Buyer: Karen Hunt
Permissions Editor: Jeanne Bosschart
Copy Editor: Lura Harrison
Cover: William Reuter Design
Compositor: Ruth Cottrell Books
Printer: Malloy Lithographing, Inc.

Printed in the United States of America

2 3 4 5 6 7 8 9 10—01 00 99 98 97 96 95

For more information, contact Wadsworth Publishing Company.

Wadsworth Publishing Company
10 Davis Drive
Belmont, California 94002
USA

International Thomson Editores
Campos Eliseos 385, Piso 7
Col. Polanco
11560 México D.F. México

International Thomson Publishing Europe
Berkshire House 168-173
High Holborn
London, WC1V 7AA
England

International Thomson Publishing GmbH
Königswinterer Strasse 418
53227 Bonn
Germany

Thomas Nelson Australia
102 Dodds Street
South Melbourne 3205
Victoria, Australia

International Thomson Publishing Asia
221 Henderson Road
#05-10 Henderson Building
Singapore 0315

Nelson Canada
1120 Birchmount Road
Scarborough, Ontario
Canada M1K 5G4

International Thomson Publishing - Japan
Hirakawacho Kyowa Building, 3F
2-2-1 Hirakawacho
Chiyoda-ku, Tokyo 102
Japan

This book is printed on acid-free recycled paper.

Library of Congress Cataloging-in-Publication Data

Wooden, Wayne S.
    Renegade Kids, Suburban Outlaws / Wayne S. Wooden
       p.   cm.
    Includes index.
    ISBN: 0-534-24012-7
    1. Socially handicapped youth. 2. Problem youth. 3 Juvenile
delinquents. Deviant behavior. 5. Suburban life. I. Title
II. Series
HV1421.W66   1994
362.7'4'0973—dc20   94-22113

Youth, though it may lack knowledge,
is certainly not devoid of intelligence;
it sees through shams
with sharp and terrible eyes.

H. L. Mencken

CONTEMPORARY ISSUES IN CRIME AND JUSTICE SERIES
Roy Roberg, Consulting Editor

Hard Time: Understanding and Reforming the Prison (1987)
Robert Johnson, The American University

The Myth of a Racist Criminal Justice System (1987)
William Wilbanks, Florida International University

Gambling Without Guilt: The Legitimation of an American Pastime (1988)
John Rosecrance, University of Nevada at Reno

Crime Victims: An Introduction to Victimology, Second Edition (1990)
Andrew Karmen, John Jay College of Criminal Justice

Death Work: A Study of the Modern Execution Process (1990)
Robert Johnson, The American University

Lawlessness and Reform: The FBI in Transition (1990)
Tony G. Poveda, State University of New York at Plattsburgh

Women, Prison, and Crime (1990)
Joycelyn M. Pollock-Byrne, University of Houston-Downtown

Perspectives on Terrorism (1991)
Harold J. Vetter, Portland State University
Gary R. Perlstein, Portland State University

Serial Murders and Their Victims (1991)
Eric W. Hickey, California State University, Fresno

Girls, Delinquency, and the Juvenile Justice System (1992)
Meda Chesney-Lind, University of Hawaii, Manoa
Randall G. Sheldon, University of Nevada at Las Vegas

Juries and Politics (1992)
James P. Levine, Brooklyn College

Media, Crime, and Criminal Justice: Images and Realities (1992)
Ray Surette, Florida International University

Street Kids, Street Drugs, Street Crime: An Examination of Drug Use and Serious Delinquency in Miami (1993)
James A. Inciardi, University of Delaware
Ruth Horowitz, University of Delaware
Anne E. Pottieger, University of Delaware

Ethics in Crime and Justice: Dilemmas and Decisions, Second Edition (1994)
Joycelyn M. Pollock, Southwest Texas State University

It's About Time: America's Imprisonment Binge (1994)
John Irwin, Professor Emeritus, San Francisco State University
James Austin, National Council on Crime and Delinquency

Sense and Nonsense about Crime and Drugs: A Policy Guide, Third Edition (1994)
Samuel Walker, University of Nebraska at Omaha

Renegade Kids, Suburban Outlaws: From Youth Culture to Delinquency (1995)
Wayne S. Wooden, California State Polytechnic University, Pomona

Contents

▼

Foreword

The Contemporary Issues in Crime and Justice Series introduces important topics that until now have been neglected or inadequately covered for students and professionals in criminal justice, criminology, sociology, and related fields. The volumes cover philosophical and theoretical issues and analyze the most recent research findings and their implications for practice. Each volume is intended to stimulate further thinking and debate on its subject as well as to provide direction for policy formulation and implementation.

Renegade Kids, Suburban Outlaws provides an in-depth look into the lives of troubled youths by allowing them to speak for themselves, particularly through the use of interviews and letters. While the findings reported from surveys and official records are quite revealing, hearing from these kids in their own words regarding how they feel about their lives and their particular situations is even more troubling and insightful. It is troubling because, given the extent of despair and anxiety and the lack of moral direction, it is clear that little can be accomplished in the near term to help "straighten out" these at-risk youths. Similarly, it is insightful because the information furnished by these young people provides such a rich understanding of the problems and the needs of those studied. This can be especially beneficial for designing future strategies to deal with preventing and controlling delinquent and criminal behavior.

Wooden has broken his study of troubled youths into two groups: those he refers to as *renegade kids*—identity seekers who are relatively socially harmless—and *suburban outlaws*—the nonconformist and rebellious youths who are prone to lawbreaking. This is a useful dichotomy in that we gain an understanding of troubled youths at the periphery of delinquency (for example, mall rats, punkers, and metalers) and those more intimately involved in serious delinquent and criminal behavior (for example, taggers, skinheads, stoners, and satanists). Included among the unique aspects of those studied is a comparison of clique structures and behavior in four suburban high schools and a cross-cultural comparison of youth culture.

There is much to be gleaned from Wooden's analysis of these troubled youths. The final chapter is devoted to how society, including the school, mental health, and juvenile justice systems, as well as concerned citizens, can attempt to respond in a meaningful manner to some of the trends established by these at-risk kids. It is his feeling that not only criminal and juvenile justice officials will benefit from a careful reading of the book; concerned citizens, and especially parents, will also gain valuable insights into recognizing and dealing with youths headed for trouble. It is clear from these findings that while society's systems for handling such at-risk youths can be improved, only limited and superficial gains will be made until families and concerned citizens become more caring and involved.

Roy Roberg

Acknowledgments

As is the case with most research projects, this study of suburban youth cultures and juvenile delinquencies has a history. I began work on this book about eight years ago when I was asked to teach a new senior seminar course, "Youth and Social Deviance." Wanting to focus on behaviors that involved youths in those middle-class suburban communities near where I reside and teach (located some thirty miles each of Los Angeles), the class of twenty students and I developed and field tested the questionnaire of one hundred items that became known as the "Youth Survey." (See Appendix A for a full discussion of the methodology of this research project. Copies of the questionnaires and the summary tables appear in Appendix B.)

Although I am listed as the sole author of this work, the study in general and this book in particular would not have been possible without the cooperation of many people. First, I must thank the numerous university students, in addition to that initial class, who have assisted me with various facets of the study. In every chapter there was considerable input from students, including assistance with administering the questionnaires and analyzing the data. On occasion, university students took directed studies with me to assist with the interviews.

I wish to acknowledge the support of my campus, Cal Poly, Pomona, which granted me one quarter leave with pay in the spring of 1993 to complete the manuscript. I also wish to acknowledge the reviewers of the manuscript for their helpful suggestions. Thanks are also in order to the entire production staff at Wadsworth who assisted with the preparation of the manuscript. And, finally, I want to express my appreciation to Brian Gore, who was the Criminal Justice Acquisitions Editor at Wadsworth and enthusiastically supported this book through its development.

Wayne S. Wooden

1

▼

Introduction to the Problem

"Pals in the Posse: Teen Culture Has Seized the Word as a Hip Name for Groups: Not All Are Harmless"

Not quite boys in the hood, it's more like boys in the halls. You go to high school. And you and your friends have this little group. You're tight. You have something in common—anything from sports to girls to parties and music. Maybe you work as a team to spray-paint your nicknames—your tags—around town. They're your boys. Your clique. Your tribe. Your crew. Your mob. Your pals. Your cronies. Your posse.

But now, authorities say, many such cliques—especially the graffiti tagging groups—are resorting to the same gang-style violence that has polarized youths everywhere, from inner-city street corners to suburban shopping malls.

This week, as investigators probe the death of a 17-year-old student gunned down Monday by a fellow teen-ager on the Reseda High School campus, police are eyeing posse rivalry as a motive.

"These posses, crews, tribes—whatever you want to call them—they may have started out innocently enough but, in growing numbers, they're starting to mimic the kind of stuff real gangs do," said Los Angeles County Sheriff's Sgt. Joe Guzman, a gang expert who lectures nationwide.

"It's the way gangs are romanticized in our culture—from the newspapers to the movies—we've pulled them out of the gutter and given them status. A lot of these other kids can't resist the attraction. They're becoming gang wanna-bes, developing turf, drawing lines on the sidewalk, crossing each other out. The dynamics are changing at a rapid pace. And what happened at Reseda may well have been an off-shoot of this" (1).

"Boys Arrested in Vandalism at Graveyard"

Police have arrested six teenage punk rockers on suspicion of damaging or destroying 65 tombstones—some more than a century old—two weeks ago at Upland's oldest cemetery, a police spokesman said Friday. The six boys, all 15 to 17 years old, were arrested at their high schools Thursday. They were booked on suspicion of trespassing and vandalism and were released to the custody of their parents.

According to witnesses, the police spokesman said, the teenagers frequently "hung out" at the cemetery. On the night of September 14, he said, "These juveniles were drinking and just got a little overzealous." Twenty of the tombstones, some of which were tall and elaborate marble markers, were destroyed, he said (2).

"'Skinheads' on Trial in Racial Terrorism"

Prosecutors opened their case Wednesday against five youthful white supremacist "skinheads," accusing them of beating up blacks and Hispanics and plotting to gas Jews by putting cyanide in a synagogue's air conditioning. Three also are accused of chasing blacks and Hispanics out of a city park that they claimed for themselves. Each of the federal charges carries up to 10 years in prison and a $250,000 fine (3).

The ominous signs are everywhere: kids bringing guns onto junior high and high school campuses and shooting each other; teenagers forming sex posses and racking up "body counts" of the number of girls they have "scored with" or "sacked"; mall rats rampaging through suburban shopping arcades, "streaming," as it is called, through the aisles of department stores and grabbing stacks of clothing before making a quick getaway; tagger crews "mapping the heavens," spray painting their three-letter monikers on overhead freeway signs. The "cry for help" of punk rockers and their offshoots, ignored, as they were, by families and society that do not take time to listen. And these are just the good kids!

And what about the others? Racist teenage skinheads plot revenge on unsuspecting fellow students at suburban high schools for no other reason than that they dislike them because of their skin color, nationality, or presumed sexual orientation. White, youthful, stoner gang members adrift, wander aimlessly with their suburban "homies," or homeboys, looking for the next high, surviving on dope and booze. Juvenile satanists, participating in a fad, find themselves caught up in a cult.

It is an examination of these youths and others that forms the bulk of this book. For the most part, the teenagers discussed in the pages that follow resided within a 25-mile radius of each other in sleepy, upscale bedroom communities of the San Gabriel Valley and the Inland Empire in Southern California. It is in suburban areas with such pleasant-sounding names as San Dimas, Diamond Bar, Walnut, Chino Hills, Upland, Claremont, and West Covina that this disturbing story, and study, unfolds.

These are not the youth of the inner city, racked by street crime, urban violence and gang intimidation, but the youth, primarily males, of more affluent, suburban, middle-class neighborhoods, situated more than a 30-minute commute from Los Angeles, that form the focus of this inquiry.

It will be my intent to distinguish between two types of troubled teens from these privileged areas. On the one hand, I am interested in the reasons or conditions under which some teenagers get caught up in the everchanging youth styles and youth cultures of the moment. These youths I refer to as *renegade kids,* identity seekers who are relatively socially harmless. On the other hand, I am interested in those teenagers who have embraced decidedly more deviant and delinquent identities and behavior. These juveniles I refer to as *suburban outlaws,* the nonconformist and rebellious youths prone to lawbreaking.

Not all youths, of course, test the limits of authority or break the law. Most teenagers, in fact, are law-abiding citizens. They do well in school, mind their parents, and come from loving, secure, and attentive families. These youngsters, fortunately, grow up to become responsible and contributing citizens. Not enough good things can be said about these types of teens.

AT-RISK KIDS

My focus, however, is on the others—those *not* so good kids. I am interested in the teens who feel isolated and misunderstood, get angry and enraged, take risks and get into trouble. For some, these behaviors are only a stage, a "kids will be kids" kind of thing. But for others, the choices made in adolescence not only label them as delinquent, but set them on a path embracing a way of life that will put them at risk for their entire lives.

Perhaps by better understanding these troubled kids, we can take steps to rectify the situation, to intervene early in their lives, and to assist in pointing out the errors of their ways. If we fail to accomplish this, then the morass that we as members of society seem now to find ourselves in can only deepen.

Society in the 1990s is held hostage by fear. We read with alarm about a 13-year-old girl getting snatched out of the security of her own bedroom in the middle of a slumber party, and then killed. Or about evening commuters gunned down by a crazed gunman on the subway. But perhaps what shocks and alarms us the most is the increasingly violent turn that our youngsters seem to be taking. More than just the senseless, and unending, drive-by shootings of urban ethnic gang warfare. More than just the mounting body count of runaway youths strung out and overdosed on drugs. It is the perception that society is no longer in control of its destiny—that this next generation of youths is not just dazed and confused, not just those *renegade kids*, but armed and dangerous as well, the more unsettling *suburban outlaws*.

The main reason for embarking on this book was to try to make some sense out of these alarming trends. This study attempts to serve several purposes. For one, the case studies and examples of different types of suburban youths presented can provide the sociology and criminal justice student with a clearer understanding of the various theories put forth over the past several decades by sociologists and criminologists that examine juveniles and delinquent behavior. Second, the variety of methodologies used in gathering the data for the study—from questionnaires to participant-observation to content analysis—offer examples to students who also intend to do studies of their own on certain aspects of modern youth culture.

For the layperson, perhaps this book can serve as a "guide to troubled teens." It is the intent that the youths examined in some detail in this study will provide parents and concerned citizens with the tools to examine their own relationships with their children. Hopefully, they will also provide others—from youth counselors and social workers to correctional, probation, and parole officers—with important clues and behavioral indicators to look for when working with at-risk young people.

UNIVERSAL YOUTH CULTURES

In no way exhaustive, this inquiry looks into some of the array of youth styles and delinquencies that emerged in these Southern California, middle-class, suburban communities in the late 1980s and early 1990s. Pioneers, innovators, and rebels of our society have been traditionally drawn to the western United States. Indeed, studying the sociological climate of California can provide insight into what is to come for the rest of the country, and in some cases, the world.

It should be pointed out, however, that behaviors observed among youths in Southern California are not unique to this locale. Although there may be *slight* differences in popular forms of deviant behavior, the problems these youths face and their modes of adaptation are similar to those in other parts of the country. Just a look at the local paper in any region of the nation will document that fact. Because many people like to "write off" folks in California as very strange and unique, it should be emphasized that youths across the nation are not that different. The underlying problems that some contemporary juveniles experience seem to span the continent.

Further, in several instances, the youth cultures played out here in suburbia, such as the punk rocker and heavy metaler scene, were ones that came late to these inland communities. Youths elsewhere in the country (such as Los Angeles and New York City) and abroad (such as London) had long embraced those particular styles. But in other aspects, the youth styles of these Southern California suburban neighborhoods have led the way, ushering in new teen fads—such as rave parties and tagger crews. All of these various trends are examined in this book.

Alienated youths, in their various guises, have long fascinated observers. Concerned parents and family members, peers, school officials, police, social workers, journalists, the mass media, and scholars alike have all attempted to understand and work with these troubled youngsters in a concerted effort to reintegrate them into society. In this regard, this book follows in a long line of other works that have examined the "youth scene" of the day.

Albert K. Cohen in his classic study published in 1955, *Delinquent Boys: The Culture of the Gang,* employed categories differentiating the

corner boy, the collegiate boy, and the delinquent boy of forty years ago
(4). I have used similar categories in differentiating their counterparts of
today. However, today the categories I employ include the mall rats,
punkers, and metalers (in place of the corner boy); the preppies and conformists (the collegiate boy); and the taggers, skinheads, stoners, and
satanists (the delinquent boy).

And like past researchers who have explored earlier youth scenes, I
made every attempt to get to know these kids, to interview them, to analyze their case files (for those who are incarcerated), and to try to understand these often troubled teens. In an ethnographic technique often used
in studies of this sort, I worked diligently to let these youths speak for
themselves. Through questionnaires and interviews, I tried to provide these
teenagers with the means by which they could express their points of view.

This approach was most successful with the punk rockers, heavy
metalers, tagger crew members, and both racist and nonracist teenage
skinheads who consented to be interviewed for this study and who completed the extensive questionnaires. Several of my university students
assisted me with these sometimes difficult interviews, and I am indeed
grateful for their input. Many, when they themselves were in high
school, had been involved in some of the youth cultures analyzed, and
their observations and insights were invaluable.

What follows, therefore, is a work that examines the youth cultures
and delinquencies of assorted suburban male youths who, for a variety of
reasons that will be made clear, chose to deviate from the paths of conformity and respectability that most of their peers followed.

A GENERATION AT RISK

In late 1993, the results of a poll that questioned 758 children between
the ages of 10 and 17, along with their parents, found a generation living in fear. No longer sharing an optimistic view about the future, nor
sharing the American Dream that their parents still believed in, this new
generation seemed to be "growing up fast and frightened" (5).

Many of the juveniles expressed concerns about guns, drugs,
poverty, and divorce—issues that their parents could not have imagined
when they were youngsters. The study noted how these fears tran-
scended locale. It was no longer just children of the inner cities that
were worried. Rural as well as suburban youths, too, feared "coming
of age in a rough world."

When specifically asked what concerns them and their families the most, the juveniles responded: violent crime against a family member (56 percent); an adult losing a job (53 percent); not being able to afford shelter (47 percent); a family member having a drug problem (38 percent); and the fear that their family would not stay together (38 percent) among other concerns.

Another recent national study also reported dire findings. In 1990, the commission formed by the National Association of State Boards of Education and the American Medical Association announced the results of their long-term study, noting with great alarm that America was raising a generation of adolescents plagued by pregnancies, illegal drug use, suicide, and violence (6).

The commission's stark report concluded that if immediate action was not soon undertaken to reverse these trends, American society would soon find itself with a failing economy and social unrest. Furthermore, according to the report, young people were less healthy and less prepared to take their places in society than had been their parents at their age.

Among the troubling items in the commission's report were such findings as the fact that one million teenage girls—nearly 1 in 10—get pregnant each year; two-fifths (39 percent) of high school seniors reported they had gotten drunk within the two previous weeks; alcohol-related accidents were the leading cause of death among teenagers; the suicide rate for teenagers had doubled in the years since 1968; and teenage arrests were up thirtyfold since 1950 (7).

The report concluded that inattention to these problems has left thousands of youngsters "doomed to failure" which for many will be a precursor to an adult life of crime, unemployment, or welfare dependency.

To remedy some of these concerns, the commission recommended that teenagers be guaranteed access to health services, and that communities set up adolescent health centers in schools or other convenient places. Schools were also urged to play a larger role in the health and sex education of these youngsters.

Renegade Kids, Suburban Outlaws shares the concerns of these studies and documents in some detail the extent and scope of the problem facing young people today. As previously stated, focusing primarily on white, suburban, middle-class, teenage males, the book attempts to differentiate those youth behaviors that are merely styles, fads, or displays of youth culture, from those that warrant broader societal responses because of their delinquent and deviant character.

THEORETICAL PERSPECTIVES

Since the early 1940s, and particularly since the end of World War II and the emergence of the "baby boomers," each generation of teenagers in American society has developed its own distinctive youth styles. Strongly influenced by the popular culture—particularly music tastes, fashion, and lingo—as well as by broader societal social changes, modern teenagers have looked to their contemporaries and to the media for clues to what is hip, fashionable, and trendy.

To gain some semblance of distinctiveness and individuality, teenagers often embrace the outrageous, testing the limits of "acceptable" behavior or dress, challenging free expression, and upsetting adults and their less rebellious peers in the process.

To give some theoretical perspective to this pattern, it can be argued that youth culture follows what might be referred to as a *linear progression*. That is, the often *fluid* nature of teenage social character dictates that it continually evolves and changes in shape and form, building an identity on, and even surpassing the extremes of, the preceding generation. It is a social character quick to challenge whatever has become the recently defined status quo. Youth culture is constantly in motion, moving onward in some mad rush to some new creation, manifestation, or reinvention.

A contrasting theoretical perspective, introduced only to provide some conceptual framework by which to discuss specific forms of youth culture, is a *curvilinear progression,* which considers broader societal trends in modern society. By looking at the patterns of social change and politics, one can explain the emergence and disappearance of distinctive youth cultures within the context of the social structure. Rather than viewing contemporary teenage youth culture as constantly evolving in some form of linear progression, embracing new forms of outrageous and even rebellious fads, a *curvilinear progression* sees youths as both shaping, and being shaped by, the broader cultural trends which, themselves, periodically shift between liberal and conservative directions due to the political whims of a given historical time period. The progression of social change that both moves forward and then curves back, to be followed by another shift forward and back once again, forms a curvilinear line. Forward movement occurs during historical periods that embrace liberal, progressive social change; backward movement occurs during historical periods aimed at restoring conservative social order and tradition.

By looking more closely at this curvilinear perspective, for purposes of this study, which examines the suburban youth cultures that emerged in the late 1980s and early 1990s, one could argue that the conservative trends of the last decade helped explain the rise of such youth groups as heavy metalers and skinheads who shared a more traditional, conservative ideology embracing the status quo. These youth groups arose, in part, in opposition to the more liberal ideologies, shared by punk rockers, which preceded them during the decade of the 1970s, and by the remnants of the more liberal, Democratic policies of the 1960s which had promoted greater racial and ethnic integration.

Employing this alternation between liberal and conservative periods, one could predict that the youth cultures of the1990s should also evolve since the broader society seems to have taken a slight turn once again in the direction of supporting social change with the election of a Democrat as president in 1992.

Both linear and curvilinear theories have legitimate claim as to which is more accurate in explaining the effects of change in society. Both perspectives, when applied to explaining youth cultures and delinquencies, have their appeal. And it is likely that both perspectives play a part in the way a given youth culture emerges at a particular point in time; why it, as opposed to another form, is embraced by troubled teens; and what accounts for its often rapid decline once the fad or its novelty has worn off.

This book examines the youth styles and identities that emerged in American society during the conservative decade of the 1980s. It focuses on a variety of youth cultures that manifested themselves for the first time in middle-class suburbia during that time period. The book also examines the more recent youth cultures and beginning trends of the 1990s, shaped by the shift in society to a new, less conservative direction.

WHY YOUTHS BECOME DEVIANT

Apart from the macrotheory that explains the broader societal, structural, and political trends that may be influencing youths in a linear and/or curvilinear fashion, *Renegade Kids, Suburban Outlaws* examines the more micro- or social psychological reasons for the conditions that lead some teenagers into the youth cultures of a given time period.

Youths often become involved in youth cultures or delinquency because of boredom and alienation. Some youths are hyperactive and need extra stimulation to keep from getting bored. These kids are motivated to become deviant because of the risk involved. They rebel from more normal, conservative, tranquil lifestyles to embrace those more on the edge. Most teenagers find excitement in mildly deviant ways, but these kids enter into more serious activities such as stealing, often graduating to even more serious offenses such as robbery and violence.

As this study will show, these juveniles commit many of their crimes under the influence of drugs, commonly used among deviant youths. These kids are somewhat intelligent, seeing through society's attempts to pressure them into becoming good citizens. Freedom, for them, is testing the limits or restraints set up by society—and getting away with it. For these middle-class youths, there is an appeal to do things that are not right, to show they are bigger than the "system."

Other youths get caught up in deviant behavior because of an unhappiness with self or with the outside world. Many of the teenagers examined in this book, such as the satanists, get involved in deviant behavior for the personal power that they can attain. Many of the risks taken are an attempt to see how good one is at something, making up for low self-esteem. Kids who are not happy with themselves either turn it inward and become depressed or turn it outward and become violent. Some youths, as Part II of this book delineates, unfortunately do both.

If you do not care about yourself, then you are not going to care about what you do to other people or their rights. This is the feeling ingrained in many gang members, those from the inner city as well as suburbia. Some youngsters from the inner city are hardened from a young age by the violence around them. With little hope that comes with economic deprivation, they become callous to others and do not really care if they kill someone or die themselves.

For those more middle-class youths examined in this book, the violence they experience in their young lives stems from parental abuse, indifference, and neglect, and less from the hardships of economic instability or deprivation. Other youths—like punk rockers, for instance—feel alienated from what they perceive as the complacency and mindless conformity of their peers. Or, their alienation may result from being excluded, taunted, and ridiculed by other teenagers for the personal convictions they embrace. Unhappiness with the surrounding culture also partially explains the presence of racist skinheads. (This will be documented in subsequent chapters.)

The punkers reject the rules enforced by parents and the community that advocate obedience to authority for authority's sake. This revolt is acted out in extreme hair, dress, music, political views, and so forth. The new rule embraced by these youths follows the principle that you do not do things because people say so, but because you want to do them. In effect, they are opting for a society that they themselves would set up.

In practice, this process usually results in a person who eventually outgrows defiance and becomes an independent thinker, one considerate of others. During their youthful stage, however, their independent thought and behavior may not be bound by what is right. Punk rockers may turn their frustration on those peers who act like hypocrites or people they believe to be robotlike, locked into the system, by using shock confrontation. More often they take out their rage on themselves, through self-mutilation, drugs, alcohol, and thoughts of suicide.

Other youths, however, are more likely to resort to acts of violence. Racist skinheads, for instance, are motivated more by the changes in racial diversity taking place in their community, and disapprove of accepting minorities into their midst. They band together to take physical steps to try to reverse such trends.

In general, youths become deviant either out of a need for different experiences—for the thrill of taking risks—or out of unhappiness with themselves or with facets of society that they feel they have no control over. Many times, it is a combination of these two factors that motivates youths to act defiantly.

Other-Directedness

David Riesman, in a popular book published in 1961, *The Lonely Crowd*, argued that the modern age has ushered in a world of "other-directedness," whereby people regulate their own behavior based on how they feel others think about them (8). For upwardly mobile, middle-class families, moving to more affluent homes in suburbia and becoming status seekers—trying to become "the Joneses"—has left many of their youngsters adrift. Dual career families, in which both parents work to pay the mortgage, have created, in some instances, latchkey children with minimal supervision.

And what happens to these kids? Many retreat—hanging out, wasting time in the malls out of a sense of sheer boredom. Many of these kids have been given anything and everything they want, from computer games to cars, and they are still not happy. Searching for an excitement that their parents cannot provide, they turn to their peers. Less affluent youths, too, are often left at home alone to care for themselves, many forced to virtually rear themselves. As a result, many do not learn the skills needed to function in the contemporary world and simply cannot cope. They become anomic, broken by society. These are the youngsters that become some of the outlaws I discuss in the book.

Although the musical tastes and styles of dress differ from group to group, these adolescents share one commonality. They are experiencing what sociologists refer to as *anomie*, a sense of rootlessness or normlessness. In part, to combat this state, they join groups and assume identities which, for many, become all-encompassing, a form of a "master status," the core way of defining themselves. And embracing or identifying with a specific group—whether it be a metaler clique, a stoner gang, or a tagger crew—provides these "tearaway" teenagers with a way of reducing their anxiety and alienation.

The other-directed youths of today face a new reality: these are middle-class youngsters raised in materialism and mindless consumer and social conformity who can see little of the future. For some, growing up in an environment of luxury and leisure has bred complacency. These kids want it all, but they have never learned the values of hard work to achieve the things they desire. Disillusionment is the result when they realize things are not always going to come to them on a silver platter, and they turn to drugs to cope with this reality.

As one of my students noted:

> I grew up in an affluent area where this (feeling) was rampant. Most teens were given everything and wanted more. There was a huge drug problem at my high school and a theft ring was uncovered where rich kids were letting friends break into their own homes to steal money and VCRs for drugs and whatever else they wanted.

The result for many of these other-directed teens is downward mobility when they realize that they must work for the things they desire. For others, the mall only serves to perpetuate the materialism of society, and so they rebel. Likewise, the suburban high schools seem to perpetuate a value system that many teens reject, leaving these youths at the bottom of the social "pecking order."

Instant Youth Culture

This, in turn, shuffles like-minded and mistreated or misunderstood teens together into groups, linked by their common frustration. Add a particular musical taste which addresses their distinctive angst, a distinctive style of dress, and you have instant youth culture. And if the home life is chaotic enough, and if the individuals and/or group are ostracized and labeled as delinquent, you have—in a phenomenon known in sociology as *labeling theory,* made popular by Edwin M. Lemert and others—a pattern that leads to secondary deviance and juvenile delinquency (9).

As Walter C. Reckless noted, without some form of internal and/or external containment, the push factors of a dysfunctional family, coupled with the pull factors of a beckoning delinquent peer group, lead many juveniles astray. Juveniles who have both strong external and internal containment are much less likely to become delinquent (10).

Joining clubs and groups fills a gap in one's life. This is definitely the case with gang affiliation. People will always flock to people who understand them. As will be documented in the early chapters of this book, the punkers and metalers want to be seen as individuals, so they abandon the traditional dress, symbolic of the conformity of their parents and the adult world, and don the Doc Martens and earrings that assert their individuality. But the irony becomes clear. After rejecting the status quo, these kids form a group where they all have similar attitudes and styles of dress. In essence, they are simply rejecting one conformist situation to enter another, with a new set of rules to follow.

Most of the middle-class youths and fringe groups examined in this book, such as punkers and skinheads, are seen as and see themselves as outsiders. As such, according to Howard S. Becker, they reject and are rejected by the larger society, and their deviant identity becomes their "career" (11). With no political power base, they cannot exert change, merely rebellion. Thus they remain on the outside looking in. Some of the youth groups, on the other hand, such as the high school jocks and the poseurs, see themselves as insiders. They conform to society, but they, too, lack the power to change. They play the game, causing their more rambunctious peers to seethe.

OUTLINE OF THE BOOK

This book is divided into three sections. Those youths whose rebellious nature has taken the form of sampling one or more of the youth styles and youth cultures of the moment are discussed in the first section. These teens are referred to as *renegade kids* because they abandoned the established norms of society, joining other youths in opposition to rules, defying—often through dress and demeanor—the status quo.

Their more delinquent counterparts—youths who are referred to as *suburban outlaws*—are examined in the second part of the book. Selecting a different path—one that seems to have led them into increasing despair and deviance—these often recidivist offenders are distinguished by a variety of offensive behaviors. They include youths who have joined a delinquent gang or a satanic cult, or become a racist skinhead. By their actions they have placed themselves outside of the norms of acceptable behavior, and society has had to intervene. By embracing a life of crime they have, in effect, become bandits or outlaws!

Renegade Kids

Part I, "Renegade Kids," includes four chapters which examine, in some detail, contemporary youths in several settings. First, there is a general discussion of the meeting ground for modern youths, namely the suburban shopping mall. This is where the array of youth cultures studied were first encountered.

Chapter 2, "Mall Rats and Life in the Mall," explores the role that the modern mall plays in contemporary society, particularly as it pertains to middle-class teenagers. For those youths who spend most, if not all, of their available time in the mall, the shopping center serves as the arena where they compete with each other, staking out their "turf" in much the same way as inner-city, ethnic gang members claim certain streets and neighborhoods as their own areas. In fact, in one of the malls examined for this study, after the mall had gone through a complete renovation, the first customers to arrive the morning of the grand reopening were teenage punkers and metalers who quickly claimed the public area near the record stores and video arcades as their social space.

The discussion shifts in Chapter 3 to an examination of the various youth identities that are present on suburban high school campuses. As many as thirteen distinctive youth identities are observed. In the chapter titled "Kicking Back at 'Raging High,'" current teenage clique structures at four suburban high schools are analyzed, noting how uniformly teenage groups are stratified. Most apparent is how the common bond of social activities, athletics, dress, music, and the like differentiate teenage groups from one another.

Of particular note is the emergence of "star athletes" as the privileged class—a distinction which for one high school in the Southern California region led to the rise of a clique of athletes named the "Spur Posse." Capitalizing on their athletic prowess, fame, and social position, they abused this special privilege by instituting morally offensive competitions of sexual conquest, and engaging in anti-social and delinquent acts.

Noted in each of the high schools studied, also, is the presence of groups of youths that are viewed as less "desirable" and less popular by the other youths. These groups of teens who were treated by the others as social outcasts or misfits included punk rockers, heavy metalers, taggers, racist skinheads, stoners, and satanists. And it is these groups of socially disenfranchised youths that later (in Part II) become the central focus of this book.

The discussion turns in Chapter 4 to an examination of the array of youth styles and youth cultures that have emerged over the past several years. In "From Punk to Grunge: Changes in the Youth Scene," the punk and post-punk scenes are explored. Although the lingo may have mutated—from "slamming" to "moshing," for instance—the teen scene basically has remained the same. Like fireflies to bright lights, these youths are still attracted to the loud music and thrashing dance styles, throwing themselves with abandon into "the pit."

An analysis of letters written to a self-help organization from teenagers involved in the earlier years of the punk scene, as well as letters from their concerned parents and other citizens alarmed at what has been happening to American youths in general, provide us with insight into the issues that so upset the modern teenager. Excerpts from these sad, often desparate letters, as well as those from the irate public, demonstrate how confusing and frustrating it has been for parents and teenagers alike to understand each other, to bridge the gap, and to open up lines of communication.

The chapter also includes a discussion with the founder of this self-help organization, begun earlier in the 1980s to assist these troubled youth. It details the current status of those kids who had been previously so heavily involved in the punk scene as rebellious teenagers.

The concluding chapter of the first section, "Youth Cultures in Cross-Cultural Perspective," looks comparatively at the results of an analysis of over six hundred completed questionnaires distributed to youths in Southern California and Christchurch, New Zealand. Similarities between those youths who self-identified as punk rockers and those who self-identified as heavy metalers in both countries are discussed. Further, both of these two groups are contrasted with other teenagers who completed the questionnaire but did not identify as punk rockers or as heavy metalers.

The concerns of both punk rockers and heavy metalers in such areas as estrangement from family, alienation, drug usage and alcohol abuse, peer group influences, and patterns of juvenile delinquency are discussed in some detail in this cross-cultural focus. The findings show that punk rockers in both countries were the *most* alienated, compared to heavy metalers and to the control group of teenagers not involved in either of these two other youth styles.

The universality of youth cultures, specifically as they pertain to those teenagers who assumed either a punker or metaler identity, is also examined. Punk rockers in both countries, for instance, had more in common with each other, with respect to attitudes and beliefs, than they appeared to share with other youths from their own respective countries. The same pattern held true for heavy metalers in California and New Zealand. Fueled by a shared popular culture, these types of youth styles cross national and geographic boundaries. Youths in one area of the world become clones of youths elsewhere, half a world apart.

Suburban Outlaws

Not all teenage behavior can be analyzed as groups of youths struggling to differentiate themselves from previous generations by adapting distinctive music, hairstyles, dress, and fads and fashion. Some recent juvenile behavior has taken on a decidedly more sinister tone, warranting response and crackdowns by school authorities, public officials, and the juvenile justice system. This behavior has crossed the line from merely being part of a youth style or youth culture, to activity that has broken the law and is clearly delinquent in its manifestation. The second section of the book, "Suburban Outlaws," examines these more criminal youth behaviors, studying those juveniles who have embraced a decidedly more deviant identity.

We begin this section with an examination of "Tagger Crews and Members of the Posse." Next, the analysis shifts to an examination of teenage skinheads, both racist and nonracist. This is followed by a discussion of stoner gang members, heavy metalers and some punkers who have defiantly acted out upon society in ways that make them a danger to both themselves and others, and who are now incarcerated in the California Youth Authority (CYA) for their crimes. Finally, we analyze those youths who seem most extreme in their acting out and alienation—teenagers who embrace satanism and are part of satanic cults.

Tagger crews, the newest form of delinquent patterns to emerge in Southern California suburbs, involve bands of youths—armed with anything from spray cans and felt pens to chiseled knives and guns—who mark the suburban landscape with their tags. Like outlaws on the lam, over six hundred such crews, according to police officials, now roam

Los Angeles County streets, competing with other posses on their "bombing" runs. Interviews with several members of one such tagger crew are presented in Chapter 6.

Chapter 7, "Skinheads: Teenagers and Hate Crimes," looks in some detail at modern skinhead youth styles. Noting the alarming rapid increase, begun in the late 1980s, of teenagers who are identifying as such, the study differentiates between several types of skinheads, including both the racist, often delinquent, skinhead teenager as well as their nonracist counterpart.

Results of questionnaires completed by both types of skinheads are presented along with excerpts from selective case files of teenage skinheads incarcerated in the CYA for criminal acts of violence against persons and/or property. As expected, racist skinheads expressed their bias and rage at minorities. Often shunned at high school by their more popular peers, mistreated and abused at home, teenage racist skinheads strike out at others such as ethnic minorities, immigrants, and gays they perceive to be "weaker" than themselves. Of particular note is the finding that *the* strongest predictor of a racist teenage skinhead is that as youngsters most had been bullies. In effect, these are individuals who, having exhibited a history of anti-social behavior, added the skinhead ideology to their already unruly nature.

Chapter 8, "Stoner Gang Members in the Youth Authority," continues the discussion of those delinquents who embrace an even stronger, more defiant, and collective youth identity. Frequently referred to by the police and law enforcement personnel as "stoners," these troubled youths have a history of violent affiliations with the punk rocker, heavy metaler, racist skinhead, and/or satanic youth styles. Typically involved with white juvenile gangs, these stoners engage in a variety of anti-social behavior, often under the influence of drugs or alcohol.

A detailed analysis of the case files of *all* teenage stoner gang members currently housed within the institutions of the CYA spells out those patterns held in common. Not surprisingly, many of these juvenile stoner gang members had traumatic childhood experiences, and have abused drugs and alcohol since they were youngsters. Likewise, their parents have a history of substance abuse. A composite profile of the stoner gang members documents their deeply troubled and alienated nature.

Part II concludes with Chapter 9, "Satanists: Devil's Children?" which looks specifically at those teenage delinquents involved with satanic cults and ritualistic behavior. Several case studies are presented from the CYA's files of adolescents who were self-proclaimed satanists. In this chapter satanic rituals are discussed—often in the youngsters' own words—and reasons are given for the increased interest by some of our nation's youths in these types of activities. A discussion with a gang specialist dealing with these youths is also presented.

Parental and Societal Responses

Part III, "Parental and Societal Responses," concludes the analysis with Chapter 10, "Reactions to Youthful Offenders," which looks at the range of societal reactions to these contemporary youth styles. From programs like Back in Control, that employs a "Tough Love" approach to "de-punking" and "de-metaling" those youngsters who have become delinquent, to the treatment approaches used in the adolescent treatment hospitals and our nation's juvenile correctional facilities, a variety of approaches are explored that have been or are being used to treat, assist, and reunite these often lost, angry, and confused youngsters with their families and with society.

In summary, *Renegade Kids, Suburban Outlaws: From Youth Culture to Delinquency* attempts to pinpoint several of the reasons why, and in what ways, some teenagers feel alienated and estranged. By examining a variety of youthful identities, we also note the commonalities and differences in their varied expressions. We listen to their pleas and try to understand their pain. Throughout the book, their voices speak loudly and clearly regarding the nature of their alienation and their need to find alternative expression to what is troubling them. Furthermore, their voices inform us about the roles conformity and deviance play in their young lives. Lastly, these troubled youths also have something to say about family, school, and modern life in suburban America.

In moving from the general to the particular, this book explores some of the patterns that distinguish those teenagers who share common youth styles and youth cultures—such as *mall rats, punkers,* and *metalers,* discussed in the first section—from those teenagers who share more delinquent identities—such as *tagger crews, racist skinheads, stoners,* and *satanists,* discussed in the second section. By examining these juveniles who embrace one of these various youth identities or delinquencies, it is hoped that society will gain greater insight into the complexity of these often rebellious adolescents.

NOTES

1. Newspaper accounts are interspersed throughout this book in edited form. In several instances, identifying characteristics such as names and locations have been altered. The exact citation, however, is given. John M. Glionna, "Pals in the Posse: Teen Culture Has Seized the Word as a Hip Name for Groups; Not All Are Harmless," *The Los Angeles Times* (26 February 1993), p. B-1.

2. Ray Perez, "Boys Arrested in Vandalism at Graveyard," *The Los Angeles Times* (27 September 1986), p. A-38.

3. "'Skinheads' On Trial in Racial Terrorism," *The Desert Sun* (11 June 1988), p. A-2.

4. Albert K. Cohen, *Delinquent Boys: The Culture of the Gang* (Glencoe, IL: Free Press, 1955).

5. Michele Ingrassia, "Growing Up Fast and Frightened," *Newsweek* (22 November 1993), p. 52.

6. "Study of Youths' Problems Finds a Generation at Risk," *The Los Angeles Times* (9 June 1990), p. A-3.

7. Ibid.

8. David Riesman, *The Lonely Crowd: A Study in the Changing American Character* (New Haven, CT: Yale University Press, 1961).

9. Edwin M. Lemert, *Social Pathology* (New York: McGraw-Hill, 1951).

10. Walter C. Reckless, "A New Theory of Delinquency and Crime," *Federal Probation* 24 (December 1961), pp. 42-46.

11. Howard S. Becker, *The Outsiders* (New York: Free Press, 1963).

Renegade Kids

2

▼

Mall Rats and Life in the Mall

"Merchants Battle So-Called 'Punkers'"

Merchants at a shopping mall here are locked in a turf battle with a contingent of self-described "punkers," teenagers who the merchants claim are scaring away business with their rowdy behavior.

"These young punkers, with their wierd hair and clothing, are scaring the customers, and it's definitely hurting business," said the manager of the El Camino Mall. "Almost every day I get a frightened old lady who says she isn't going to shop here anymore."

The teens, often bedecked in leather pants, spiked bracelets and wildly coiffed hair, deny that they stir up trouble, and say they convene at the mall because there is no other place for them to go.

The problem, merchants say, began a year ago, when the F.W. Woolworth Co. opened a video arcade known as the Fun Center. Since the arcade opened there has been a 900 percent increase in "incidents," according to the mall manager, which he defined as complaints from merchants and customers and calls for security guards.

The police chief said officers at the mall have seen punkers "littering, spitting on each other, washing up in the mall's fountain, begging for coins," and engaging in horseplay near the Fun Center. At

Hickory Farms, across the corridor from the arcade, employees said the teens "come in in mobs, swipe all our samples and steal our beef sticks. They're obnoxious and intimidating."

Another merchant said punkers once formed a human chain across the mall corridor and refused to let a pregnant woman pass. Woolworth officials contend that the arcade is being unfairly blamed for the problems. Manager Brian Shaps said an informal survey found that 6 percent of arcade patrons fit into the punker category, while 75 percent were off-duty Marines.

Nonetheless, at the urging of 68 mall merchants who signed a petition calling for the closure of the arcade, the local Planning Commission voted 4–2 last week to revoke the Fun Center's conditional use permit.

Mike Brady, 16, said closing the arcade will not change the situation. He said the punkers will continue to meet at the mall because there are no centrally located clubs, parks or recreation centers where they can gather. "It's a nice safe place where we can just be," said 15-year-old Doug Henry, who roams the mall every afternoon. "We were there before the arcade, and we'll be there after it's gone" (1).

"2 Hurt in Gang Gunfire at Mall in West Covina"

What began as a toe-to-toe argument between two groups of teenagers escalated into a wild shooting incident inside a West Covina (California) shopping mall Monday night, leaving one bystander and one gang member injured and sending more than 50 horrified shoppers ducking for cover.

The melee, one of a number of violent incidents that have plagued Los Angeles-area shopping malls and theaters, broke out between members of two warring gangs about 6:30 p.m., during peak shopping hours at The Plaza, police said.

Like other malls, The Plaza in the San Gabriel Valley has become a magnet for young people—some of them gang members who engage in occasional arguments and shoving matches. Until Monday night, it was mild violence that the mall's unarmed security guards could usually handle, merchants said" (2).

THE MALLING OF SUBURBIA

The opening of the Mall of America in August 1992, in a suburb of Minneapolis, Minnesota, follows more than three decades in which malls have transformed the way people shop and entertain themselves. At 4.2 million square feet, the nation's largest enclosed mall is not the world's biggest mall. That distinction belongs to the West Edmonton Mall in Alberta, Canada. However, the new megamall has supplanted the Del Amo Mall in Torrance, California, for that distinction in the United States.

The Mall of America's retail and entertainment center boasts a $70 million, 7-acre version of a Southern California theme park, a golf course, a fourteen-screen movie theater, nine nightclubs, numerous comedy clubs, sports clubs, and forty restaurants. As a recent *New York* article noted,

> (The mall) can hold five Red Squares, 32 Boeing 747 jumbo jets, or 34 average American shopping centers: Some locals call it "megadeath." . . . The Mall of America was conceived in the consumption-is-king days of the mid-eighties, when many Americans professed to enjoy shopping more than sex (3).

According to recent figures, even with the recent recession, at least once a month 94 percent of all adults in the United States visit a mall to make a purchase, see a movie, browse, or even date. Since the first enclosed shopping mall opened in 1957 in Edina, Minnesota (also outside Minneapolis), malls have accounted for an increasing share of all retail sales—amounting to $627 billion in 1989, more than half of all retail purchases other than cars and gasoline (4).

Survey data for 1990 showed that in Southern California, shoppers averaged eleven trips to the mall every ninety days and spent $45 per visit. At the Glendale Galleria—long famous as a mall where teenage trends in clothes and hairstyles are first spotted—shoppers visited about nine times per quarter, spending $65 on each occasion (5).

Major suburban shopping malls now number about 17,000 in the United States and, on average, each attracts between 100,000 and 150,000 people on a typical weekend. The suburban shopping mall has long replaced the town square as the mecca for commerce. According to one figure, the average person spends 2.6 hours and $84 during a typical visit, compared with 55 minutes and $34 at other shopping centers. Further, 19 percent of visitors to a mall purchase something and nearly all (97 percent) state they plan to return (6).

The Mall of America opened to capitalize on such consumer patterns. Ten times the size of the malls most people are accustomed to shopping in, the initial phase of this megamall was big enough to hold 78 football fields. Furthermore, 800 specialty shops line four indoor streets on three levels, and one must walk a quarter of a mile along one street to get from an anchor store in one corner of the complex to the next. Another distinctive feature is a 300,000-square-foot indoor amusement park that features a roller coaster, flume rides, and merry-go-rounds (7).

Developers of the megamall have been proven correct. In its first six months of operation, 16 million people "shopped 'til they dropped," including tourists on excursion trips from England and Japan (8).

California Shopping

Sociologists have charged malls with everything from "draining downtowns to becoming new town centers to making trends," according to one observer (9). But in Southern California, there is no mistaking the fact that malls have transformed the social landscape for hundreds of thousands of people, including suburban youths.

Three of the nation's five largest shopping centers are located in Southern California: the Del Amo Fashion Center in Torrance with 3 million square feet; South Coast Plaza in Costa Mesa with 2.6 million square feet (the fourth largest mall after The Galleria in Houston, Texas, with 2.8 million square feet); and Lakewood Center in Lakewood, California, with 2.5 million square feet (10).

In a detailed economic study of the South Coast Plaza shopping mall in 1992, on its 25th anniversary, several interesting patterns were noted. For one, between 1967 and 1992, the number of stores increased from 70 including 2 anchor stores to 250 with 8 anchor stores.

The top name stores also changed, reflecting an upscaling of the mall to fit its new higher-income shoppers, drawn from newer, higher-income residential areas built in Orange County during the intervening years. Sears, Woolworth, and the May Company anchored the mall in 1967. But by 1992, the presence of Chanel, Tiffany, Gucci, Cartier, and Emporio Armani had long booted the "riffraff" in favor of stores that would attract the free-spending trendies, including both the young adult yuppies and their teenage preppies counterparts. The annual number of shoppers increased as well in that time period. In 1967, 500,000 shoppers were drawn to the mall; in 1992, that number had risen to 18 million (11).

VIOLENCE IN THE MALL

Trouble in shopping malls—such as the 1992 account of shootings in the West Covina mall noted at the beginning of this chapter—has been much in the news of late. A front-page story in *The Wall Street Journal*, for instance, featured this headline: "Shoppers Beware: Malls May Look Very Safe, But Some Lure Crooks as Well as the Shoppers."

In discussing crimes that can "plague" a mall, the *Journal* article examined police records of fourteen major crime incidents that occurred in just one North Miami Beach, Florida, mall over a three-year period. Crimes reported included several incidences of shoplifting, armed robbery, indecent exposure, disorderly conduct, and attempted rape (12).

The article also went on to cite several other serious incidents at other suburban malls across the country, including the following two reports:

In northern New Jersey, packs of teenage thieves carry how-to manuals for pillaging shopping malls. In one recent sweep, police arrested 65 youths aged 11 to 14 for allegedly stealing an estimated $250,000 in merchandise.

In the Northland Mall outside Detroit, police tallied 2,083 crimes in 1985. Of these, 1,041 crimes were serious, including murders, assaults, rapes, robberies and car thefts. It could have been worse, police say, had it not been for the mall management's tough approach: Northland's guards receive 240 hours of police training and have full arrest power, which eliminates any waiting for local police to arrive (13).

According to police officials, suburban malls—though not as crime-ridden as inner cities—are not as safe as one would expect. Besides being convenient for consumers, they also entice the criminal element as well, including muggers, rapists, car thieves, and shoplifters. Crime, it appears, is occurring more frequently in "nice places, like suburban malls" (14).

The actual numbers or rates of incidents of violence in malls are difficult to obtain. National crime statistics on mall crime (or on mall security litigation, the more technical term) are not tabulated, so that the actual numbers are not available. Also, most police statistics are organized according to geographical areas that often do not isolate crime rates at a given locale such as a mall.

Furthermore, malls change over the years as the demographics of the surrounding community change, as with the South Coast Plaza.

Officials do note, however, that as crime in general spreads to the suburbs, malls—particularly older ones in formerly white-collar areas—are
increasingly vulnerable (15).

One criminologist refers to malls as the new "main streets of
America," arguing that they get more crime per capita than the old
main streets used to. Malls, in his opinion, have become a "no man's
land" (16).

Other communities' crime statistics for malls are equally alarming.
In the New Jersey community of Paramus, for example, 90 percent of
crime occurs in the city's malls. A police study showed 1,670 reported
crimes at the malls—including 79 assaults and 346 stolen cars as well as
shoplifting and robberies—in the first seven months of a recent year.
The police chief attributed this 20 percent increase over the year before
to an escalating drug problem (17).

In south Florida, one upscale mall reported 10 sex offenses, 176
assaults, 64 holdups, 597 burglaries, 445 stolen cars, and about 2,000
larcenies, including shoplifting, within a two-year period in the late
1980s (18).

"Child Thieves Plague Malls"

A "charismatic" shoplifting mastermind organized about 75
New York City boys into a gang of thieves and gave them a
manual that concentrates on expensive designer clothing at
suburban malls in four states, authorities said.

New Jersey and New York City police said children from a
Brooklyn neighborhood made weekend trips to shoplift up to
$800 worth of clothes apiece in exchange for money and drugs
from the ringleader.

The latest arrests came when 10 boys were nabbed at the
Paramus Park mall, where 42 children have been arrested, and
at Willowbrook Mall in Wayne 50 boys have been arrested.
The police chief described the boys as "streetwise and slick"
and said they work in groups of 10 on Saturdays, either taking
a bus or being driven to New Jersey (19).

Such criminal patterns are not unique to the United States. During
the Christmas holiday season in London, England, in 1991, fashionable

department stores reported the occurrence of "streaming"—bands of juveniles racing through the aisles, grabbing what they could get their hands on, then tearing out of the stores before they could be apprehended.

An Inviolate Place

In fact, although the original concept of the mall dates back to ancient Greece, the actual term *mall* (as in "shopping mall") started out in old England as nothing more than a strip of green grass where a croquet-like game called "pall mall" was played. Today, malls in England are referred to as "retail markets" (20).

The inviolate feel of a mall—somewhere between a living room and a park—makes any violent disruption such as crime and assault seem all the more shocking and alarming. Malls are among the few common areas where people from different ethnic backgrounds, social classes, and neighborhoods cross paths willingly.

According to one urban anthropologist,

Violence would be exactly what you would not expect in malls. Their major design is safety, to provide strangers with a safe place to exchange goods. It's very much a symbolic ground for safe space and a violent transgression on it is a collective violation (21).

Violent incidents at malls shatter this sense of security. Although not all incidents involve youths, many mall operators see teenagers as a major problem. In a 1990 poll by the International Council of Shopping Centers, 37 percent agreed that large groups of teenagers were bothersome. Keeping the malls safe presents a paradox because, at the same time, the shopkeepers want teenagers around because they are frequent shoppers. There is a lot of "teen buying power" (22).

SOCIAL FUNCTIONS OF MALLS

In recent years several excellent books and magazine articles have been published on the social phenomenon of teenagers and suburban shopping malls. William Severini Kowinski, for instance, in his book, *The Malling of America: An Inside Look at the Great Consumer Paradise,* describes the mall as the modern version of "Main Street USA."

Kowinski, in fact, has an entire chapter devoted to youths: "Kids in the Mall: Growing Up Controlled." The author contends that the majority of American youths today have probably been going to malls all of their lives, spending more time in the mall than anywhere else but home and school.

One could argue that just as lower-income youths get their "street smarts" from hanging out on inner-city street corners, their middle-class counterparts, hanging out in these suburban shopping meccas, get (more or less) exposed to the larger world and gain a sense of "mall smarts."

Kowinski sees the mall as a "university of suburban materialism, where Valley Girls and Boys from coast to coast are educated in consumption" (23). Noting the economic and social ramifications of suburban youths' buying power, Kowinski views this as but another reflection of the changes taking place in family life and sexual mores. Concurring with child psychologist David Elkind, Kowinski feels that the pressure on teens to buy the array of products presented in the mall probably exposes these youngsters to too much of the adult world too quickly, hurrying the child to become an adult (24).

In another important book, *The Mall: An Attempted Escape from Everyday Life*, Jerry Jacobs presents an ethnographic account of a midsize, enclosed suburban shopping center. Jacobs notes how the mall serves different age groups, including teenagers, and social classes in their search for meaning and as a "flight from boredom."

The modern mall, Jacobs argues, provides three things for its participants. First, it offers people entertainment or just plain diversion. Second, it provides the public with convenient shopping. And, third, the mall offers public, social space—a place to meet and interact with others. In other words, the modern shopping center has become an "indoor street corner society" (25).

Karen Lansky's article, "Mall Rats," for *Los Angeles* magazine discusses what it means for teenagers when they "just hang out" at these "indoor shopping palaces." Lansky contends that kids spend so much time in the mall partly because parents encourage it, assuming it is safe and that there is adult supervision. The structured and controlling environment of the mall is ideal for them. According to Lansky,

> True mall rats lack structure in their home lives, and adolescents about to make the big leap into growing up crave more structure than our modern society cares to acknowledge" (26).

Lansky also believes that the mall has become *the* focus of these young people's lives.

Malls are easy. Food, drink, bathrooms, shops, movie theaters—every part of the life-support system a modern kid needs is in the mall. Instant gratification for body and senses—and all of it close at hand, since malls are designed to make life more comfortable by eliminating parking problems, long walks, heavy doors, hot sun, depressing clouds. It is ironic, in fact, that the mall is becoming all that many kids know of the outside world, since the mall is a placeless space whose primary virtue is that it's all inside. Kids come in from the cold (or heat) for a variety of reasons, of course. But the main reason kids seek the mall, especially in the summer when school's out, seems to be because they can't think of anything better to do (27).

Lansky sees mall rats as kids with nowhere else to go.

Their parents may drink or take drugs, be violent or just gone. Whatever, the mall becomes the home they don't have. For them, the mall is a rich, stimulating, warm, clean, organized, comfortable structure—the only structure in some of their lives (28).

In gathering research for her article, Lansky interviewed several adolescents. One male expressed the belief that the mall "belongs to the mall rats." Arguing that the mall is *his* property, his mission in life, he said, is to become "top mall rat," adding, "Without the mall, we'd be street people" (29).

Another female mall habitué interviewed by Lansky complained that the only place in the mall that is "theirs" is the arcade. She and her friends get kicked out of the other places. Security warns them to keep moving if they are not buying anything. It is these kids, according to Lansky, that the mall owners do not like. The managers resent having to set limits for these kids—limits that should be the responsibility of the community or the family. The owners discourage these kids because they often do not have much money to spend, yet drain the resources of the mall (30).

"A DAY IN THE LIFE OF A MALL RAT"

At the beginning of my study in 1988, it was decided to contact teenage youths in suburban malls since they were so readily accessible there, easy to approach and to interview. A detailed questionnaire, titled the "Youth Survey" (see Appendix B), was developed.

Although teenagers in several high schools would be approached as well, the vast majority of the interviews and surveys gathered for the Youth Survey portion of this study were completed by over four hundred youths contacted in Southern California malls. The initial focus of this study, therefore, began with my meeting and talking with these so-called teenage mall rats.

One of the first young men so contacted was "Bob Bogan," or "Skidd Marx," as he preferred to be called, who allowed me to spend several afternoons with him as he wandered through the Brea Mall. Seventeen and 5'10" tall, Skidd struck a mean pose. With his black hair spiked all over with three separate 1-foot tails in back, Skidd also sported eye makeup, a leather jacket studded with spikes, a white T-shirt with a punk band logo on it, black Levis rolled up high, and black Converse high tops. Skidd also sported four hanging earrings in each ear and a loop pierced into his right nostril. Skidd, decked out in full punk regalia, cut the swaggering image of the "young man about the mall."

Skidd, like all of the teenagers studied in this book, resided in suburbia. He came from a middle-class background. Both of his parents worked. He defined himself as "a suburban punk bordering on the punk funk." Skidd, in true mall-rat fashion, spent much of his free time and social life in the Brea Mall.

Q: When did you first define yourself as being into punk or punk funk? How did the process occur?

A: It was in my third year of high school. I really wasn't feeling that good about myself at the time. I felt very self-conscious at school. I always kind of dressed differently. Being tall, people usually looked at me physically, and I used to be very insecure about that. So I kind of had the attitude, if I do something a little bit different, then that would be the reason why they're staring at me. I can't do anything about the fact that I'm tall.

Q: So it gave you a rationalization?

A: Right. The punk thing is when I just didn't care what I looked like. My parents were always saying, "You're such a nice looking young man. Why do you want to do that?" That really used to bother me.

I remember that when I'd get depressed, I'd go into the bathroom, and I'd just start butchering my hair. I look back now on those days when I was "hard core punk" and kind of laugh at it. But I cut all my hair off, and I would just dress really crappy all the time. I didn't want anyone to know that I was from a middle-class family. My parents have a Mercedes and I didn't even want to drive around in it.

Q: Who was the first person to label you as punk, or did you label yourself?

A: Yeah, I just labeled myself. I had some friends then that were punk, and I was really into skateboarding and a lot of people that were into punk were into skateboarding. That's how we would come to the mall—on our skateboards.

Q: Did defining yourself as punk solve some issues for you?

A: I thought so at the time. But I don't really think it did. At the time I thought of these things very differently than I think of them now. That was three years ago when I was fourteen. At the time I thought, oh, this is great. I liked the attention, and another reason was that my girlfriend's parents were very middle-of-the-road. I never really liked them and I kind of liked to piss them off.

Q: What does punk mean to you now?

A: I don't know because it's really lost its focus now, I think. To me, I still consider myself a punk on the inside, if we still go by the definition of punk as doing your own thing. I still go to a lot of the gigs (concerts), and I hang out with my punk friends here.

Q: Why is society threatened by, or indifferent to, youths like you?

A: I think a lot of it is that they don't have the balls to do it themselves. I heard a real interesting thing in a punk movie. This guy says—and he used to dye his hair a different color every other week—a lot of people don't like it because they look at him and wish they could dye their hair blue or orange or yellow or whatever, but they're in their jobs or locked in to certain things, and they're pissed at him because they can't do it themselves.

Q: The anger that you experience, where does it come from?

A: A large part of why I still insist on being a little bit different is because it really bugs me when people can't get past what people look like on the outside. That's one of the arguments I have with my parents. When I used to cut my hair up,

I would say, "Look, I haven't changed on the inside any, so what should it matter what I look like on the outside?" And that's still one of my big battles with them. They say, "You're going to have to conform. You're going to have to do this if you want to get ahead in society, and first impressions are a big part of it."

Q: You don't have the same middle-class aspirations as your family?

A: No, I don't. They're into making money. My dad told me he was going to become a millionaire within the next year and a half. And I believe he will because he's damn good at what he does. He's vice-president of investments at a major financial firm. You know, "Get a piece of the rock."

Q: Do you ever see yourself changing into something like that?

A: Sometimes I feel that I want more money. Like right now I do want more money. I need money to pay insurance on my car, and fix it up. Whatever I can do to keep it running. It's a piece of shit. It's an old '73 Nova. But, you know, I want to have money so I can go see bands, so I can go party, so I can buy my girlfriend nice things, like take her out to dinner maybe once now and then, and buy her a gift on her birthday.

Q: Why do you spend so much time at the mall?

A: It's weird, this place, the Brea Mall. I've been coming here since I've been in sixth grade. I've lived in Brea for almost eight years now. I've always come here. Even when I was a kid. Whenever I don't have anything to do I come to this mall.

Q: You just come here to hang out?

A: Yeah, just because there's nothing else to do. You go to the arcade. You walk around. This is where all your friends hang out. Talk to people. I know everyone that works in this mall. I work in this mall. I know all the people that work in here. I know everyone that hangs out and stuff. We have a bad image now because there are people that come to this mall with an attitude like, "We're so great. If you don't hang out here, you're not cool." That's not the way I feel. I've never felt that way. It's just a place for me to go when I'm bored. There's nothing to do now. I've really no place to go. I've got school, I've got work, I've got band, and I've got a girlfriend. I'm always busy, but I always seem to be bored. There's really never anything exciting to do.

"Nothing to do?" "Go hang out at the mall."

"What are you going to do today?" "Like hang out at the mall. Hang out with everybody else who's bored."

"I've got no money. Let's hang out at the mall."

A guy we know who comes from Boston came here about two years ago. Off the Greyhound from Boston. He left Boston because the scene was dead. In L.A. he said, "Where do all the punks hang out?" They go to the "Brea Mall." He got on a bus that said "Brea Mall," came here, and we met him. And he's been here ever since.

Q: Why are you at the mall today?

A: I got out of school at 12:20 p.m. I didn't feel like going home and doing my homework. Nothing else to do. I didn't want to sit home watching the TV set. It's stupid. TV sucks. So I come here. There's nothing to do. I come here and I talk to my friends. What the hell. Or I go to work. Or I have band practice. Or I go see my girlfriend. It's just something to do. And you can tell everybody this, "Punks are not all scum-balls. A few of them are. And I'm graduating with honors from high school. I've always been a straight A student, and I still am."

Q: What's it like working in the mall?

A: I don't dress totally punk while I'm at work. I work at May Company. I used to do a lot of little experiments on people. 'Cause when I used to have my hair cut really short, people can't tell if you're trying to be punk or you're just conservative. They can't tell. So I'd be waiting on them all along. Then we'd get up to the counter and I'd go to sign their check or whatever and I'd put my arm up on the counter and I'd have a dog chain for a bracelet. All of a sudden, all the rules changed. Their perceptions of me, all of a sudden—bingo—"punk" jumped into their mind. So I could have been the nicest guy in the world, but as soon as they thought I was a punk, then I was a piece of shit. Just like that.

Q: How would they express that change?

A: They were just really standoffish. All of a sudden. You could just watch them recoil. A lot of times I would wear a safety pin for a lapel pin. A safety pin with a padlock hanging off of it. People would always ask me, "What does that signify? What is that?" People always want to know the rules, and I wouldn't give them to them.

Q: Isn't that what punk's about? Isn't that the statement you are making dressed today like you are and roaming the mall?

A: Oh, yeah, exactly. A lot of it is taking symbols that people are so accustomed to and distorting them. That's the way with the swastika. They'll take a swastika and put it next to a happy face. Just really destroy things. Just designify and resignify things so they don't mean anything anymore.

People want the rules so badly. That's another thing I noticed while working at May Company. People are basically cattle. They feel very comfortable in a line. Because they don't have to think. And they feel safe. So as a punk, when you question that, and you look them straight in their faces and say, "I'm not going to stand in line. And I'm not going to be afraid to think." That kind of scares them off.

Q: Are you very streetwise?

A: I was never streetwise at all, until I got into punk. I was always so at home—so sheltered. I never was even kicked out of my house. But being a punk, you always learned how to be streetwise. Spending time watching people here in the mall I've learned the things of the street—how to act, what to do, what's a good move, and all that. 'Cause I've stayed a week on the street. I spent some time at this person's house and you just go off and have fun. Live wherever. It was fun. I don't think I could do it though all the time. But I had a good time.

As this interview with Skidd Marx demonstrates, what many of these youngsters in the mall suffer from is boredom. Lansky noted this sad pattern as well:

> Ask the kids in the malls and they'll talk about boredom: great, yawning, empty stretches of boredom against which they don't know how to marshall their undirected energies. Boredom that neither their families nor their communities nor their schools are prepared to acknowledge and help them with (31).

Lansky also views sexual posturing as another element that attracts these kids to the mall. No one expects these youths to follow through on their sexual impulses, but this very absence of expectation provides the kids with the opportunity to indulge in their wildest fantasies. In the mall,

> They cluster about like pigeons looking for a handout. They are a pastiche of multicolored bandannas tied around

jeans and heads, earrings, leg warmers, flats and miniskirts,
sheared sweatshirts, spiked haircuts, garish makeup, pirate shirts
and juliette nails—symbols of the boredom and voyeurism that
are a modern adolescent dilemma (32).

Malls have become our contemporary town squares. Not just the
preferred place to shop, they are also popular teenage hangouts and ren-
dezvous arenas for singles on the prowl. Shopping malls have become
our fantasy cities.

The sociological and cultural ramifications of the shopping mall have
been well documented. For some observers, young people's values have
shifted away from the family. With parents taking a less active role in
rearing their children, middle-class teens are looking outside the family
for some form of structure. The malls are one place they find it. For
some youths, the mall helps to fill a void left by churches, schools, and
families when they fail to provide centers of ritual and meaning.

For many teens this means a muddling of traditional middle-class
values. Life in the mall with its endless array of material goods leads
some of today's teens to become more materialistic, less realistic, and
harder to motivate than teens of previous generations.

Sociologists also worry that malls help create kids' illusions that they
will never have to suffer from want. Under one giant roof, malls
demonstrate the same endless conspicuous consumption fed to these
teenagers on television. Only two generations removed from the Great
Depression, today's middle-class youths, even with the recent down-
turn in the economy, are generally ignorant of poverty or the potential
for it.

In closing, perhaps this observation best sums up the mall experience:

For the young and restless, the mall is a mating group. For the
retired, the fired and the just plain tired, it is a sanctuary. For
the newly prosperous, it is a candy store. For the children, it's
an education (some actually do their homework here, while
others learn how to smoke cigarettes and play video games).
For the bored, it is a human carnival. For the destitute, it is
forbidden fruit (33).

And for the mall rats, it can be said, the mall is like an endless con-
veyor belt, moving some youngsters aimlessly around-and-around-and-
around. No wonder for some adolescents, life in the mall can be a form
of "megadeath!"

NOTES

1. "Merchants Battle So-Called "Punkers,'" *The Progress Bulletin* (6 November 1984), p. A-8.

2. Vicki Torres, "2 Hurt in Gang Gunfire at Mall in West Covina," *The Los Angeles Times* (26 February 1992), p. A-1.

3. Bernice Kanner, "Mall Madness," *New York Magazine* (29 March 1993), p. 18.

4. Isabel Wilkerson, "World's Biggest Mall to Have 800-Plus Shops," *The San Francisco Chronicle* (14 June 1989), p. B-7.

5. Peter Bennet, "Malls Offer a Walk on the Mild Side," *The Los Angeles Times* (20 December 1990), p. E-19.

6. Kanner.

7. Wilkerson.

8. Kanner.

9. Jennifer Lowe, "A Mirror of OC Life," *The Orange County Register* (15 March 1992), p. B-1.

10. Ibid., p. B-4.

11. Ibid.

12. Ann Hagedorn, "Malls May Look Safe, but Some Lure Crooks as Well as the Crowds," *The Wall Street Journal* (10 September 1987), p. A-1.

13. Ibid.

14. Ibid.

15. Magagnini, Stephen, "It's a Mall World," *The Sacramento Bee Magazine* (25 May 1986), p. 7.

16. Hagedorn.

17. Ibid.

18. Ibid.

19. "Child Thieves Plague Malls," *The San Francisco Chronicle* (22 April 1989), p. A-2.

20. L. M. Boyd, "The Grab Bag," *The San Francisco Chronicle* (20 March 1988), p. F-7.

21. Pat Morrison, "Violence Mars Malls' Image as Safe Places to Shop, Relax," *The Los Angeles Times* (1 March 1992), p. B-1.

22. Ibid., p. B-4.

23. William Severini Kowinski, *The Malling of America: An Inside Look at the Great Consumer Paradise* (New York: William Morrow and Company, 1985), p. 351.

24. Ibid.

25. Jerry Jacobs, *The Mall: An Attempted Escape from Everyday Life* (Prospects Heights, IL: Waveland Press, 1984).

26. Karen Lansky, "Mall Rats," *Los Angeles* (August 1984), p. 250.

27. Ibid., p. 254.

28. Ibid., p. 257.

29. Ibid.

30. Ibid.

31. Ibid.

32. Ibid.

33. Jeffrey Zaslow, "Children's Search for Values Leading to Shopping Malls," *The Wall Street Journal* (12 September 1989), p. A-1.

3

▼

Kicking Back at "Raging High"

"Truancy Soaring: Why Go to Class When Mall Beckons?"

On a typical day last month, nearly one of every three Sacramento County high school students—more than 10,000—missed one or more academic classes.

The problem is reaching crisis proportions at some schools, where nearly half the students skip class each day, *The Sacramento Bee* learned by examining attendance records in the county's five largest school districts.

"It's easy enough—you just walk out," said Rachel, a 15-year-old sophomore at McClatchy High School. "They have hall monitors, but if you skip every day, you know what you're doing. It's easy to get away with it."

Rachel said most of her classmates skip about 10 periods a week. Typically, they forge their parents' signatures on notes to get back into class, she said (1).

"Campus Styles Rekindle Debate on School Codes"

Shawn Peters, a 16-year-old junior at South Whittier High School, hardly thought twice about wearing a gold stud earring on his left ear.

"It's a form of identification and I like the way it looks on me," he said.

But school officials were chagrined when Peters, who favors Judas Priest T-shirts and a leather jacket, appeared on campus last December wearing the earring. Saying earrings on boys are not appropriate for campus, school officials gave Peters an ultimatum: Take it off or be suspended.

He refused, touching off a battle between school officials and the American Civil Liberties Union.

Shawn missed three days of school but was allowed back on campus—with the earrings—after the South Whittier school board decided that it could not afford a costly court fight to uphold its position (2).

"Where 'Boys Will Be Boys,' and Adults Are Befuddled"

It was lunchtime at Lakewood High School and the big men on campus were strutting their stuff at the local Taco Bell.

Eric Richardson, a 17-year-old football star, swaggered in, a T-shirt reading "No Crybabies" stretched taut across his pectorals.

"I got the power! I got the finesse! I got everything!" Eric declaimed to no one in particular.

Eric and eight of his friends, members of a group called the Spur Posse, had spent the last few days in jail, accused of molesting and raping girls as young as 10.

Now all but one had been released, while investigations continued. And the boys returned to school this week to a heroes' welcome, their status enhanced and their scrapbooks thicker by several press clippings.

The tale of the Spur Posse in some ways sounds like an old story about bad boys and fast girls, about athletes who can do no wrong and the people who fawn over them. But it comes as codes of sexual conduct are colliding with boys-will-be-boys mores and as unemployment and broken marriages are troubling the still waters of this piece of suburbia southeast of Los Angeles (3).

THE FOSTERING OF
LOW SELF-ESTEEM

According to material collected by a gang prevention and intervention project located in Southern California, Turning Point, the major key to resolving the "social ills" of our junior high and high school campuses is to focus on how to improve and bolster each student's self-esteem.

This view is supported by the recent findings of "The Report of the California Commission for Reform of Intermediate and Secondary Education," which contends that a person's education should contribute to self-understanding and self-esteem. Both of these organizations and other groups agree that by teaching self-esteem, our public schools will help students overcome their negative ideas about themselves and discover their unique potentials (4).

According to one study, 2 out of 3 Americans suffer from low self-esteem. Although 80 percent of children entering school in kindergarten or the first grade feel good about themselves, by the time they have reached the fifth grade, the number has dropped to 20 percent. And by the time they become seniors in high school, the number has dropped to 5 percent! (5).

Furthermore, according to this report, students endure the equivalent of sixty days each year of reprimanding, nagging, and punishment. During twelve years of schooling a student is subjected to 15,000 negative statements. That is three times the number of positive statements received.

In a recent National Institute of Education study, 1,000 thirty year olds were asked if they felt that their high school education had prepared them with the skills they needed in the real world. Over four-fifths answered, "Absolutely not." When asked about the skills they wished they had been taught in high school, they answered:

> Relationships skills such as how to get along better with the
> people they live with; how to find and keep a job; how to
> handle conflict; how to be a good parent; how to understand
> the normal development of a child; skills in financial manage-
> ment; and the "meaning of life" (6).

In a related study, 2,000 youths in 120 high schools were asked the following two questions:

> If you were to develop a program for your high school to help
> you cope with what you're needing now, and what you think
> you will need in the future, what would the program include?
> And, list the top ten problems in your life that you wish were
> dealt with better at home and at school (7).

The respondents listed the same skills as the thirty year olds in the National Institute of Education study. They further suggested that the skills training would have to include assuming responsibility for one's actions; respecting one's self and others; gaining a better sense of reality; and improving relationship skills. The two top problems they listed were *loneliness*, with even the most popular kids stating that they felt lonely, and *not liking themselves*.

The Consequences of Low Self-Esteem

Students who hold themselves in low self-esteem frequently resort to anti-social and delinquent behavior. When such behaviors are expressed within the school context, as they often are, they can take many forms. On the personal level, these frustrated students frequently engage in acts of truancy; experience despondency or depression; resort to drug and/or alcohol abuse; attempt or commit suicide; show disrespect for their parents, teachers, and authorities; become disruptive and inattentive in class; and/or fail to perform up to their academic potential.

According to the National Center of Health, one adolescent attempts suicide every 70 seconds. Furthermore, over 6,000 students per year take their own lives. In California, the state superintendent of schools estimates 1 of every 10 adolescents will make a serious attempt at suicide before graduating from high school (8).

Other alarming statistics from the National Center of Health include the following:

- Every 20 minutes an adolescent is killed in an automobile accident. Over 50 percent of these accidents are attributed to alcohol or drug abuse.
- Every 30 seconds an adolescent becomes pregnant. Fourteen adolescents per day have their *third* child.
- One-half of all high school seniors have used illegal drugs; 90 percent have used alcohol.
- One-fourth of the current high school population is judged to have a serious problem with alcohol or drugs. (Serious drinking is defined as going on a binge once every three weeks, and drinking away from the family on a regular basis.)
- Dropping out of school is now considered seriously by 50 percent of *all* high school youths in America. The dropout rate is now 27 percent nationally and 50 percent in urban settings (9).

These teenagers' frustrations may not end with acts of self-destruction. Some students who are unable to cope with the pressures of home and school may take out their hostility on the teaching faculty, administrators, and staff of the schools that they attend; on other students; or on school property. Such delinquent behavior may include committing acts of violence against teachers and staff; bullying or intimidating fellow students; participating in acts of vandalism against school property, including arson (as my book, *Children and Arson: America's Middle-Class Nightmare* conclusively documented); and/or joining gangs and participating in "gang-banging" activity.

SOCIAL CLIQUES AND YOUTH CULTURE

The modern high school campus is frequently the locale where teenagers are most critically judged and evaluated by their peers. It is in high school that students establish a social hierarchy. One's position within this hierarchy plays a major role in shaping one's self-esteem. Popular students who are placed high in the status hierarchy frequently express high self-esteem, while less popular students who are placed lower on the scale often express lower self-esteem.

The positioning of one's *clique*, or social group, relative to the other cliques and students on campus also affects self-esteem. Not fitting in with any clique is bound to produce unpleasant experiences. Being identified with a less popular clique is apt to negatively affect a youngster who may have a fragile ego.

Several researchers have looked at the impact of cliques on adolescent behavior. Cliques—defined as small, exclusive groups made up of three or more individuals who share similar interests and strong loyalties toward one another—provide their members with a refuge from the pressures of home and school (10).

As early as age 8, same sex, close-knit groups or cliques take shape. During the teens, almost all of both sexes become involved in cliques. A clique's members are usually of similar social status, although someone of a different background may be included if they share attributes such as attractiveness, personality traits, or athletic prowess that are highly valued by that particular clique (11).

All adolescent groups, including cliques, constitute the so-called peer or *youth culture*, which presumably possesses a distinct social identity. One observer views the youth culture as not always explicitly anti-adult, but as belligerently nonadult. This peer culture is usually independent of the larger society and has its own distinctive values and behaviors (12).

Youth culture in general serves several functions. It helps the adolescent define her or his values and behaviors. Most youths today do not follow in the footsteps of their parents. They face an array of alternatives concerning career choices, moral codes, and lifestyles. As a result, they find refuge in their own culture until they have developed their own identity. They use their peer group to sort themselves out.

One sociologist sees cultural differences in this pattern, with adolescent peer groups assuming more importance in some societies than in others. Such groups are most important in nations, like the United States, where the family unit fails to adequately meet youths' social needs due, in part, to parents and other family members having their own set of priorities (13).

Although not all sociologists are in agreement about whether there is such a thing as a "common" youth culture, most observers of contemporary youths would concur that there are distinctive youth styles that differentiate the various peer groups. They would also concur that youth cultures share values that distinguish them from adult culture. As one observer of youth cultures noted, "(They) can be defined only in terms of distinctive life styles which are to a great extent self-generated and autonomous" (14).

Several people have commented on the various factors that encourage the growth of youth cultures. One has argued that the affluence of Western society accounts for these distinctive youth styles:

> Only a wealthy society can afford a large leisure class of
> teenagers not yet in the labor force but already consumers on a
> large scale. What adolescents earn, besides what they succeed
> in wresting from their elders, they spend chiefly on themselves,
> for such items as records, cars, travel, clothes, cosmetics, and
> recreational paraphernalia. Meanwhile, this same affluence
> demands, for its support, a high level of training which itself
> prolongs the transitional period to adulthood (15).

Up to age 12, and after age 19, parents generally have more influence on their offspring than peers. But from ages 12 through 18, what peers say often matters more than what parents say.

Not all teenagers participate equally in the youth culture. In fact, the vast majority of youths are basically "conformist-oriented," to apply one of the five cultural adaptations observed by Robert K. Merton (16). Such youths shy away from assuming a "total identity" or "master status" of any particular youth style—whether that be an identity of a punk rocker, a heavy metaler, or a racist skinhead. Instead, conformists opt to be just the typical, average teenager who, although affiliating with the general youth culture because of their age, choose not to affiliate with any one distinctive youth culture.

The other adaptations according to Merton include innovators, ritualists, retreatists, and rebels. Such a typology is useful in examining the array of youth styles that will be discussed in this book. In fact, punk rockers, for instance, can be categorized as innovators in that from their perspective they see themselves as trying to change and improve their social environment. On the other hand, others might categorize their behavior as one of the other three groups: ritualists in that they mimic the behavior and dress of other youths like themselves; retreatists because many have seemed to drop out of society; or rebels in that some espouse anarchy and civil disobedience.

Study of Collegiate Subcultures

Categorizations of youths are not just limited to the general youth culture. One study of the college world by Trow and Clark found four subcultures of students. Representing clusters of attitudes and modes of behavior rather than specific groups of people, they found that university students frequently moved in or out of these subcultures and often were marginally members of more than one of the groupings (17).

The Trow and Clark categorization of collegiate subcultures included four models: *collegiate, vocational, academic,* and *nonconformist students.* Each will be briefly discussed. Then, after I have presented the high school youth cultures, I will apply the Trow and Clark classification in a different way, grouping the various high school cliques using their four models.

The *collegiate* culture, according to Trow and Clark, comprised fraternities and sororities, football games, cars, and drinking while the academic part of college life occupied "a dim marginal background." Members of the collegiate culture concentrated on campus activities, partying, and having fun. They generally did not aspire to graduate or professional school. As Trow and Clark noted, "This culture is not hostile to the college; it is merely indifferent and resistant to any serious demands."

The *vocational* culture comprised working-class students who were interested in college because they desired skills and a degree. They viewed college as *the* means for upward social mobility. Frequently, these students had to work part- or full-time and so were unable to afford, financially or timewise, the activities that the collegiate culture engaged in.

By contrast, the *academic* culture group included students who were involved with academic coursework and strongly identified with the college as an institution of higher learning. This group attended the university because they wished to learn. Often they identified with their professors and became involved with their research.

Finally, the *nonconformist* culture involved the intellectuals, radicals, and alienated, bohemian students whose style, according to Trow and Clark, was not always intellectual. "Its members are rebellious and realistic, detached from the faculty, and primarily involved with seeking an identity" (18).

Further, Trow and Clark distinguished between the academic and the nonconformist, arguing that the academic subculture linked its interests to the curriculum and classroom setting, while the nonconformist subculture pursued its intellectual interests outside the curriculum and the classroom.

Studies on High School Campuses

Several sociologists have studied the teen status hierarchy and teen life in high schools. Schwartz and Merten, studying an upper-middle-class high school in 1967, found two distinctive youth styles—the *socies* and the *hoods*—as well as a third, residual category composed of students who identified with neither of those two types (19).

The socies represented the top stratum of the prestige system and established the values that determined high or popular school status. The hoods, on the other hand, were from lower socioeconomic statuses than the socies and included the "out-of-its," such as mentally handicapped and slow learners; the rebels; as well as the intellectuals, and those who somehow deviated from the prestige group. Schwartz and Merten described "the others" as just ordinary students who did not fit into the other two cliques.

Gary Schwartz, in *Beyond Conformity or Rebellion: Youth and Authority in America*, analyzed the distinctive youth cultures present in six different communities throughout the United States. In one of these communities, which he named Patusa—a small, conventional, midwestern American town—Schwartz noted that the teenage clique structure in the high school closely reflected the socioeconomic status and prestige of the students' parents (20). These patterns were similar to the findings of the classic *Elmstown Youth* studies done by A. B. Hollingshead on a community in Indiana in the late 1940s (21).

Schwartz, in examining the "peer group world" of Patusa High School, observed four broad categories. In descending order in terms of popularity and prestige, they were: *youth elites, religious youths, fashionable freaks,* and *greasers.*

The *youth elites* comprised three distinct subgroups: the student politicos, the athletes, and the "brains" of the high school. Each of these groups had different bases for high status. As Schwartz noted,

> Seen from below, they are all beneficiaries of official privilege. Seen from within their own ranks, they are three separate groups who do not associate with and do not even particularly like one another (22).

Due to the rural character of the small town, the *religious youths* in Patusa High School had the second highest level of prestige. The town Christian church, for instance, with 2,000 members, had the largest youth club, and this social contact carried over into the high school campus. Although the youth members were generally passive, according to Schwartz, they did accept authority and were average students at school.

The *fashionable freaks*, on the other hand, had as their reference point the larger youth culture from the outside world. As Schwartz observed, "The social sources of (their) form of peer sociability are rooted in cosmopolitan culture." These youths, who dressed in the latest urban fashion and listened to the newest recording artists, merely were marking time until they graduated from high school and could move to more cosmopolitan areas.

Finally, the *greasers*, a term synonymous with working- and lower-class youths, clustered heavily in the remedial classes. They frequently socialized in public meeting areas such as the local pool halls, behind the welding shop at school, and the bowling alley in town. Although alcohol and drugs such as marijuana would be used by some of the youth elites and fashionable freaks, the greasers were the ones most suspected of substance abuse.

The heavy drug users, known in Patusa as "freaks" or "burnouts," were highly visible due to their demeanor, appearance, and group activities. Although such heavy drug use did cross socioeconomic and clique lines, in general, according to Schwartz, the greasers were the ones most frequently apprehended and expelled from school for possession and drug usage (23).

CLIQUE STRUCTURES IN FOUR
SUBURBAN HIGH SCHOOLS

Patusa High School was located in a small-town, middle-American, rural setting. For the purposes of this study, I decided to examine the teenage clique structures of several suburban high schools located in the Southern California area. Of particular interest in this analysis would be the following five issues:

1. Were the teenage status hierarchies similar in each of these Southern California high schools, including the terminologies used to distinguish one social clique from the other?
2. Were the status hierarchies in the Southern California schools similar to those found in Patusa High School, or were there differences in the rank ordering of the different youth groups because of differences in geographic region or locale?
3. What was the demeanor of some of those youths at the top of the clique structure in terms of how they handled their special status, and how they treated some female students?
4. How did those students who were part of less popular cliques feel about their position, and how were they treated by the other cliques in their school?
5. And could the various youth cultures found in these Southern California suburban high schools be grouped according to the four subcultures observed by Trow and Clark in their study of collegiate subcultures?

Of the many studies of local high schools submitted to me by my students, four "typical" suburban high schools were selected for comparative analysis with the Patusa study. With the assistance of several of my university students who had attended these particular high schools as recently as three years preceding the analysis, the clique structures and status hierarchies of the four high schools were examined. The study analyzed the senior yearbooks of each of these four schools. For purposes of discussion, each graduating senior was classified into his or her respective social clique and group.

All four of the high schools examined shared similar characteristics. They were large, cosmopolitan, and located in the suburban areas that served as "feeder schools" to California State Polytechnic University (Cal Poly) in Pomona. The students who attended these high schools were predominantly Caucasian and from middle- to upper-middle-class socioeconomic backgrounds. As part of the research, each of the four schools was visited, and the clique structure was discussed with representatives of the school administration such as senior counselors who commented on, and validated, the findings.

Similarity of Status Hierarchies

As the summary table, "Southern California High School Clique Structures," depicts, the status hierarchy of cliques was generally similar in each of the four high schools analyzed, although the students in the schools often used different names or terminology to distinguish one social clique from the other. Each group is listed in *descending* order of popularity.

Table 3.1

Southern California High School Clique Structures

1	2	3	4
Jocks	Jocks	Jocks	Jocks
Cheerleaders	Socs	Partiers	Surfers
Tweakies	Cheerleaders	Cheerleaders/ Barbie dolls	Trendies/Preppies
Trendies	Death rockers	Preppies	Punks/Metalers
Drama freaks	Cha-Chas	Burners	Death rockers/ Dance clubbers
Bandos	Brains	Band members	
Smacks	Metal heads	Geeks/Nerds	Cholos
Dirtbags	Asians	Brains	Brains
Sluts			
Punks			
Loners			

High School Case Study I

Jocks. The jocks at this school consisted of boys who actively participated in many of the sports on campus. They strutted the campus in letterman jackets to prove to all other students their athletic ability. Most were self-centered and egotistical. At parties jocks could be seen participating in beer-drinking contests and smoking marijuana. They had no problems finding dates, and they tended to choose cheerleaders as their girlfriends. For jocks, high school was fun—a positive part of life, increasing their self-image.

Cheerleaders. The cheerleaders were attractive, school-spirited, and popular. They were constantly being elected homecoming and prom queens. Unlike the jocks, the cheerleaders acknowledged other students who were not as popular, wanting to be everyone's idol and friend. They had high self-esteem and confidence.

Tweakies. The tweakies were boys who had an extremely "laid back" attitude toward school. They often skipped class to go to the beach, and they consumed alcohol whenever they had the chance. Surfboards and girls were more important than school. They had their own slang, including words such as "bogus" (terrible), "righteous" (out of sight, the best), "gnarly" (cool), and "sweet" (perfect). They wore baggy clothing and sandals.

Trendies. The trendies were desperate to fit in and spent their time shopping for the latest trends in clothing. They constantly changed their looks in hopes of finding a style that would make them popular. To be labeled a "trendie" was not good. It meant that you were "hard-up" for friends and would do anything, other than be yourself, to become popular.

Drama Freaks. The drama freaks were students who were completely engrossed in acting. Constantly practicing for upcoming plays and musicals, they were viewed by others as an extremely loud and obnoxious group. The majority of students considered "drama freaks" to be fake. They dressed in high fashion, and the girls wore brightly colored makeup. Many of them were excellent actors, but they could never draw a distinct line between fantasy and reality.

Bandos. The bandos were similar to the drama freaks, but instead of being centered on acting, they were centered on band. Students viewed them as "nerds" and thought of them as "uncool." Bandos spent the majority of their time practicing their instruments and were never seen at any of the weekend parties. They were very conservative in dress.

Smacks. The smacks were students who had extremely high GPAs. They were overly friendly to all teachers and always had their hands up in class. They spent many hours studying while their peers were shopping, partying, or playing sports. Only those students who were not popular were labeled smacks. A few students in the popular cliques who received high grades were not labeled as smacks.

Dirtbags. The dirtbags came from middle-class families, but they were considered the "lowlifes" of the campus. They roamed around school constantly brushing long hair out of their eyes. They were always skipping school to smoke marijuana or party at a friend's house. Many of the dirtbags were enrolled in remedial level classes, and many were held back from graduating or dropped out because of failing grades. Their typical dress consisted of heavy-metal-band T-shirts and jeans.

Sluts. Some girls were labeled sluts because of their provocative clothing, such as tight jeans, high heels, and no under garments. They usually had bleached hair and wore a lot of makeup. They were popular merely for sexual purposes. They loved to party and had sex with many fellow male students.

Punks. The punks dressed in torn jeans, combat boots, and wore Mohawks. They were harmless, merely making a statement of their individuality. Many of them were intelligent and enrolled in honors classes. They could be found on the outskirts of campus. Fellow students did not see them as a threat and respected their uniqueness.

Loners. The loners had no peer group to socialize with, and they were always in a corner eating lunch or studying. Everyone tended to ignore them, and the loners avoided contact with any of the cliques. They were very introverted and never talked in the classroom.

High School Case Study 2

Jocks. Similar to the status hierarchy of high school 1, the jocks in this second high school were also the most popular students. The jocks were bonded together by their sport and Friday night parties. They always ended the week with a huge party and five kegs of beer. The jocks were very cocky and obnoxious. They were not very successful with grades. In this high school there were no African-American or Asian jocks; they were mainly Anglo with some Hispanics.

Socs. The socs were rich, white students and the metal heads' worst enemy. The typical "soc" always wore the latest fashion—Guess jeans, a

Gennera shirt, and Reebok tennis shoes—and their hair was always neat and clean with a salon look. The soc community was very exclusive.

Cheerleaders. The cheerleaders were usually part of the soc clique. They were involved in student government and many were scholastically intelligent. They did use drugs but often tried to hide their addiction from parents and teachers.

Death Rockers. The death rockers were bonded together by music, which was generally an alternative Hollywood underground type, bordering on punk rock. Their clique was entirely open and nondiscriminatory. They wore black clothing, black makeup, and dyed black hair. Their appearance challenged, "Like me for who I am, not for where I live or what I wear." They were seldom athletic or extracurricular, but they were very scholastic.

Cha-chas. The cha-chas were mostly Hispanic and wore "GQ"-type outfits. The boys styled their hair in pompadours and the girls teased theirs to resemble a lion's mane. They drove lowered mini trucks with huge speakers that created incredible bass sounds, listening mainly to rap music. The only sport they played was soccer. Most cha-chas dropped out of school or failed to earn enough credits to graduate.

Brains. This group was bound by the classes they took: math, biology, chemistry, physics, computer programming, and honors courses. They never were invited to any parties and had a reputation for never touching any alcohol or drugs. They did not thrive on fashion and had no set dress code nor hairstyle. They ate lunch in the cafeteria and studied in the library when finished. Tennis was the only sport that a brain would consider playing. They belonged to the science club and the California Scholastic Federation.

Metal Heads. They were the students who idolized Van Halen, bonded in their clique by hard rock music from the 1970s, and heavy metal music from the 1980s. Their dress consisted of old Levi jeans, concert T-shirts, cowboy boots, and long hair. They never denied the use of drugs, and often flaunted it. They did not participate in sports and were not involved in student government. The metal heads did not usually excel scholastically, and the only thing they could see as a profession was stardom in the music industry.

Asians. This clique included groups of Vietnamese, Chinese, and Filipinos. Anybody who could not speak their language was automatically rejected by them. They rarely spoke English except to teachers. Asians excelled in math and computer classes, but lacked the verbal ability to excel in the English and social science classes. Because they were different, the jocks and socs ridiculed them no end.

High School Case Study 3

Jocks. They were the most predominant clique, and they ran the school. They always knew what was going on and were always at the center of attention. Underclassmen stayed away from jocks because they had the power and ability to force them to do what they wanted. Jocks wore their letterman jackets to remind everyone of their status. They also sometimes received preferential treatment from teachers after intervention by their coach.

Partiers. The partiers were mostly in the average track, able to party without sacrificing their grades enough to avoid being placed into any remedial classes. The partiers included a group called the "Lunch Club" who met at lunchtime on every Thursday to drink heavily at the home of a student whose parents were working. To be accepted into this group you needed to play an assortment of drinking games that usually made you sick. They frequented parties during the weekend and always brought alcohol into the football games.

Cheerleaders or Barbie Dolls. They were the girls that all the guys desired. When they were not in their cheerleading uniforms, they wore all the fashionable clothes. They partied and hung out with the athletes. If you were seen with a cheerleader, you were perceived to be popular.

Preppies. The preppies arrived at school in flashy new sports cars that their parents bought for them soon after they turned 16. They wore plaid pants or shorts, along with an Izod or Polo shirt, penny loafers, and matching argyle socks.

Burners. Often placed into the remedial track, burners appeared to be stoned most of the time. This group included the rocker crowd, along with some punkers. Their territory was the school-provided smoking area and a park across the street from school called "Toke" Grove, instead of Oak Grove, because of the constant drug activity there.

Band Members. On the surface they were perceived as squares who enjoyed playing music, until sporting events when their playing abilities focused positive attention on them. In actuality, they were the most rowdy group. They had privileges others did not have such as being in parades or going to special events, but they often partied and got into trouble more often than any other group.

Geeks or Nerds. These students were not accepted into any group, so they formed their own. They were often the target of many practical jokes. Geeks retaliated by throwing soda, water balloons, or rotten fruit off the third floor onto targets in the quad below. They were avid members of the Science Fiction Club, and they were also among the few people who actually ate lunch in the cafeteria.

Brains. These were the people who threw the GPA of every class off the scale. Brains usually spent their lunch in one of the labs or in the library working on their homework. They preferred not to socialize with anyone.

High School Case Study 4

Jocks. They were the most influential group on this campus as well. Unfortunately, there were numerous instances in which jocks beat up people at parties or in public places for no apparent reason. The assaults were committed gang-style, with three or four jocks beating up on one person. A few of them were convicted and sent to jail or juvenile hall. It was later learned that their aggressive behavior had been caused by steroid use.

However, most of the jocks were not like this; they were nice "All-American" boys who dated cheerleaders—but were not especially intelligent. Another group of jocks were labeled the "502 Crew." This group prided themselves on their drinking ability. Still another group of jocks, the "TKE" (Tappa Kegga Encinitas), were the rivals of the "502 Crew."

Surfers. They were the second largest group on campus. Surfers tended to keep to themselves merely because their lifestyle was so different. They had their own lingo and a laid-back attitude—"Smoke some pot, drink some beer, kick back, eat some Mexican food, and catch a wave." They were hardly ever at school because they were at the beach.

Trendies or Preppies. These were the mainstream kids. They were the homecoming and prom queens, the associated student body officers, and the student leaders. On the surface, they were every parent's dream. But, they were just as into drugs as everyone else.

Punks and Metalers. They were the devils and did whatever they wanted, not caring who knew. They got wasted before, during, and after school. They sold drugs on campus, and they were often kicked out of their classes and put on detention. In reality, they were not any worse than anyone else. They just chose not to hide their beliefs and attitudes or drug use.

Death Rockers or Dance Clubbers. They were known as the "wall people" because they hung out at the wall in the center of campus. They had a "holier than thou" attitude that turned people off. They were too soft-core for the punk, yet too strange for the mainstream kids. Everyone usually ignored them or teased them.

Cholos. No one really knew much about the cholos because there were so few of them at school. Being a white, middle-class suburban high school, these lower-class Mexican-Americans did not fit in here. They had their gangs and every once in a while they fought rival gangs. Usually, the only sign of their existence was some occasional graffiti written on the outside school walls or in the bathrooms.

Brains. While they occasionally drank, they were the only group on campus who did not do drugs. They were not respected for their high intelligence and grades because they felt that they were superior to everyone else and they formed an elite. Usually, brains are considered nerds and ostracized, but these people ostracized everyone else. They were the most isolated group because they felt they had no need to socialize with others.

Beyond these four "typical" high school clique structures, our study turned up even more groups, often with derogatory names. Some of these other high school cliques included:

- *Black cockroaches*: kids that wore all black such as the death rockers
- *BAs*: students of Native-American ancestry or "bows and arrows"
- *Skanks*: girlfriends of the heavy metal groups
- *Motorheads*: guys who drove old Mustangs or Camaros
- *Water jockeys*: swimmers and water polo players

- *Kickers*: cowboys and sons of cowboys
- *The tuna barge*: fast girls
- *Daddy's girls*: spoiled rich girls
- *Puppy power*: those freshmen and sophmore males who were popular partly due to being good in sports
- *The shadows*: students who were into death rock
- *Disco biscuits*: youths who liked to party and drink and did not care for school at all
- *Dog squad*: girls on the drill team that wanted to be cheerleaders but were less attractive and less coordinated, and came from lower socioeconomic backgrounds

Finally, one of my students, looking at the entire clique structure at her high school, summed up the various groups in this fashion: "The first clique was the trendy, the second was the 'worker bees,' the third was intelligent, and the last was simply lost."

Implications of the Findings

As the clique summaries indicate, the teenage status hierarchies in these four Southern California suburban high schools were generally similar. However, each high school—apart from the categories for jocks, cheerleaders, and brains—used different terminology to describe the other cliques on campus. Furthermore, in two of the high schools (1 and 3), the terms used to refer to some of the less popular cliques were downright cruel. In the first school, derogatory terms included "smacks," "dirtbags," and "sluts"; and in the third high school, the derogatory terms used were "burners," "geeks," or "nerds."

In most instances, the top clique comprised the jocks, followed closely by either the cheerleaders or the wealthier students who were part of either the socs or the partiers cliques. The clique structure of Patusa High School, however, also grouped the brains—along with the athletes and student politicos—into the top clique, or youth elites. By contrast, the brains in the Southern California cliques were much lower on the hierarchy. In fact, in two of the four schools, the brains were the *least* popular of the student groupings.

Perhaps the greatest difference, however, between the Southern California schools and Patusa High School was the placement of the religious group. Whereas the religious youths played a major role in the rural, midwestern high school, religious youths were less of a visible, collective group on these suburban, West Coast, public high school campuses.

More similar in status hierarchical placement was the middle-to-lower range positioning of the fashionable freaks (or their equivalents) in the two regions. Likewise, the greasers (and their equivalents) held comparable lower status in both geographical sections (and time periods) of the country.

Of particular interest to this book (and the topic of chapters to follow) are these latter two groups at the bottom of the suburban high school clique hierarchies: those fashionable freaks who engaged in the popular youth cultures of the day (such as punkers and metalers), and the modern equivalent of the greasers or teen rebels: taggers, racist skinheads, stoners, and satanists. But, first, let us examine the rowdy and immoral behavior of some of those youths at the top of the high school clique hierarchy: the jocks.

THE LEADERS OF THE PACK

As our analysis denotes, there is no doubt that the high school athlete—particularly those males who letter in such prestigious sports as football and basketball—are given special privileges at high school. But what happens when such status goes to their heads and they begin to act indifferently and insensitively toward others in their school and community?

This issue reached national debate with the shocking case of the Spur Posse that unfolded in spring 1993 at Lakewood High School in Southern California, a suburban community located just thirty miles from Cal Poly, Pomona. The nation's news media were quick to focus on this alarming incident as the excerpt from the front page of *The New York Times* at the beginning of this chapter demonstrated.

Perhaps one of the leads from *The Los Angeles Times* best delineates the scope of the problem—"A Stain Spreads in Suburbia: Issues of teen promiscuity, forced sex and parental neglect rock Lakewood, once a bastion of morality. Many see the town and its unrepentant Spur Posse as symbols of a declining America" (24). This comment from an article in *Newsweek* further laments the problem: "Mixed Messages: California's 'Spur Posse' scandal underscores the varying signals society sends teens about sex" (25).

As *The Los Angeles Times* article pointed out:

All of a sudden, in a glaring media spotlight, Lakewood stands as a reluctant symbol of declining America. Sex sprees, violence and turmoil were about the last things many residents might have expected in the mostly white middle-class community—

the prototype of the modern California suburb when it was laid out on nine square miles of sugar beet fields in the early 1950s. What the founders created—a verdant sprawl of parks, ball diamonds and quiet streets—seemed all but immune to today's spreading plague of gang warfare. If any city could make the claim, Lakewood remained Norman Rockwell's America, a family place, as solid a bastion of traditional ethical values as might be found.

But no more. The innocence has given way to hard questions and self-searching. Residents talk fearfully, and some escort their teen-agers to school because of recent street fights and alleged threats of retribution—all involving mostly white youths raised without financial hardship, the products of fine schools. Issues of promiscuity, forced sex and parental neglect are out in the open (26).

What concerned this community (and the country as a whole) was the disclosure that a clique called the "Spur Posse," most of them top athletes at the local high school, told investigators that they had kept tally or scores of the number of young girls they had bedded. Founded in 1989 as a sort of high school fraternity, many juveniles of the Spur Posse, which counted twenty to thirty boys as members and was named for the San Antonio Spurs professional basketball team, brashly claimed they had sex with as many as sixty girls.

It appears as if one of their main activities was "hooking up," or having sex, with as many girls as possible. Furthermore, because of their local hero status as athletes, the boys took turns having sex with the same girls and later boasted about their conquests, labeling some of the girls as "sluts" for "putting out" for them and their friends.

Eight members of this high school boys' clique were arrested on charges of lewd conduct, unlawful intercourse, and rape allegedly involving seven girls from 10 to 16 years of age. Other charges filed by the authorities included burglary, assault, intimidation of witnesses, and other crimes.

But what also shocked the community was the staunch support these athletes received from other students who denounced the Spurs' accusers as "whores" and "promiscuous girls who got what they asked for." Furthermore, many of the parents of those accused were equally unrepentant. The "boys will be boys" attitude of some of the parents was particularly bothersome. One father *boasted* to reporters about the virility of his three sons, one of whom had been a founder of the Spur Posse.

Teenage sex without responsibility—and without precaution in this time of AIDS and other sexually transmitted diseases—is serious business and foolhardy, to say the least. But in truth, the most striking thing about the Spur Posse, as one reporter noted, was that these juveniles' actions appeared to be more about "scoring" than about sex, about conquest rather than intimacy. Sex, like the athletic field, had become yet another arena in which these teenagers competed (27).

Such alarming behavior is not just found in Southern California. In October 1993, in Rockville, Maryland, a 16-year-old son of a Washington-area school superintendent was one of five juveniles charged with rape in connection with a gang named the Chronics whose objective was also to have sex with as many girls as possible (28).

Sex, and sexual promiscuity, has become another fact of adolescent life. And over the past few decades, the age of initial sexual experience has been declining. According to a 1990 survey by the Centers for Disease Control and Prevention, 7 out of 10 high school seniors and over half (54 percent) of ninth through twelfth graders have had intercourse at least once (29).

The extraordinary attention given the Spur Posse, according to one commentator in the Los Angeles area, was partly due to the increased interest in sexual harassment on campus. Citing figures from a recent magazine survey which found that almost 90 percent of 2,002 high school-age girls had been sexually harassed, he notes that the Lakewood High School incident has been but another case in which girls continue to submit to sexual aggression when they do not want to. And if these girls complain afterward, they are told they wanted it and are mocked by unsympathetic peers (30).

Sadly, the community of Lakewood was left with many unanswered questions in the wake of the sex scandal and all of the negative publicity that it generated. But as our previous discussion of four other Southern California suburban high schools pointed out, Lakewood High is obviously not alone in these matters.

The Byrds

One student in one of the other schools examined for this study spoke about the top group at her high school, a group known as the "The Byrds," of which she was a member.

The group consisted of approximately twelve guys and eight girls. "The Byrds" were established when we were juniors by four of my guy friends. When I look back now at what The Byrds stood for, it really sickens me. Only the guys could be a "Byrd." It was formed by them, but as they got more and more recognition, the name just became applied to the rest of the group.

The guys in my clique were all drop-dead beautiful. I guess you could say that they were the big men on campus. They were desired by every girl. Well, of course, they knew it, and The Byrds were born.

They were like a nonviolent gang. They had a full initiation ceremony to become a Byrd, and the quest was sex. It was by no means forced sex, and they did not keep tabs either. To become a Byrd, a guy must first be accepted by the rest of the guys. Then the "pledge" would have to find a girl that was willing to have sex with him. The actual initiation ceremony consisted of a Byrd and a pledge having sexual intercourse with two girls at the same time, in the same room. They called this "going side by side." This, of course, was the one aspect of our group that the other girls and I were not proud of. We thought they were so disrespectful.

The girls in the clique were never used in the initiations. We were like their sisters, and were completely off limits to any kind of activities like that. Our clique was special. We were like one big family. We differed from the other cliques in school because ours was not based on superficial friendships and egoism. We looked out for one another and took care of each other. We loved to drive into Los Angeles and the club scene. That was our way of life outside of campus. We were always aware of the latest trends and fashions and were one of the first to sport them at school.

Obviously, the behavior exhibited by certain males of the Lakewood Spur Posse and The Byrds is reprehensible. With the prestige that comes with being a star athlete or a popular student should come the responsibility of setting a good example, of showing respect and restraint. If not their parents, then teachers and other persons in authority have their task cut out for them: to instill in these youngsters some rules of conduct and some good common sense.

Comments by Students Who
Have Been Ostracized

Another issue raised in our analysis of the four suburban high school clique structures was the impact on the student of being placed in a less prestigious position or social clique. What pressures were placed on the student to be selected or accepted into, and remain within, a particular social clique?

As the following statements of students who were ostracized by their high school peers indicate, being taunted and experiencing ridicule and discrimination were not pleasant experiences.

One male Asian student recalls his high school days, and explains why he chose to become a punk rocker.

> Like many other Vietnamese teenagers, I began to question my identity. Although I had made some American friends in school, they did not treat me the same as others. I was often made fun of because of my slanted eyes and my accent. Feeling left out from everybody, I started to go out frequently and was introduced to other Vietnamese teenagers who were having the same problem. A community of Oriental punkers was formed, and they fought and stole as a daily practice. I joined these teenagers and became a punker. Being one of them gave me a sense of belonging and security. It gave me an identity. In school and at home I paid little attention to anybody.

One of the so-named fashionable freaks in high school recalls her experience.

> We were shunned and made fun of. We were called freaks. We were different and not well liked. We were harassed. We had food thrown at us and we were spit upon. The attackers were primarily the jocks. We were treated worse as a group than as individuals. An example of this is how I was treated by my former "friends."
>
> When I was with my fashionable freak friends, my former friends and other cliques ignored me, but if I were alone they would talk to me as if I was still their friend. This angered me and I eventually cut off all ties with those type of people. I think the reason we were treated so badly is because people were jealous and envious of our individuality and they felt threatened by us because we were different.

A female student recalls the process of becoming a member of the punk social clique during high school, as well as the attending consequences this decision had for her.

Being new in school was hard, and I started to hang around with the "weird" kids. I had always been a straight "A" student, but suddenly grades became unimportant to me. I began to slowly get into more and more trouble. I had no curfew and stayed out all night. I met a lot of new people who introduced me to crystal, coke, acid, and other various drugs. I ditched all of my classes, and for the first time in life, I began failing in school.

I had also turned punk and my appearance was strange. I wore all black, including my makeup. My hair was short in some places, long in others, and ranged from white to orange to pink to black. I wore chains, crosses, and skulls. After getting arrested for possession of cocaine, I soon became tired of the whole punk scene—tired of people laughing at the way I looked, staring at me, and making fun of me.

Another Cal Poly college student remembers his high school experience, and his heavy involvement with drugs and alcohol.

Upon entering high school, I was exposed to many new people. In order to maintain my status of being a leader and high achiever, I strived to be the biggest drug addict on campus. All that was required of me to be in this drug group was to experiment with different drugs. It is just amazing what one will do in such a group situation. One example is drinking tequila every day for a couple of months in order to be with your friends. Another example is burglarizing houses, including neighbors and family friends, in order to obtain money and alcohol to party with. I know that these decisions would never have been made by myself, but with the help of "friends," the answer didn't seem to be very hard to come by.

During the time span from freshman to junior year in high school, I had become a complete idiot. My education assumed the lowest space on my priority list, and selling drugs and having a good time were at the top.

One college student recalls his rambunctious high school days as a "stoner."

Like many presumptuous teenagers, I was thoroughly convinced that I knew what life was all about, and anyone who didn't see reality as I did was a fool. I was basically a loner, ostracized by my peers; but I did have a handful of friends, most were in one faction of the "stoner" clique.

Stoners (at my school) cultivated the reputation of being wild, self-destructive, party animals. Our motto was SFB—shoot for a buzz. Most of us would snort some coke or drop acid on occasion, but for the most part, pot was the drug of choice, followed closely by beer. Stoners were, in my judgment, second in the social hierarchy.

Although the occasional drug bust would occur, a good percentage of us—myself included—would get stoned nearly every day. What was taking place in the parking lots and in the field by the gym was common knowledge. I remember one particularly brash incident: two students actually lit up a joint while a film was being shown by a substitute teacher. As I recall, the only penalty they suffered was not being able to finish the whole cigarette.

Another college student recalls his high school days and the "punk phase" he went through in this way, as he describes a typical high school punk party scene.

The people gathered were of various ages and interests. Several people, for the most part fellow high school students, were present who didn't display punk dress or hairstyle. Although not directly associated with the punk movement, they seemed to enjoy the social aspects of punk music or had friends who were punkers. The true high school punks made up the largest part of the crowd. Appearing in similar style and dress, they constituted the most visible and active of all present.

Many people, especially high schoolers, embrace the social, stylistic, and musical aspects of the punk culture without abandoning traditional forms of livelihood. They gain financial support from their families and in most cases continue their education and pursue a career. They seem to find in punk an identification with a cause, a quality which may be lacking in their lives. They seem to find refuge in the adoption of a style of dress and taste which provides an identity and enables them to stand out. This type of punk—which I was—is apt to look back at their affiliation with the movement as their "punk phase."

Still another college senior majoring in psychology examines what punk has meant to him.

> I was a "hard–core" punker throughout high school. I was the typical stereotype of a punker. I became a punker for individualistic reasons. I wanted to form my own identity and be different. Now that I am in college I have "grown up" after being a punk. In many of my thoughts and ideals, I still think along those terms. Instead of exploiting myself externally, I have tried to internalize my youthful rebellion and transform it into positive and helpful actions. I think that's one reason why I want to counsel people.

And, finally, one college student summed up her experience in high school and its relentless pressure to conform.

> Would I relive my high school years if I could? No, thanks! I really had a hard time in high school. The courses were interesting, but the peer pressure was just too much. High school in America is not really about academics. It's pretty much learning social skills. How someone interacts in a social setting is the main focus of secondary education. I feel this needs no further explanation because any high school graduate probably understands my point of view.

The Clustering of High School Cliques

There were similarities between the high school youth cultures in our study and those uncovered by Trow and Clark in their collegiate study. That is, as the following summary depicts, high school cliques in Southern California—based on this small sample of four suburban high schools—could be grouped or clustered in ways comparable to the four distinctive groups of collegiate, vocational, academic, and nonconformist subcultures found to exist among college students.

The first group is the *collegiate* student. These high school cliques would include the jocks, cheerleaders, socs, partiers, surfers, tweakies (laid back), and Barbie dolls. These students attend high school not just for academic reasons—most do plan to or hope to attend college—but for athletic and social reasons as well. Their activities give them popularity. This group also includes those "wannabes" or "poseurs" who try to gain popularity by associating with the more popular students.

The second category is the *vocational* student. They include the cholos, cha-chas, dirtbags, burners, beaners (Mexicans), rap groups, and sluts. In high school, moreover, these students are frequently tracked into the noncollege preparatory vocational classes such as woodshop, auto mechanics, and other vocational and agricultural programs for males; and typing, homemaking skills, and general secretarial programs for females. Vocational students also include those from traditional ethnic backgrounds who dress according to their (sub)culture's expectations. This group would include many of the ethnic gang members as well (although few gang members were present in the more affluent high schools analyzed for this study), and females who have reputations for being sexually active and available.

The third group found in high school are the *academic* students. These include a wide variety of high school cliques, including the brains, geeks or nerds, ugly pets, smacks, drama freaks, and bandos. The academic group affiliate strongly with the high school in terms of academics as well as specialized group activities or interests. These students generally excelled in some aspect of school life, but were not in the mainstream, popular high school cliques. These students would eventually go on to college, often getting admitted to prestigious public and private universities because of their top scholastic records.

Finally, the *nonconformists* were present in high school but they differed from the nonconformist of the college setting in important ways. In high school, the nonconformists, located often near the bottom of the school hierarchy, include the punk rockers, heavy metalers, death rockers, loners, and skinheads.

Although many of the punk rockers and heavy metalers in high school could be compared to the radicals, intellectuals, and alienated students of college, other high school youths in the nonconformist category would not be college bound. These include the more delinquent punkers, metalers, taggers, skinheads, stoners, and satanists. Furthermore, often their exploits as teenagers, both in and out of high school, would eventually bring them to the attention of the authorities and the juvenile justice system.

These *nonconformist* youths are the main focus of this book. But for now, the discussion turns to a more in-depth analysis of teenage youths who embraced some aspect of the changing punk youth culture. This discussion is followed by a subsequent chapter that presents a cross-cultural comparison of punkers and heavy metalers in Southern California and Christchurch, New Zealand.

NOTES

1. Jim Sanders and Patrick Hoge, "Truancy Soaring: Why Go to Class When Mall Beckons?" *The Sacramento Bee* (11 June 1989), p. A-1.

2. George Ramos, "Campus Styles Rekindle Debate on School Codes," *The Los Angeles Times* (25 December 1984), p. B-1.

3. Jane Gross, "Where 'Boys Will Be Boys,' and Adults Are Befuddled," *The New York Times* (29 March 1993), p. A-1.

4. *Turning Point: Gang Prevention and Intervention Project* pamphlet (12912 Brookhurst Street, Suite 385; Garden Grove, CA 92640).

5. *For Instructors Only* 9 (July 1987) (Emerson, NJ: Performance Learning Systems).

6. *Turning Point*, pamphlet, p. 4.

7. Ibid., p. 5.

8. Ibid., p. 6.

9. Ibid.

10. D.C. Dunphy, "The Social Structure of Urban Adolescent Peer Groups," *Sociometry* 26 (1963), pp. 230–246.

11. Ibid.

12. Ibid.

13. Peter L. Berger, *Invitation to Sociology: A Humanistic Perspective* (Garden City, NY: Doubleday/Anchor, 1963).

14. Ibid., p. 396.

15. R. E. Grinder, "Distinctiveness and Thrust in the American Youth Culture," *Journal of Social Issues,* 25 (2) (1969), pp. 7–19.

16. Robert K. Merton, *Social Theory and Social Structure* (New York: Free Press, 1957).

17. L. S. Lewis, "The Value of College to Different Subcultures," *School Review*, 77 (1), (1969), pp. 32–40.

18. Ibid.

19. Gary Schwartz and Don Merten, "The Language of Adolescence: An Anthropological Approach to the Youth Culture," *American Journal of Sociology* 72, pp. 453–468.

20. Gary Schwartz, *Beyond Conformity or Rebellion: Youth and Authority in America* (Chicago, IL: University of Chicago Press, 1987).

21. A. B. Hollingshead, *Elmstown Youth* (New York: Wiley & Sons, 1949).

22. Schwartz, p. 101.

23. Ibid., pp. 71–105.

24. David Ferrell and Somini Sengupta, "A Stain Spreads in Suburbia: Issues of teen promiscuity, forced sex and parental neglect rock Lakewood, once a bastion of morality. Many see the town and its unrepentant Spur Posse as symbols of a declining America," *The Los Angeles Times* (6 April 1993), p. A-1.

25. David Gelman and Patrick Rogers, "Mixed Signals: California's 'Spur Posse' scandal underscores the varying signals society sends teens about sex," *Newsweek* (12 April 1993), pp. 28–29.

26. Ferrell and Sengupta.

27. Gelman and Rogers.

28. "School Chief's Son in Sex Scandal," *The Arizona Republic* (30 October 1993), p. A-21.

29. Gelman and Rogers, p. 28.

30. Robin Abcarian, "Spur Posse Case—the Same Old (Sad) Story," *The Los Angeles Times* (7 April 1993), p. E-1.

4

▼

From Punk to Grunge:
Changes in the Youth Scene

"Arrest Made in Slaying at Rave Party"

Acting on a tip from anonymous callers, Los Angeles County sheriff's deputies on Monday arrested the half-brother of a 17-year-old boy who was shot and killed as he used his body to shield two girls from gunfire at a pay-to-enter party, authorities said.

The organizers of the house party in Lancaster said they had been determined to make it safe. Security guards frisked everyone who entered, and organizers said pit bulls were stationed in side yards to keep people from sneaking in.

But despite the precautions, Ray Love was fatally wounded while shielding two teen-age girls—one 14 and the other 17—authorities said.

His death has focused renewed attention on the popularity—and dangers—of pay-to-enter parties. Since 1990, two other deaths and numerous injuries have occurred in the Antelope Valley at such get-togethers, where minimal supervision and the mix of alcohol, drugs, weapons—and strangers—can lead to deadly confrontation.

Authorities say such roving gatherings—known as "raves" in many areas of the country—often operate outside the law. Organizers will advertise them by handing out flyers at schools and other places where young people gather. Targeting teenagers or young adults, the organizers charge a $3 to $10 entrance fee for parties, usually in a rented warehouse or hall, though private homes in quieter suburban areas may also be used. A disc jockey commonly plays music, and alcoholic beverages are usually served (1).

EVOLUTION OF YOUTH CULTURES

Welcome to the world of suburban rave parties! "Dance 'til you drop" parties are only one of several new trends to entice contemporary youths. Changes have taken place in the 1990s in their musical world as well.

In August 1992, a popular weekly entertainment magazine ran as its cover story, "The New Rock: Inside the Thrash, Grunge, and Punk-Funk Sounds That Are Turning the Music World Upside Down" (2). Discussing the current status of youth-oriented music—described alternately as "fresh," "abrasive," and "sounds like teen spirit"—the article noted that post-modern pop, or "alternative rock," was not a new phenomenon at all. It was merely an extension of music first introduced in the punk scene of decades past.

The detailed article went on to elaborate on several of the so-called new musical scenes shaping the youth culture of the 1990s such as: dream pop, death metal, alternative rap, goth, grunge, industrial, jangle pop, pranksters, thrashcore, and funk and roll, as well as UK dance pop. The article discussed each of these forms, listing their origins and current musical groups and songs that illustrated their special qualities.

In a discussion of *death metal*, for instance, the article stated:

> The aptly named death metal (a.k.a. hardgore) spits in the face of the blow-dried, power-ballad metal of the last decade. In bands like Carcass and Deicide, the front man isn't singing, he's belching. The guitars and drums imitate the rapid heartbeat of someone looking up as the guillotine blade falls, and the songs are obsessed with decaying corpses, the nuclear immolation of the earth, blood-drenched massacres, and other everyday situations. . . .

Goth music was described in this way:

> Goth may be the only genre that makes dream pop sound upbeat. *The New York Times* dubbed goth "mope-rock," a not

entirely inappropriate description for music whose archetypical fan is a depressed, lonely blob pondering desolation, suicide, and . . . maintains that spiky hairdo. The music matches that mood; dark and brooding, it is often built around sulking guitars and synthesizers—but with just enough spring to show that some desperate form of hope is up around the bend.

Another style, *grunge*, was noted for its strong similarities to punk.

Along with punk-funk, grunge is the style of alternative rock (that depicts) splattering guitars, aloof lyrics (and) unvarnished yelp(s) (that) are staples of the genre. Born out of '70s punk, the movement took hold in Minneapolis in the early '80s and has since migrated to the Pacific Northwest. Although grunge remains male-dominated, a wave of female-led grunge bands . . . show that women also can exorcise their demons and pummel their guitars with snotty abandon.

Finally, *industrial*, a sound that is getting a lot of air play, was described in this fashion:

Industrial sprang out of an early-'80s movement in Europe where bands . . . actually used shopping carts, pipes, and metallic odds and ends to create, er, music. Eventually, industrial became a little more polished and electronically driven . . . . As a result, many hard-core danceheads consider industrial to be dead, replaced by even more mechanized forms as house and techno. Still, there's nothing quite like it—the sound of a horrible accident on an assembly line, with a beat you can dance to (3).

All of these current post-punk forms seem to owe their allegiance, in part, to the earlier punk rock scene. And although by the early 1990s, few youths still dressed in the style of "Skidd Marx" detailed in the second chapter, the remnants of the former punk and heavy metal scene—albeit redressed, retooled, and renamed in one form of "alternative rock" or another—remain forces to be reckoned with when discussing disenfranchised youths in society. Classic-style punk rockers may have vanished only to be replaced or resurrected by a new form, drawing similarly alienated youths to its core, in this post-punk or alternative rock era.

Of all the youth styles to emerge in the past fifteen years, the early punk rock scene and its evolutionary manifestations have been the most mystifying and difficult to comprehend. In an attempt to understand this phenomenon, this chapter looks back at the punk rock scene as it manifested itself in Southern California during the decade of the 1980s. Hopefully, by gaining a clearer insight into the experiences that drew dissatisfied teenagers (or "slackers" as one movie dubbed them) into the movement at that time, we can better understand the issues that continue to affect the newer generation of teenagers who are similarly alienated today, and who continue to be drawn into the various segments of the post-punk scene.

We begin this discussion by examining some of the teenage punk rockers and their families who got involved with a self-help organization, Parents of Punkers, in the early to mid-1980s. This is followed by an analysis of selected letters written by youth and other citizens who responded to the appearances by these punk rockers on several nationally syndicated television shows.

Continuing, we cite and discuss a few of the letters that teenagers have written over the years to *Flipside*, a prominent Southern California-based "fanzine," or magazine, devoted to followers of the contemporary punk and post-punk scene. And, finally, we conclude this chapter with a discussion of what happened to some of the youth who had been involved with the punk scene in Southern California in its early years, a decade ago.

PARENTS OF PUNKERS

Serena Dank, a community counselor in the greater Los Angeles area, first became aware of the problem of teenagers turning to the punk movement while she was working in the early 1980s with violent youths and youth gangs in the city of Norwalk. School counselors had referred young punkers to her at the nonprofit Community Counseling Associates she and a colleague had formed.

During the course of five years from 1981 through 1986 Dank met with over four hundred families in the Southern California area. She also conferred with numerous other families across the country who were concerned about their rebellious offspring and had sought her out for counsel and advice.

Parents of Punkers was formed to help parents whose children were involved in the punk style, as well as the children themselves. The organization took no position on what should be the appropriate public policy toward punk although Parents of Punkers believed that many of the values and behaviors promoted by punk ran against the grain of almost all concerned parents.

According to Dank, when punk rock came to the United States from England in the late 1970s, punk rock's raw, aggressive sound "caught the ears of youth on the west coast" (4). Overnight, punk groups were formed in the Los Angeles area, appearing in a variety of teenage nightspots such as the Stardust Ballroom, the Starwood Nightclub, Vex, Club 88, Cathay De Grande, the Whisky-A-Go-Go, and Madame Wong's.

From the very beginning, the philosophy of hard-core punk rock appeared to be one of total anarchy. Youths were quick to "hold a beef" against anybody and anything that reeked of the establishment. The words of punk music often summed up the violence-oriented, uncaring feelings of many hard-core punkers. One such song of this early period, "No Values," proclaimed that one should not insist that everything in society is all right. Otherwise, youths might resort to violence and "start destroying" everything in sight, and "blow(ing) you away" (5).

According to Dank, not everyone who associated with punk fit the aggressive mold. Many punkers, including the poseurs or wannabes, were on the periphery of the main punk culture and enjoyed the music and the dress without embracing the total philosophy. For these young-sters, punk was "dressing up" on the weekends to attend the gigs at the clubs.

It was the "hard-core punkers" who were "totally into" the punk sound and philosophy that went along with it that Dank treated, and whose families she assisted. In interviews with the news media at the time, Dank gave examples of the violence and senseless aggression that were the standard trademarks of the hard-core punker:

> They'll go to great extremes to do anything that offends and
> defies society. I know of one girl who wore Rosary beads
> around her neck with a skull attached to offend Catholics. The
> friends of another girl I knew celebrated her 21st birthday
> party by slamming twenty-one holes in the wall (6).

Early critics of the violent aspect of the punk style drew attention to the "slamming" that took place on the dance floor of the gigs. When serious punkers got down and danced to their music, they did the "the slam." Much of the aggressive behavior observed at concerts occurred in the slam pits close to the stage where rockers would get tossed around.

Such rituals continue today, but the names have changed. Now, instead of slamming, teenagers engage in "moshing"—jumping up on stage, being thrown off onto the crowd, and passed around the tight band of fans that are close to the stage where the dance pit is located.

Moshing, like slamming, starts off with bouncing light on one's feet. The dancer begins moving to the left and right, then smashing—hard—into the person next to him. Usually, the dance amounts to nothing more than playful pushing and shoving. But at other times, fists are thrown, fights break out, and people get hurt. Some bands even pride themselves on the fights and ensuing violence created at their gigs.

In America, punk by the early 1980s had become the general banner under which everything from "Christian punk" to "devil music" and "art music" was lumped, spreading philosophies of anarchism and nihilism, along with a million different "isms" along the way. From the very beginning the punk rock scene appealed to the young. Both the bands and their followers were frequently juveniles barely into their teens. Even today, alternative rock concerts have fans in attendance who are 13 and 14 years of age, if not younger. Some of the members of the bands are barely older.

As Dank noted at the time,

> The abundance of crazy-colored hair cut in bizarre shapes, death shades of makeup, and the outlandish punkers' dress— along with the reported violence and self-abuse incited by the music—had many parents at a loss.
> Parents and kids were unbelievably alienated. Many kids had virtually no relationship with their parents, while the parents couldn't relate to punk at all and didn't know where to turn (7).

As with most youth cultures, their music was the glue that held the entire group together. Commenting during the early years of the punk rock movement, one observer noted:

> The music brings a lot of turmoil at home. It's almost like subliminal advertising. It has such an undercurrent of hate—it can be playing and you get bombarded with it. You read the words, and it's all negative. It upsets your entire life (8).

For Dank, an early concern with the punk music was the potentially negative effects it had upon younger children who internalized the lyrics and embraced the philosophy of punk without understanding the irony or parody in much of the music.

> Kids were initially attracted to punk because of its music and clothing, but they stayed in it because they liked the attention, even if it was negative.

The hardcore punk—in contrast to the poseurs—was the type of punk that parents were afraid (all) their children would become. The hardcorers were the ones made infamous on television and in newspapers. The only rule they lived by was that there were *no* rules.

There were punks who fell somewhere in between the hardcorers and poseurs. In full regalia, this middle-type, nevertheless, aroused concern since frequently they appeared harsher than the simple statement they were trying to deliver: "It's all right to be yourself and do what you want" (9).

For some parents, punk was merely a phase their children were going through. According to one mother who was involved with Parents of Punkers for several months:

> I did not mind when my 16-year-old son first started looking punk, although I questioned his Mohawk hairstyle. Punk is part of the maturing process for some kids. Kids in the 1930s wore long fur coats. I'm sure those parents went crazy, too, but it goes away (10).

Some of the adolescents, however, involved with Parents of Punkers did not agree with this view that their youth style was merely a phase. One punk rocker, interviewed while she was still involved with the movement, claimed:

> I don't picture myself dressing like this at 30. It's a phase, but not one that I'm going to grow out of. It's more a phase that I'll grow with (11).

Through the Parents of Punkers organization, Dank acted as a facilitator, educating parents on punk and eventually helping them to form support groups or networks of knowledgeable mothers and fathers whom others could turn to for assistance. She also conducted parenting workshops.

Dank's advice for parents of punkers is appropriate today as well for those families that are having difficulty understanding other youth styles that their children may be involved with.

Parents should know what their kids are into. To start off, read the words from one of your son's or daughter's record albums. Discuss what the words mean with your child. Hear what he has to say and don't condemn him. Try to get to know your kid.

Many children do things because of a need for attention or a cry for help. To gain a clearer understanding into the world of punk, parents should visit a punk club—or at least stand out-side—to see what is going on and what it's all about.

Parents need most, however, to learn to set limits that are compatible with the values they feel should be instilled in their children. Parents still have the right to set limits on their children. Love and limits convey security. And love will allow the limits to spread out (12).

VOICES FROM THE FRINGE

Parents of Punkers received much publicity during the years of its operation. Besides being the subject of countless interviews by the press, Serena Dank and her group were the focus of an extended article in *US* magazine. The novelty and success of her program also brought her to the attention of the television media. On two occasions she and several of the teenage punkers that she was counseling appeared on "The Phil Donahue Show" to discuss the punk youth culture. And Dank, along with both the parents and their punk offspring, were the subjects on such national and local network shows as the "Today" show on NBC; "Hour Magazine," a nationally syndicated special features show; and three segments of "Eye on LA," an ABC locally affiliated show aimed at the Los Angeles market.

Whenever the group appeared on television, the program and the topic elicited a great deal of response from the viewing public. Teenage punk rockers wrote in either in support of what Parents of Punkers was trying to accomplish, or in opposition to Serena Dank and her views on some of the dangers of the hard-core punk scene. Furthermore, other concerned citizens wrote in, voicing their opinions on the topic and on the kids that embraced a punk identity. In all, Dank estimated she received close to one thousand letters from persons who had seen one or more of the television shows, and who felt strongly enough about the subject that they took the time to write to her care of the television stations that carried the shows.

Copies of 105 of these letters were made available to me for analysis purposes. As the following edited excerpts from 20 of these letters indicate, the American public held wide-ranging views and attitudes concerning the entire punk youth culture.

Letters from Punk Rockers

Forty-five of the letters (43 percent) analyzed were letters written by punk rockers themselves. Thirty-six of these (80 percent) were supportive of the punk movement and youth style. The rest discussed parental problems. One letter from a male punk rocker discussed his efforts to escape the punk scene. One female punk high-school student wrote to denounce the stereotyping of punkers.

> I wish to criticize you for your generalizations and grotesque stereotypes of "punk" teenagers. I find it appalling to see that in our supposed modern thinking world, prejudices would still be based on a person's taste in music and clothing. Have you people any sense of originality in style? In these desperate times, we teenagers are searching for some way to hold on to our "selfs."
> I attend a school in an upper-middle-class area. I am enrolled in advanced academic courses, am an honor student, and am a representative in the Junior Class Council. I am heavily involved with the marching band, track, and *I am a punk*. From the shoes, to the hair, to the polk-a-dot leotards, I am punk. Most of the punks at school are on an unusually creative mode. Many are top athletes, musicians, valedictorians, artists, and cheerleaders. And most have a high academic standing. We are creative, fun-loving, and mentally and physically healthy people. And, I resent the implication that we are bizarre, warped cult-members. I hope you reevaluate your position.

A 16-year-old male punker defended his lifestyle.

> I am a "punker." I love life. I love my girlfriend, and I want to see my children grow up to be free from peer groups, death and many other things that face me today. I want you to understand something. I didn't become a punker to make friends. I became a punker to be free from trying to be someone I'm not. When I was a "rocker," I did drugs and alcohol. I fought my parents a heck of a lot more than I do now. And from listening to the music, I was depressed. Now I'm free from all of that. But one thing that makes me mad is that people won't accept me for what I am, and I mean "normal" people like the clones who run this world today. People stare at me because my hair is shaved on the sides.

One older teenager expressed concerns for the evils of a campaign against the punk youth culture.

> I have been listening to punk for five years, and I attend punk concerts at the local clubs regularly. Admittedly, punk has grown more violent in the last few years as "pogoing" has gradually been replaced with "slamming," but I never heard of, or saw, violence at a punk concert until it began to receive massive media exposure. In fact, I have yet to actually see a fight at a punk concert. It seems to me that punk is the least violent of all musical movements.
>
> Alcohol and drugs are sometimes present in these halls. But the pressure to imbibe is not stressed among punks as it is among businessmen and football players. Young people should be allowed to express distaste for the values and mediocrity of modern America.
>
> The violence associated with punk rock is the direct result of media exposure which draws thrill seekers to concerts. You are creating mayhem by attracting jocks, red-necks, and plain idiots to our clubs. Please, in the name of sanity, Stop! Please stop your media campaign which is destroying the good intentions of a once self-respecting movement. Punk is passe, but you are making it dangerous.

Many letters from punks, however, were written by teenagers literally "crying for help," as the following excerpt from a 16-year-old female indicates.

> I am a punk. I cut my arms, and recut the cuts to make scars. When I get angry or upset I have these urges to hurt myself. I love playing with fire and seeing how much pain I can bear. I guess I punish myself by hitting walls, and digging into my arms with glass. I guess I like pain or something. I mean I don't but I do. Do you understand?
>
> I picture myself doing all kinds of destructive—even suicidal things. Like running red lights into cars, taking a .22 and shooting myself in the head, opening the car door and jumping out while it's moving. The thing is, I'm afraid maybe I'll do it sometime.
>
> A year ago I started a new high school. I had a hard time fitting in basically because I'm shy and don't have much—none really—self-confidence. Well, the punks accepted me. I could

become a part of something. I cut my hair, wore the clothes, and listened to the music. All my friends were punks. I was sort of into the self-mutilation before and I fit right in. A year before that I was into a lot of drugs.

Another 14-year-old female, who signed her letter "Vomit," also discussed inflicting pain upon herself.

I am a so-called punker. I enjoy listening to the music I listen to, believing in what I believe in, and even self-inflicting pain. When I see the first drop of blood I actually feel a sense of relief and definitely no regret for what I am doing. Maybe it is not the best solution to my problems, but as of right now I have nothing to stop me from doing it except myself, and I don't want to stop.

I have a set goal for when I am a mature adult which is to be a psychiatrist (I bet I didn't even spell it right). It is probably a stupid thing for a person in my position to want to become because I probably need one myself but my mom and dad think it's a start.

Another teenage female wrote in to discuss how becoming part of the punk youth culture assisted her by providing her with a social group.

All of my life I've been a bit of a social outcast, with few friends. I have always dressed unusual, always been a brain, and always asked questions when others acquiesced. My depression and isolation hit a peak at the end of my fourteenth year and I started to cut up my arms with razor blades, and even burn my wrist to a pulp with cigarettes. This was all *before* I became involved with the punk scene. While I was trying to stop, or at least decrease my self-mutilation, I made good friends with punks at my school, and thanks to them and the other friends I met at the local punk club, I have managed to keep my suicidal and self-deprecating feelings in check most of the time.

Other youths requested assistance in dealing with their parents who did not understand the punk youth scene. One male wrote:

I would like some more information about how to relate to my parents better, and tell them I am not throwing my life away. I actually am not a bad kid. I get good grades, am straight-edge, and yet my folks are scared that I am becoming a derelict of society just because of my choices in music and clothing. I am so afraid of what my parents would think, that I can't even bring my friends over to my house without the thought of giving my parents cardiac arrest.

Likewise, a female wished her mom would support her more.

Can you help me get my mom to understand me? She doesn't know why I "have to do this" to myself, and doesn't get why I "haven't outgrown this stage yet." She doesn't understand that this is how I am. During these "discussions," I'm the one keeping my voice down and making sensible statements. But that doesn't matter because she doesn't even hear me.

I have friends whose parents accept and even support them. I'd settle for being able to leave the house without my mom having an ill look on her face!

One high school junior wrote in to complain about his parents' indifference.

My parents have decided that ignorance is bliss. If they ignore their kids' problems, things will be great again on middle-class "Respectable Street" (my dad's a doctor). Let me tell you this. I have been a follower of John Lennon's ever since I was a little kid. He was like a modern Christ to me. When he was assassinated, my parents didn't care—my dad even expected me to go to school the next day! They acted as if nothing happened, and they knew it was a turning point in my life. I tried to commit suicide but they didn't notice. My mom is an invalid, at home all the time, but she was too busy watching TV to care. I doubt if she would have even taken it seriously if she did find out.

Another 16-year-old female punk rocker wrote about her parents' failure to listen to her.

My parents don't seem to care. They say that people like me are sick and that we need to be put in mental institutions. They have not thrown me out of the house yet, but they are ready to. I had decided to try to leave punk after being in it for two years. I went to my mother and told her that I wanted to talk about getting out. You know what she said? She said, "Well, I am glad you finally came to your senses. I hope that you're fed up with that trash." I tried to tell her what was causing me to turn to punk. She said, "Never mind. I don't want to hear anything else about it. At least I don't have to send you to a mental hospital." That really did it. It did not help me one bit. It only pushed me deeper into punk.

Letters from Parents, Other Family Members, and Friends

Nearly all of the thirty letters examined that were written by parents of children who were involved in the punk youth style, or by other family members or friends, were letters quite critical of the entire punk movement.

One mother wrote a lengthy letter, pleading for help with her delinquent son.

We have a son that's been getting into trouble since he was 6 years old. Nothing serious at first, just his behavior in school. Without help it got serious. He was finally kicked out. We couldn't get him into any local schools, so we had to send him away to schools for kids with behavior problems, where he was supposed to get help, but he never did.

Anyway, the older he got, the more of a punk he became. The way he dressed, earring in the ear, the whole bit. We argued a lot. I tried to reason. I punished. Nothing helped. I remember when he was about 8 years old, I spanked him, and he ran away. Oh, he came back the next day.

My husband is a minister. We have prayed. He's gone to church with us. Our son was never interested. My husband has counseled numerous children and teens, and was able to get through to most of them. We both are really hurt, because nothing we've said or done has helped our son.

We took him to a psychiatrist, against our son's wishes. He said he didn't need a shrink. There was a big argument, but he went, after his dad insisted. The doctor's finding was, that he couldn't tell the difference between right and wrong all the time. That he was so very angry inside. When he could tell the difference, he was not able to stop himself from doing wrong.

He soon started getting in trouble with the law. It started with him stealing a bike. He joined a gang of boys later on in his life, boys that stole bikes. The guys were glad to have our son because he's very good with his hands. He can fix almost anything.

He seemed to get into trouble after each argument. We felt he was doing it to get even or to hurt us. He never realized that he was hurting himself. You see, he had gotten to the place where he didn't love himself, and yet he didn't know it. He still doesn't know it.

From the behavior schools, he finally went to jail, a detention school for boys and girls. He served 1 1/2 years without getting any help from a doctor. He came home after serving time. For a while he was alright. Then he started going out looking for his old buddies.

Our son smokes pot, drinks, steals, sleeps with girls, the works. Only 16 years old—you name it and he's done it. We have raised 12 children. He's the only one we never could reach.

Would you believe me if I told you, that he and his friends went out and stole a car. Well, he's in jail. His friends ran. He couldn't get out of the car so easy as he was driving. It was his turn to drive. When the police stopped them, he wouldn't name his friends.

I have a guilty feeling for feeling glad that he's in jail. My husband is always in court with him, and he's pastoring a church. I feel guilty because when he's out and the phone rings, I think it's the hospital to say he's been shot.

You're doing a very fine job. I sure wish there had been an organization like yours that could have helped our son. He used to be so nice. His trial is tomorrow. I hope you don't mind my writing. I needed to talk some way, so writing really helped.

One concerned father of a 12-year-old boy wrote the following:

Our son got into punk rock about a year ago. At first, my wife and I didn't mind it because all he did was listen to punk music. The only thing we did mind was the lyrics to some of that music.

One day he shocked us both by coming home with blue hair and a pierced ear. I didn't like it and I expressed my disapproval to him. He told me not to worry about it. Now, he has both his ears pierced (one of them is pierced three times) and he wears trashy clothes. He pierced his ears without our knowledge because he knew that we wouldn't have allowed it and no matter how much we plead with him, he refuses to change his style of dress. My wife and I are pretty liberal and therefore do not force him to change his appearance, but we do wish that he would listen to us.

He is a good boy but we are getting worried. He has started breaking his curfew and his grades have slipped from straight As to Bs and Cs. We are also very worried that he may be getting into drugs. We are hoping and praying that he hasn't taken any drugs and never will, but still, the anxiety is there. Our relationship with him has diminished quite a bit since he has become a punker, and I'm afraid. Afraid that he will start doing things that are bad and wrong. Afraid that we'll grow farther apart. I don't want that to happen. I want us to be close. Help us, please.

A concerned mother wrote the following:

My son has taken to spending his time with a rather unappealing group of fellows. They claim to be "into" the punk scene and have embraced what I define as clearly anti-social behavior. My son is a good boy, but he appears to have become carried away in his attempt to be a full-fledged member of the movement of the day. He looks and acts as if he were raised in a subway and has never seen the light of day. His music even exudes the monophonic drone readily found in a subway tunnel. Needless to say, I am concerned about his well being.

One parent wrote about how his son's punk behavior might be (mis)interpreted as a reflection of how poorly they, as his parents, had raised him.

Our son's involvement in punk rock has put a lot of strain on my wife, essentially because many of her friends have noticed his change in character. One of them even asked if he was using drugs. We feel positive that he would not misuse drugs. We are more concerned with how his behavior reflects upon my wife and I. His obvious change in behavior puts us in an awkward position when we try to explain it to friends. We are afraid that our friends may interpret his radical behavior as the result of the way we brought him up.

One mother wrote of her fear of her own son.

> I have been having trouble with my fourteen year old since his father died two years ago. I first thought he was just going through the regular teenage rebel stage, but then he turned very cold toward me. I can't talk to him anymore without him swearing at me and threatening me. I'm afraid of my own son! I don't even dare talk to him about counseling anymore. I had mentioned it one night after finding pot in his room. He just blew up. I was actually afraid he was going to kill me or something. It was a terrible scene.
>
> I just don't know who to turn to. I don't belong to a parish, and don't have any real close friends who I can talk to. I come home at night and just cry. I don't know my son anymore. He never speaks to me.

Letters from Other Concerned Viewers

Many people wrote in to express their concern about the punk rock movement and the punks that had appeared on the television shows. Thirty such letters were analyzed.

One self-proclaimed born-again Christian wrote the following:

> Punk rock is no good at all. Punk rock is of the devil. It is the parents' fault the way the kids act. The parents are out in some bar with some other man or woman, and their kids are on the street getting into trouble.

A woman wrote in, "greatly appalled" at what she had seen on the television show.

> The punks! Those rejects of society and no wonder. What a bunch of uglies. What a decay of our society they represent. They claim that they are dressed and made up as they are because they feel comfortable that way. I feel comfortable in my nightgown, too, but that does not mean that I wear it for work or play.

Their outside betrays their sick and evil inside. I denounce the "Donahue Show" for even putting those "uglies" on his show where youngsters can easily watch them and may follow their misguided attitude.

Not all the letters were from people critical of punk youths. One elderly couple in their sixties wrote to say they were in "partial sympathy with the crazy kids" they had seen on television.

Many young people are confused (to say the least) when people tell them "things are great—times will be better"—when they know they are not better and won't be better. I think patriotism is difficult to muster when you see that governments turn their backs on the needy and are more interested in building a great army and beautiful warships and a fascinating defense force than in their people.

Maybe it helps to dye your hair purple, wear arm bands, or fantasize. Maybe then you can feel like you are protesting the bad things you see, hear or feel.

A supportive grandfather declared, "If I were 17 instead of 77, I would be a 'punkie,'" and made these observations:

I know a woman who kicked her son out of their house because of his long hair and beard. She was ashamed of what neighbors would think. However, she did not mind that her husband cheated on his income tax, broke speed laws or took towels from hotel rooms. She does not mind that her church accepts money from a Mafia member. She is an anti-abortionist while favoring war. I prefer any punker to her.

My son's two children are punkers. Both graduated from high school in three years with honors. They are both welcome in their parents' home and in our home.

Finally, one letter voiced a concern of a different sort.

I have a problem like the "Parents of Punkers" have except that it's my mom that's the punker. I'm embarrassed to go to town with my mom because she colors her hair all weird. My mom tries to be with the "in" crowd, and it's embarrassing if some of my friends come over. Is there anything that you can send me so that I can show my friends that my mom isn't crazy?

LETTERS TO THE FANZINES

Fanzines are magazines that began in the early 1980s by catering to the punk youth culture. They continue to be published in several different countries around the world. Today, the magazines' appeal has broadened to those youths involved in the post-punk scene as well.

In the United States alone, there are over 150 such magazines, published on either a bimonthly or quarterly basis. The most famous of the fanzines, at least on the West Coast, include *Flipside*, *Ink Disease*, *Maximum Rock 'N' Roll*, and *Propaganda*.

Other fanzines that have been published throughout the United States include *Animal 'Zine* in St. Lawrence, Kansas; *Bad Meat* out of Bartiesville, Oklahoma; *Basket Case* published in Staten Island, New York; *Bloody Mess* from Peoria, Illinois; *Choose Your Fate* in Etters, Pennsylvania; and *United Underground* published in Houston, Texas.

Fanzines are also popular in other countries. For instance, *Alternative Punk* is published in Quebec, Canada; *Antrim Alternative* in Belfast, Ireland; *Pig Paper* in Ontario, Canada; *One World* hails from Auckland, New Zealand; and *Sub* is printed in Skannege, Sweden.

In each of the magazines, a typical issue includes the following sections: letters to the editor; advertisements for rock or punk bands soon to play in the area; comic strips depicting punk characters; advertisements for albums or record stores; feature articles on new or popular bands along with interviews; a pen pal section; a lengthy classified section; and many pictures of band members or fans standing in line at gigs or slam dancing or moshing in the pit.

One of the most long-lasting and consistently popular such fanzines, *Flipside*, out of Whittier, California, began publication in summer 1977, and is still in publication with January 1994 marking its eighty-seventh issue. Usually sixty to eighty pages in length, each issue is crammed with articles and letters from punk and rock fans involved with the current scene. Topics raised in the fanzine are often well-crafted and reflect the concerns of the day.

All of the following quotations are taken from one early issue of *Flipside*, published in 1982 (13). One young writer, for instance, bemoans the way the media have "ruined the movement."

> It really is a shame that punk has been so exploited by the
> media. I think that is where the whole violence bit started.
> The news was always saying it (punk) was "weird" and
> "bizarre." They treated it as if it was a Devil's cult or some-

thing. They flat out lied about it, saying that the people involved were violent, sadomasochists, who only wanted to riot all the time.

Such a thing couldn't have been further from the truth. We only wanted to be left alone and free to listen to the music we loved and what was wrong with that? They had to keep nosing around until they were sure they had it all analyzed in their little black books. Only what they didn't realize is that by that time there was a new generation of punks who were never into it until they read about it in the papers. So, thinking that it was all violence, (they) acted accordingly. Brainwashed, the media had won again.

Frequently teenagers write in to *Flipside* trying to explain what punk is or what it means to them. This young male fan described his affiliation with punk in this way:

Punk is people. People tired of shit getting shoved in their head. Conform. It's a fucking attitude, a lifestyle that allows (for) individuality and creativity. So I don't want to wear an alligator on my tit and prefer green lipstick to red or pink. That's my trip. I'm happy and my appearance reflects why, who and what I am.

People like to reassure themselves I'm going thru the rebellion my youth entitles me to. I went through my rebellion last year. I was a partyer (sic), took all sorts of drugs, and screwed up my head and life. Well now I'm 15 and got my shit together good, got a job, moved out, and still get myself to school. No, this is no fuck'en rebellion. There's no one to rebel at, except society in general. This is a lifestyle I've acquired, that relates to me, and caters to my individual needs.

Other youths write in voicing their disappointment with the direction the punk movement has taken.

This whole movement started with youth sick of what society had to offer. Now it's not that. It's changed to how many gigs have you been to? How many symbols do you know? Did you slam at that gig? Well, I think that's bullshit!

Another youth is critical of the punk scene as it manifested itself in California.

I'm beginning to think that California is like another country, all that bullshit about the "Cal Lifestyle" is almost true. Kids here seem to be affected by peer pressure more than other places. Being cool is the most important thing. Right now it's cool to be a punk in high school, so all the otherwise "loadies" and "too hip" people are "into" the punk scene. They're not punks and they blow the whole image.

Some youths see the punk culture as a continuation of earlier rebellious youth movements.

The revolution didn't start with punk. It didn't start with the hippies. And it didn't start with the beatniks. It started with the Pilgrims feeling the oppression of their countries and coming to the "New World." All the movements since then have just added to the momentum.

Another youth describes his involvement more succinctly:

I'm a punk rocker cause there's nothing left in American culture to conform to and we're all bored.

Or punk has been described in this manner:

Punk is chip on the shoulder, burden on the back, boil under the armpit music—indulgent, sniveling and essentially youth-obsessed.

Some youths use the fanzines to discuss what some of the components of the punk culture mean to them. One such male discussed his first experiences "slamming in the pit."

I was shocked to see the slam dance. So I thought, well I'll try slamming. I went there with a couple of my friends and we did it and it was so cool. It was so totally different than anything that the media had said. I can see how they (the media) have exploited what it looked like, but it was totally different.

That's what the media does. Unless they experience it, they don't know what it's like. They think that when you go in there and you're bumped real hard, that it hurts. It really doesn't hurt because you're on such a rush. You're just bouncing around.

Another explains his views as to why punk is primarily a male phenomenon and how females are treated at the gigs.

There is a lot of macho kind of things to do along with punk. The slam dance is kind of a macho thing. Even girls that participate in the slam usually do so by creating their own maleness. They are not out there in their spiked heels slamming. They give up their femininity and take on all the masculine characteristics.

I don't see a lot of the things that go on at gigs, so my girlfriend points them out to me. They are playing the same old games. The girls are there to pick up guys and the guys are there to pick up the girls. It's a lot more forward, I would imagine. I've been at gigs where guys would just ask girls when they walked by if they would give them "head."

In summary, the fanzines like *Flipside* have provided youths with the opportunity to express their feelings on a wide range of subjects of concern to them (as we have seen with just this small sampling). Over the years these magazines have come to serve as the rallying cry for the entire youth culture.

INTERVIEW WITH THE FOUNDER OF PARENTS OF PUNKERS

By the mid- to late 1980s, the punk youth culture had "peaked" in terms of its influence on contemporary youth culture. Although youth would continue to define themselves as punkers, much of the media interest in the punk movement as a *new* youth movement had long since passed.

One question remained, however. What happened to those youths—particularly the hard-core punkers—who were involved with the youth culture during its most visible, and perhaps most violent, period of the early years? What had happened to the youths that were counseled and assisted by Parents of Punkers? Had the punk movement been merely a phase for them that they would outgrow? Had these youths—several years later and now part of the twenty-something generation—readjusted to society? Or did they still view themselves as outsiders and feel alienated?

To address some of these questions, I reinterviewed Serena Dank, the founder of the organization, in 1991.

Q: How many youths and families did you treat and/or work with during the five-year period that Parents of Punkers was in existence?

A: I treated about five different families a week throughout the entire five-year period. In fact, I treated families from all over the country. There was one wealthy family from New York City whose daughter I treated for three months.

Q: How did you get started?

A: I had been working with Hispanic gang members, and female delinquents—mostly teenagers that nobody else could deal with. These were high-risk kids. Many had tried to commit suicide. Because I got a reputation of having some success with these kids, school counselors began referring their students who were involved with punk to me.

Q: Why hadn't these children been referred to other types of treatment programs?

A: They all had. Most of the kids had already gone through $60 to $80,000 worth of psychiatry. Their parents had run out of money. They had to turn to a nonprofit organization that was basically free for assistance.

Q: Were you successful?

A: Not one single kid I worked with ever committed suicide. Yes, I felt that I was successful with these high-risk kids.

Q: What were the reasons for this success?

A: I think it was due to the fact that I showed genuine concern. I made contact with these kids. There were not many people out there who could connect with them or with whom they could connect. The therapy these kids had received in the past was cold. These kids could always call me if they needed help. I was accepted by them because I was genuinely non-judgmental and noncritical.

Q: Have you kept in touch with any of those kids or their families?

A: Yes, particularly those who traveled with me across the country and who participated on the television shows. I just recently had lunch with Oliver's mother. Oliver's is not a happy story. A couple of years after I had worked with him, he got into trouble with the police for severely beating up two other young men at a party. For a while he dodged the police, even going to London to hide out. But he came back, surrendered to the authorities, and did one year in prison. He seemed to straighten up, but he never entirely got off drugs. He is now serving time and doing a drug-rehab program, Cry Help. It is a nine-month residential treatment program. Oliver is now 23. He was 15 when I first worked with him.

Karen (another former punker who was featured on several of the television shows) is 22 now and works for her mother. She didn't go to college. She, too, later went into a residential treatment program. She has been in and out of trouble over the years. According to her mother, she has not entirely given up drugs.

Karen's concerned older brother, Kevin (who, on the televised show, was the epitome of a well-rounded, stable adolescent), has gone off the deep end. The parents have since separated. (On the show the parents had appeared to have a strong relationship and be united in their efforts to help their punk daughter.)

On the whole, however, most of the kids did okay. Two of the kids that were on the "Donahue" show have done alright. One has had a baby, and the other, though not living at home, has a steady job and is off the street. All have survived. Only thing is that they didn't really change.

Punk wasn't the real issue in their lives. It was drugs. Punk was just an umbrella that these people ducked under. Drugs was the real problem. Punk is what brought them to me. Punk was the common line but there were other issues. Punk, it seems, just made them lost in time.

Q: Any thoughts about the whole punk movement and what it has meant?

A: What did punk mean? It was a way of expressing one's self. A way of saying, "I'm not happy inside or outside." A way of saying, "I didn't want any restraints or controls whatsoever." It was a form of rebellion for the '80s. Over the years each youth rebellion has become more dramatic.

Q: Punk, though, seemed to last the longest.

A: Not exactly. Hippies are still living in many areas.

Q: What attracts youth today? Are kids today on a new offshoot of what was the punk movement?

A: There is nothing like that group today. Everybody then knew that there were punks. But not everyone knows what is

fashionable today. Punks were the most extreme in the early
'80s and no real offshoot of it could survive. Society turned
away from punk because they were disgusted with it. These
kids were showing the atrocities of society whereas hippies, for
instance, had issues that others could relate to. No one could
relate to punk.

Q: Why did you close down the organization in 1986?

A: I couldn't get any support or money to run the operation because people were disgusted with punks. People were
appalled about the group. I stopped because I couldn't survive
financially. As a nonprofit organization I was dependent upon
outside funding sources. These dried up. Parents couldn't pay
me for my services. They ran out of insurance and their kids
had been kicked out of mental institutions.

Q: In the long run, did these kids plug back into society?

A: Of the kids I worked with, they have nearly all made an
attempt to plug back in. There were tolls, however. Two mothers of the core group that I worked with died young of cancer.

Q: Do you think their cancer was tied to their children's
involvement with punk?

A: Yes. Their deaths, I believe, were tied to stress and the
constant worry about their kids.

Q: How did the kids feel about that?

A: One had a baby out of loneliness, I suspect. The other
one moved away. He was devastated by his mother's death. In
their own ways, they each loved their mothers.

Q: Were any of the kids you treated confused about their
sexual identity?

A: Not really confused. But some of the punks who were
homosexual felt like outcasts. Not feeling accepted by society
because of their sexual orientation, they went and got a label of
punk.

Q: Do you miss working with the punk kids?

A: No, because of the pain. These kids were hurting and I
had the continual fear that I was going to lose one through
suicide. I wondered, "If one did away with him- or herself,
how would I survive?" The stress made me get out of it.

Actually I stopped the organization when I had been working with one kid for about a month, but his parents wanted
quicker improvement and so had him institutionalized. The

parents had brought a broken object and wanted a quick fix.
But I couldn't work that way since some of the pieces were
already missing. The parents 'wanted me to put the pieces
together but I couldn't create a perfect person. With time, possibly, I could have, but they wanted it all right away.

Q: Any other thoughts?

A: One other kid recently revisited me. She had done well,
going on to college. But, generally, my cases were extreme.
My kids had been sexually molested, had gender identity crises,
had slept with a brother. They were a different punk population. But all are still alive today which was something I didn't
think would happen.

What comes across from both the letters written by punkers and the
reflections by Serena Dank on the youths she treated is the loneliness,
sadness, and frustration that these youngsters experienced. As discussed
earlier, these juveniles are classic examples of anomic individuals—
almost broken in spirit by their sense of hopelessness and pain. It is truly
a great tragedy that so many people, including our youths, feel this level
of despair. For many of these youngsters being involved in punk at least
gave them a focus and a support group even if, as we have seen, such a
group in certain ways merely exacerbated their problems.

But to what levels do these alienated youths feel such pain? And
where does their dissatisfaction come from? What accounts for their
personal upheaval? To answer these and other questions, the study now
turns to a detailed examination of the Youth Survey and those youths
who self-identified as punk rockers or heavy metalers. In an attempt to
note whether or not these feelings are limited to youths in the Southern
California area, a cross-cultural, comparative sample was drawn that
examined similarly self-identified youths halfway around the world in
Christchurch, New Zealand. Their stories come next.

NOTES

1. Phil Sneiderman and Chip Johnson, "Arrest Made in Slaying at Rave Party,"
The Los Angeles Times (21 December 1993), p. B-3.

2. "The New Rock: Inside the Thrash, Grunge, and Punk-Funk Sounds That
Are Turning the Music World Upside Down," *Entertainment* (21 August 1992),
pp. 17–25.

3. Ibid.

4. Ina Avonow, "Parents of Punkers Learning to Cope with Problems," *The Los Angeles Times* (12 March 1982), p. V-2.

5. Jeff Goldthorpe, *Intoxicated Culture: A Political History of the California Punk Scene* (San Francisco State University; San Francisco, CA: Unpublished dissertation, 1990), p. 205.

6. Nicole Yorkin, "Where to Turn When Your Son Dyes His Hair Green and Blue: Parents of Punkers Attempts to Bridge the Gap," *The Los Angeles Herald Examiner* (28 December 1981), p. A-7.

7. Ibid.

8. Faye Zuckerman, "Punk Rock Sparks This Era's Generation Gap," *Daily News* (22 November 1981), p. A-8.

9. David Figura, "Group Advocates Parental Limits on 'Punker' Children," *Huntington Park Daily Signal* (24 September 1981), p. B-1.

10. Aronow.

11. Ibid.

12. Figura.

13. *Flipside* 39 (Summer 1982), (P.O. Box 363, Whittier, CA 90608).

5

▼

Youth Cultures in Cross-Cultural Perspective

"Who Cares What Parents Think? I'm a Punker"

Tina Terror leaned against a car in front of the Starwood nightclub and took a long drag from a cigarette.

"Yeah, man, that's my *real* name, Tina Terror," she said, running a hand through her hair, which was dyed in blond and black splotches.

"What do my parents think?" she said, repeating a reporter's question. "Who cares what they think? I'm a punker, man. That's where it's at, you know. Punking and slamming. That's the world."

Tina Terror took one last drag from her cigarette and crushed it out in the palm of her hand. Then she turned and walked over to her boy friend, whose bleached blond hair was cut Mohawk style and whose left earlobe was pierced with a giant paper clip.

Tina and her boy friend, Tommy Venom, both barely 14, then squatted on the pavement in front of Southern California's most popular punk rock club and shrieked obscenities.

Tina wore scuffed work boots, faded blue jeans and a white T-shirt with the word "KILL" emblazoned across the front in black four-inch-high letters. Tommy was dressed in black pants, shoes and beret.

His black T-shirt was decorated with the word "ME" painted in white four-inch-high letters.

When Tina and Tommy sat side by side, their message was difficult to miss—violent, self-destructive, negative (1).

"Punks in Christchurch"

It was mid-afternoon and getting chilly as I approached a group of punks and skinheads sitting on steps in front of Christchurch Cathedral. With their spiky hairstyles, frayed clothing and lace-up boots, they were a harsh contrast to the towering holy place.

Would they mind if I had a chat to them?

"I wish more people would stop and talk to us," said one of the group. "Usually they insult us, stare at us, and try to cause trouble."

"We are just people," piped up one of the men in ripped jeans, mohawk haircut and assorted badges.

Some of the group had held jobs, but lost them when they went to work with unusual hairstyles or wearing their particular style of clothing. Some still had jobs, and all wanted to work. None gave me any aggro.

"We are just the same as everyone else, but we just have different appearances," said one young woman. "We like listening to rock and roll music with a message, doing what we want, but boredom is a big thing. We just want to be accepted for what we are" (2).

Every youth generation since World War II has developed its own subculture set apart by distinctive styles and identities. The bobby-sox-ers and fans of Frank Sinatra, for instance, were visible in the 1940s. The Beatniks, Elvis Presley, and the beginnings of rock 'n roll influenced the movements of the 1950s. The Beatles and the hippie counterculture marked the youth subcultures in the 1960s.

For the past several decades, punk rockers, and more recently, heavy metalers, defined a sizable portion of the contemporary youth scene—at least as it pertained to middle-class, white males (see the discussion of high school cliques in Chapter 3).

What made both punkers and metalers distinctive youth cultures on an international scale were both groups' willingness to deviate from the norms of conventional society in terms of dress, hairstyles, speech, and music, as well as code of conduct. This was most true for the punk rock-ers who, in the early years of the movement, sported bizarre hairstyles and clothing that made them easy targets for public ridicule and abuse—often by the heavy metalers who, in their own way, were equally unconventional.

To much of adult society, these two teenage groups appeared to be indistinguishable. Both punkers and metalers represented a rebellious style, a rejecting of mainstream values and goals. Both groups seemed to represent a rejection of the more preppie, conformist choices of their peers—choices that reflected the conservative decade of the 1980s.

Even as recently as the late 1980s (when the research discussed in this chapter was conducted), punk rockers and heavy metalers remained two clearly distinguishable youth identities. By then, these youth cultures had lost much of their novelty and had diminished in shock value; nevertheless, their continued presence and activities remained disturbing and controversial to much of mainstream society.

In fact, much of the standard appearance of the heavy metalers (concert T-shirt, long straggly hair, and ripped or torn blue jeans) had become a conventional mode of dress for a wide variety of teenagers, regardless of identities. These standards of dress would continue to be embraced by the grunge and post-punk youth of the 1990s as well.

Even so, for those youths who self-identified as punk rockers (or "punkers") or heavy metalers (or "metalers"), that identity became all-encompassing; it defined their entire being. It often meant, also, that they would be treated by others in a stereotyped manner.

PUNKERS AND METALERS
IN TWO COUNTRIES

To explore to what extent such youth identities do create such problems for teenagers, a detailed study of youths in two countries was undertaken. Some 623 teenagers between the ages of 15 and 18 participated, completing an extensive three-page, 100-item questionnaire. (See Appendix B for a copy of "Youth Survey 1.")

Youths were contacted in both the Southern California region where 419 teenagers completed the questionnaire in 1988 and 1989, and in Christchurch, New Zealand, where 204 teenagers participated in the study in 1988. A comparative, cross-cultural focus was selected in order to determine to what degree significant differences might exist between punk rockers and heavy metalers in each of the two countries.

Further, the comparative analysis was undertaken to see if there were major differences within categories between the two countries.

That is, did punk rockers share similar attitudes regardless of locale? Likewise, did heavy metalers share comparable views regardless of whether they lived in Southern California or New Zealand?

New Zealand was selected as the comparative country because it was English-speaking, and, more importantly, the country also had teenagers who were highly visible—at least in the Christchurch area—in both the punk rock and heavy-metal youth scene.

METHODOLOGY

Teenagers in both locales were contacted in a similar fashion and asked to complete the questionnaire. Youths in both countries were approached in shopping malls—including video arcade areas, fast food restaurants, record shops, and other youth-oriented service areas; in and near high school campuses; in concert areas; and in other public locations where teenagers congregated.

Of the 419 surveys from Southern California, 117 youths identified themselves as punk rockers, 57 youths identified themselves as heavy metalers, and 245 teenagers identified themselves as not belonging to either the punker or metaler group. This latter group served as the "controls" or comparative group for purposes of the study.

For the New Zealand sample, 17 youths self-identified as punk rockers, 33 identified as heavy metalers, and 154 teenagers identified as not belonging to either of the groups, again serving as the "control" group.

Several hypotheses were formulated to test whether differences existed in the attitudes of the punk rockers and heavy metalers. These hypotheses included:

1. Punk rockers, compared to heavy metalers, would have greater difficulties in society, and admit to having more interpersonal problems, regardless of locale (California or New Zealand).
2. Punk rockers, in general, would share similar identities regardless of locale.
3. Likewise, heavy metalers, in general, would share similar identities regardless of locale.
4. Where differences in youth identities did exist between locales, such differences might be explained in terms of the more rural, traditional, and conservative nature of New Zealand society.

To test these four hypotheses, an analysis of the responses to questions from the Youth Survey was completed. The findings are discussed in the following sections under the headings of *background information, family relations, alienation and isolation,* and *school relations and juvenile delinquency.*

Background Information

Gender. Males composed the vast majority of youths who identified as punk rockers and heavy metalers in both the Southern California and New Zealand samples (see Table 5.1). In fact, over 80 percent of each of the three groups of California heavy metalers, New Zealand punk rockers, and New Zealand heavy metalers were males. And males composed two-thirds of the punk rockers in Southern California as well.

Racial Identity. Caucasians were disproportionately represented in the California and New Zealand punk rocker and heavy metaler groups. In fact, over four-fifths of the teenagers in these groups in both countries were Caucasian (94 percent of the heavy metalers in the New Zealand sample).

Table 5.1

Background Information

	CP	CHM	CC	NZP	NZM	NZC
I am a male.	67%	88%	48%[1]	82%	81%	59%[4]
I am a Caucasian.	86%	81%	66%[1]	81%	94%	75%[3]
I have no religious affiliation.	44%	30%	19%[1]	73%	66%	54%[3]
I am a Catholic.	23%	35%	38%[1]	20%	10%	10%
I am from a blue-collar background.	42%	35%	29%	71%	52%	33%[2]

[1]sig. <.001
[2]sig. <.004
[3]sig. <.01
[4]sig. <.04

Code: CP = California Punk Rockers; CHM = California Heavy Metalers; CC = California Controls; NZP = New Zealand Punk Rockers; NZM = New Zealand Heavy Metalers; NZC = New Zealand Controls

Religious Affiliation. The New Zealand sample indicated less interest in organized religion compared to the California youths. Three-fourths of the New Zealand punk rockers and two-thirds of the New Zealand heavy metalers reported no religious affiliation. This was nearly twice the percentages of the California punkers and metalers.

Even with regard to the California group, however, the punkers and metalers reported no religious affiliation in much greater numbers than did the control group. When religion was reported, a sizable percentage in the California group identified themselves as Catholics.

Socioeconomic Status. The New Zealand punk rockers and heavy metalers were much more likely to come from working-class or blue-collar backgrounds compared to the California sample. Nearly three-fourths of the New Zealand punkers and half the New Zealand heavy metalers reported parents' occupations that would affiliate them with the working class.

By contrast, more of the punkers and metalers of the California sample listed parents' occupations that placed the family in the white-collar, middle class. Perhaps the California sample's more affluent family backgrounds reflect the differential economic levels of the two countries.

Career Choices. When questioned about their own career choices, over half of the New Zealand punkers and metalers planned to hold jobs that would maintain a blue-collar status. In California, by contrast, only one-third of the punkers, and very few of the metalers, declared blue-collar jobs as their future career choices. The California sample was decidedly more middle-class oriented with regard to career choices.

Not surprisingly, therefore, the New Zealand punkers and metalers indicated they were not planning to attend college. In fact, over three-fourths of the youths sampled in Christchurch who identified as being a punker or metaler indicated they were not college bound. By contrast, nearly two-thirds of the New Zealand controls were planning to attend college.

For California, a much lower percentage of punkers and metalers indicated they were not going to college. The patterns for those youths not planning to attend college were consistent with the blue-collar occupations they had also selected as future career choices. Much more of the California sample in general indicated they were planning to attend college.

Family Relations

Table 5.2 makes it quite apparent that the punk rockers in each of the two countries felt more estranged from their families when compared to the heavy metalers and the control groups. The punkers in California and New Zealand indicated they spent a lot of time away from home and that they had nothing in common with other family members.

The punkers in both countries also were more likely to admit that they did not like their parents. In fact, one-fifth of the punk rockers in both countries stated they felt this way about their elders.

Punkers were also more frequently likely to state that they did not get along with their mothers; one-fourth of the punkers in both countries expressed these feelings. This was a much higher percentage than the heavy metalers or control groups in both locales.

Both the punk rockers and the heavy metalers were likely to report they did not get along with their fathers (compared to the control groups). Over one-third of the California punkers, California metalers, and New Zealand punkers reported that they were estranged from their fathers.

Table 5.2

Family Relations

	CP	CHM	CC	NZP	NZM	NZC
I spend a lot of time away from home.	79%	70%	62%	88%	55%	56%[2]
I have nothing in common with my family.	62%	40%	33%[1]	77%	30%	44%
I do not like my parents.	21%	11%	5%[1]	19%	10%	9%
I do not get along with my mother.	23%	14%	7%[1]	24%	16%	13%
I do not get along with my father.	33%	37%	14%[1]	38%	21%	17%
My parents do not approve of my lifestyle.	50%	28%	13%[1]	18%	17%	19%
My parents disapprove of my friends.	34%	33%	10%[1]	27%	17%	11%

[1]sig. <.001
[2]sig. <.01

Code: CP = California Punk Rockers; CHM = California Heavy Metalers; CC = California Controls; NZP = New Zealand Punk Rockers; NZM = New Zealand Heavy Metalers; NZC = New Zealand Controls

Accordingly, for the California sample, a greater percentage (compared to the control groups) of both punkers and metalers reported that their parents did not approve of their lifestyle, and disapproved of their choice of friends. Half of the California punk rockers stated that their parents did not approve of their lifestyle. Patterns for New Zealand were less clear cut. Fewer parents of punks and metalers in New Zealand disapproved of their offspring's lifestyle and friends compared to the California group.

One explanation for these cultural differences might be that California youths in this study were much more likely to still reside at home under their parents' scrutiny, and therefore act out more defiantly against this dependency and parental authority. By contrast, in New Zealand, many of the teenage punkers and heavy metalers had moved away from their parents' homes, which were located in the more rural farmland areas, and had migrated to the urban area of Christchurch where they could live more independently. More New Zealand youth had also dropped out of school. Thus, they were under less adult supervision and control.

In summary, with regard to family relations, the punk rockers in both locales were the most estranged. Although the heavy metalers in both California and New Zealand reported some degree of problematic family relations, it was the punk rockers that expressed the most discontent with their family situation.

Alienation and Isolation

Family estrangement was not the only form of conflict expressed by the punkers and metalers in these surveyed groups. Patterns of alienation from one's self, from one's significant others, and from society in general were also noted (Table 5.3).

Self. Addressing attitudes about one's self, the punk rockers in both locales were twice as likely to agree with the statement that they sometimes felt like committing suicide. One-third of the California punkers and two-fifths of the New Zealand punk rockers reported that they had felt suicidal (compared to 14 percent of the California metalers, and 20 percent of the New Zealand metalers).

Punkers were also slightly more likely to agree with the view that life was rather boring and that they were not happy with their lives, compared to the metalers and controls. In New Zealand, a greater percentage of youths expressed feelings of boredom. When questioned

Table 5.3

Alienation and Isolation

	CP	CHM	CC	NZP	NZM	NZC
Sometimes I feel like committing suicide.	34%	14%	14%[1]	41%	20%	16%
Basically life is rather boring.	29%	26%	14%[2]	40%	32%	20%
I am not happy with my life.	15%	12%	8%	18%	7%	7%
I do not have many close friends.	29%	33%	27%	24%	17%	19%
I only get along with people in my own group.	25%	16%	17%	31%	13%	5%[4]
There will be a nuclear war in my lifetime.	36%	34%	27%[3]	24%	17%	19%
I do not want to get involved in society.	18%	13%	14%[6]	24%	23%	16%
I would not fight in a war to protect my country.	48%	16%	26%[1]	47%	43%	25%
It is good for people to be rebellious.	55%	43%	54%	47%	43%	25%
Females are equal to males.	71%	55%	57%[5]	71%	80%	70%
It is not important to me that I fit in with some group.	74%	56%	57%	53%	53%	32%
I am a loner.	20%	17%	17%[3]	6%	37%	27%

[1]sig. <.001
[2]sig. <.002
[3]sig. <.01
[4]sig. <.02
[5]sig. <.04
[6]sig. <.05

Code: CP = California Punk Rockers; CHM = California Heavy Metalers; CC = California Controls; NZP = New Zealand Punk Rockers; NZM = New Zealand Heavy Metalers; NZC = New Zealand Controls

further, they said there was nothing to do in New Zealand. These feelings perhaps reflected the lack of diversity available within their more slow-paced, traditional culture (compared to Southern California at least).

For youths in New Zealand who identified as either punkers or metalers, there were fewer opportunities to participate in their chosen youth culture as well since there were fewer people involved in it, and fewer public places such as concerts and gigs to go to and be with others who shared a similar youth style. By contrast, in Southern California, one's weekends could be filled with activities catering to the punk rocker and heavy-metaler youth cultures.

Others. Reflecting their attitudes toward others, youths in the California sample, in general, had fewer close friends than did youths in the New Zealand group. One-third of the California metalers, for instance, (which was twice the percentage of the New Zealand group) reported they did not have many close friends. One-fourth of the punkers in both locales also reported few close friends. Further, one-fourth of the punkers in both countries expressed the view that they only got along with people in their own group. This was a larger percentage than that of the heavy metalers in both locales.

Society. Responding to questions about their attitudes toward society, over one-third of the California punkers and metalers felt that there would be a nuclear war in their lifetime. This more nihilistic view expressed by the California teenagers is possibly due to the greater presence of a nuclear threat in the United States compared to the more geopolitically neutral, and more remote, region of New Zealand.

Slightly more teenagers in New Zealand compared to California expressed the view that they did not want to get involved in society. One-fourth of the New Zealand punkers and metalers shared this sentiment. Quite possibly these New Zealanders were expressing discontent and an unwillingness to conform to, and accept, the more traditional strictures of their society.

Nearly half the punk rockers in both countries said they would not fight in a war to protect their country. A similarly high proportion of New Zealand metalers expressed an unwillingness to fight in a war. Among California metalers, however, only a very small group expressed an unwillingness to fight for their country. This was one of the major differences between the California punkers and metalers, reflecting their different political philosophies—with punkers more typically liberal and metalers more uniformly conservative in their views.

Nearly half of all the sampled groups expressed the belief that it was good for people to be rebellious. Interestingly, this view was also shared by the California control group who, it appeared, also valued teenage independence and autonomy, if not some youthful rebelliousness. Only the New Zealand control group expressed some reservations in this area with just one-fourth agreeing with the statement.

A more egalitarian view with respect to females being treated equal to males was shared by the punk rockers in both countries, and by New Zealand youths as a whole. For instance, four-fifths of the New Zealand metalers agreed that females were equal to males compared to only slightly more than half of the California heavy metalers. The California metalers, it appears, were the most chauvinistic.

In summary, with regard to alienation and isolation, the punk rockers' estrangement from their families also extended to an alienation from self, others, and society. Punk rockers in both countries expressed views that reflected the greatest degree of estrangement (they had contemplated suicide, had few close friends, and shared a belief that there would be a nuclear war). The California punk rockers expressed the highest degree of alienation and isolation of all groups studied.

School Relations and Delinquency

Several statements on the questionnaire detailed the youths' attitudes toward school, peer pressure, patterns of delinquency, musical tastes, and social issues (Table 5.4).

School Relations. A much higher percentage of the New Zealand sample in all groups expressed a dislike for school compared to the California groups. Close to two-thirds of the New Zealand punkers and metalers expressed a strong dislike for school compared to two-fifths of the California punkers and metalers.

Punk rockers in both countries also were more likely to feel that their teachers treated them poorly compared to the metalers and control groups. A greater percentage of all the New Zealand respondents, moreover, felt that their teachers treated them poorly compared to the California sample.

More California respondents in all three groups (punkers, metalers, and controls) felt that schools should not have dress codes compared to the New Zealand group. (It should be pointed out that in New Zealand, uniform dress in school was often the norm.)

Peer Pressure. One-fourth of the punkers and metalers in California and metalers in New Zealand felt pressured by peers, expressing the view that they were easily influenced by others. However, only a small percentage of the punkers and metalers in both countries expressed the view that they were put down by their peers if they did not do drugs. These percentages are somewhat lower than what might be expected based on the public's common perception of these youths as being subjected to intensive peer pressure.

Table 5.4

School Relations and Delinquency

	CP	CHM	CC	NZP	NZM	NZC
I do not like school.	42%	44%	20%[1]	69%	62%	28%[1]
Teachers treat me poorly.	35%	15%	5%[1]	46%	33%	8%[1]
Schools should not have dress codes.	96%	74%	68%[1]	53%	66%	39%[4]
I am easily influenced by others.	24%	26%	15%	12%	23%	17%
I am put down if I do not do drugs with the group.	12%	12%	4%[6]	10%	10%	5%
Other people my own age consider me to be a troublemaker.	34%	11%	5%[1]	35%	14%	9%[3]
In the past I have been in trouble with the law/police.	49%	37%	14%[1]	53%	36%	19%[4]
I am an aggressive person.	38%	46%	38%	44%	45%	38%
My friends are involved with drugs or alcohol.	71%	58%	35%[1]	80%	57%	44%
Kids today are more streetwise than their parents.	78%	68%	58%[2]	70%	71%	74%
Punk rockers are delinquents.	18%	44%	25%[1]	12%	29%	38%[5]
Punk rockers are a new form of gang.	37%	18%	22%[1]	20%	27%	28%
I listen to messages in my songs.	74%	48%	67%[3]	50%	52%	56%
Sex plays a role in the music I listen to.	54%	49%	40%[1]	47%	50%	29%[5]
My music is violent.	44%	23%	8%[1]	29%	45%	8%[1]
Kids who break the law should not be punished like adults.	47%	42%	29%[3]	53%	66%	39%
Marijuana should be legalized.	43%	54%	29%[1]	65%	60%	26%[1]
The drinking age should be lowered.	58%	55%	28%[1]	44%	50%	29%
Parents should not set dress codes for their children.	72%	54%	37%[1]	35%	42%	41%
The death penalty is not a good way to deal with criminals.	32%	27%	35%	38%	24%	47%

[1]sig. <.001
[2]sig. <.003
[3]sig. <.01
[4]sig. <.03
[5]sig. <.04
[6]sig. <.05

Code: CP = California Punk Rockers; CHM = California Heavy Metalers; CC = California Controls; NZP = New Zealand Punk Rockers; NZM = New Zealand Heavy Metalers; NZC = New Zealand Controls

Patterns of Delinquency. One-third of the punk rockers in both countries agreed with the statement that other people consider them to be a troublemaker. This was three times the percentage of heavy metalers in California and over twice the percentage of heavy metalers in New Zealand. Punk rockers, therefore, were statistically much more likely to agree with the view that others think of them as troublemakers.

Half the punk rockers in both countries also indicated that they had been in trouble with the police or law in the past. By contrast, just over one-third of the metalers in both countries indicated they had prior run-ins with the law.

Although the majority of youths sampled did not consider themselves to be aggressive, an alarmingly high percentage (nearly 40 percent) in each group for each country did view themselves as being aggressive.

More punkers expressed the view that their friends were involved with drugs and alcohol compared to the metalers and controls in both countries. In California, 71 percent of the punkers, and 80 percent of the punkers in New Zealand, agreed with the statement, "The kids I hang around with are involved with drugs or alcohol." For the heavy metalers, over half of the youths sampled in each country also shared this view. And for the control groups, over one-third expressed this view. In other words, a sizable portion of the total teenage sample had friends who were involved with drugs and/or alcohol.

This awareness and involvement with drugs and alcohol may help to explain the high percentage of youths in all categories for each country who agreed with the statement, "Kids today are more streetwise than their parents were at their age." Close to 70 percent in all categories agreed with this perspective.

Musical Tastes. Over half the youths sampled stated that they did listen to messages in their songs. Furthermore, nearly half the youths sampled in both countries for all groups agreed that sex did play a role in the music they listened to.

However, concerning the issue of whether their music was violent, some distinctive patterns emerged. More California punk rockers and New Zealand heavy metalers agreed with the statement that their music was violent compared to the other groups. As a whole, punk rockers and heavy metalers in both countries, compared to the control groups, viewed their music as violent.

Social Issues. No sizable differences by locale emerged for this last set of statements. Punk rockers and heavy metalers shared more liberal views, compared to the controls, with respect to the following social issues: delinquents should not be punished like adults (with close to half of the punkers agreeing with the statement); marijuana should be legalized (with over half of the heavy metalers and nearly half of the punkers agreeing); and the drinking age should be lowered (with half of the heavy metalers in both countries and half of the punk rockers in California agreeing).

California punkers and metalers were more likely to agree with the statement, "Parents don't have the right to tell their kids how to dress," compared to the New Zealand sample. Twice the percentage of California punkers compared to New Zealand punkers agreed with this view. And, finally, the heavy metalers were the most likely of all the groups to agree that the death penalty was a good way of dealing with violent criminals. Again, this reflects the heavy metalers' more conservative views on broader social and political issues.

In summary, based on their responses to the questionnaires, punk rockers in both countries were the most delinquent and alienated of the three groups studied. Compared to the metalers and controls, punkers shared the following statistically significant characteristics:

- had more troubled relationships in school
- believed that others saw them as troublemakers
- reported a higher percentage of trouble in the past with the police or law
- were more likely to have friends who were involved with drugs or alcohol

The teenage years, it can be said, are ones in which youth are sensitive about their appearance, lack self-confidence, and strive for acceptance and approval. With parental insensitivity to these concerns, friction often develops at home, and youths become vulnerable to the pull of their peers whose youth styles often offer excitement, unconditional acceptance, and creative freedom. As youths become steadily more influenced by a negative peer group, their problems seem to exacerbate. This, in turn, causes further estrangement from, and rejection by, family members and peers who do not share similar identities and values.

No society, it appears, is immune to such patterns unfolding. What is unique, perhaps, is the different forms that youthful identities take as well as the similarity in patterns that develop throughout the world. As this small cross-cultural study indicated, youth styles and fads—fueled by exposure to a common popular culture including movies, music, rock groups, and television—transcend national boundaries. And as the results of the Youth Survey demonstrated, youths who identify as either a punk rocker or a heavy metaler in such varied settings as Southern California and Christchurch, New Zealand, seemed, more often than not, to share a similar world view.

NOTES

1. "Who Cares What Parents Think? I'm a Punker," *Daily News* (22 November 1981), p. A-8.

2. "Punks in Christchurch," *The Weekend Star* (7 June 1986), p. A-4.

▼

PART II

Suburban Outlaws

6

▼

Tagger Crews and
Members of the Posse

"Complex Dynamics Shape Local Graffiti Phenomenon"

On a backyard wall, 17-year-old Shawn Carter and fellow taggers crackle mixing balls of Krylon spray paint cans and fill the air with hiss and vapors of red and black, turquoise blue and cream white.

"It's addictive, once you get started, it's like a real bad habit," said Danny Canas, 17, of his "tagging"—scrawling on everything he can find. "I quit because I've got to go to college."

Canas, a Cleveland High senior who plans to attend California State University, Northridge, said he has left his tagging crew CMF—Criminals Murdering Families. But he visits his friend's house where Carter's mother lets him spray "pieces"—short for masterpiece—in peace on the backyard wall.

The addiction has drawn thousands of teen-agers—who call themselves and their rivals "toys," "taggers" or "piecers"—to devote their time to "getting up" to attain "fame" by tagging poles, benches, utility boxes, signs, bridges and freeway signs in the San Fernando Valley with graffiti.

The taggers "battle" to see who can damage as much property as possible in a set period and area to achieve greater fame (1).

"Life's an Exciting Game of 'Tag'
for This Valley Youth"

As the war on graffiti escalates, so does the rhetoric. It thundered inside a Riverside convention hall Wednesday when about 400 frustrated and angry parents from across the county spent the whole day strategizing against presumably frustrated and angry teen-agers. "I have a problem with the term 'taggers,'" said one sheriff's deputy. "Visual terrorism is a more accurate term."

The adults shared tips on stopping the terrorists. Impose tougher sentences. Take away their driver's licenses. Show them healthy ways to find adventure. Teach their parents how to raise them.

If 18-year-old Paul had been there, he would have been a damper. Paul is convinced that adults can't do a thing about tagging—conference or no conference.

Paul was 13 when he began tagging, but the real rush came in high school where he found plenty of competition. "I'd say: I can do better than that. Then I made a crew. Me and a friend of mine. We went bombing together. . . . You just go out with your can. The bigger the letters, the better the bomb. The best place would be an intersection where everybody's going to pass and no one's going to miss it." Then came his arrest. "I was like, bummed. I still didn't stop though." On he sprayed, right up until he was sent to juvenile hall. "Before I left, I was one of the best writers in this town."

"The whole point of being a writer is to be up the most. To be up more than everybody else." Up. As in: up on walls. Up on billboards. And not just up. Up with style. The best taggers practice on paper, over and over, doing justice to their obsession. "Half of them are in it to do the right thing—the way it's s'posed to be."

Style or no style, it's vandalism. Paul doesn't deny it. But he regards it as you might regard driving. It pollutes the air, but you do it anyway. An unfortunate but unavoidable reality of modern life. Besides, "I never write on anyone's house. Or on a church."

The payback of tagging is respect. "Respect from your crew and respect from everyone in the valley. That's what it's about. *Respect.*" And good times. "You know people are looking for you, but they'll never get you. It's night. You're undercover. You're slick."

He hated juvenile hall. He hated boarding school. He hated disappointing his parents. Yet . . . "I still would like to be up." Especially when he sees the competition. "Every morning when I drive to school. I look up and say: Ooooo. That's a good hit! I could be there! I wanna go out and burn 'em."(2)

Welcome to the hip-hop culture of the 1990s. Once mostly the work of street gangs staking out their turf, graffiti, or tagging as it has come to be known, is now considered sport by youth from every type of neighborhood. The newest youth culture on the suburban horizon is that of tagger crews and posses.

According to police officials, as of 1993 there were 422 active crews in Los Angeles County, with names such as NBT or Nothing But Trouble that claim 400 or more members. More alarming, there were about 30,000 taggers countywide (3).

Referred to by a variety of names—including "graffiti bands," "tagger crews," "posses" (or mob or tribe), "piecers" (because they draw masterpieces or works of art), "housers," or "snappers,"—taggers have sprawled their three-letter monikers over the landscape of Southern California. And as their fad gains more fame, the markings of taggers will likely spread across the country as well.

Dressed in the standard garb of cockeyed baseball caps, flannel shirts, hoop earrings, and low-slung, often oversized trousers, the taggers— armed with spray-paint cans, which they often shoplift, or Mean Streak marking pens—are ready for play. Some taggers, according to police officials, even carry beepers to call for backup if they are challenged by rival tagger crews.

Some parents, knowing their kids are into tagging, let them tag the walls of their room, or the inside of a backyard wall. According to one press report, one mother, whose son was in the eighth grade, told her he had joined a tagging crew. She indicated that setting aside the wall meant that her son and his friends would have a safe outlet to express themselves.

> My first reaction was to be really upset. I had just heard of graffiti. I'm a cool mom, is what I am. I allow them to express themselves within boundaries. Parents don't understand what tagging represents. I didn't understand it at first. It took me a long time to understand it. It's their identity. It's who they are, it's what they are all about (4).

THE DYNAMICS OF TAGGING

Why do youngsters tag? Similar to standard explanations for the presence of traditional, inner-city ethnic gangs is the view that tagging provides these suburban youths with a form of status. It is a declaration of "here I am." Being a member of a group or crew and splashing their tags on overhead freeway signs—referred to as "mapping the heavens"—for instance, tells others "who we are" in a big way. Another view explains the presence of suburban taggers as a response to the ethnic gangs that may be spreading into their geographical areas. To more middle-class youths, tagging becomes a symbolic defiance of inner-city urban gangs—a stark means of saying, "I'm (or we're) not afraid of ethnic gangs!"

But tagger crews are not merely the newest form of youth culture. On the contrary, according to police, their behavior has moved beyond being a simple fad. Older taggers now carry guns for protection and to be "cool." This is referred to as "tag-banging." Yet, most taggers insist they are peaceful and they do not want to "tag bang," or escalate the use of weapons to attack tag rivals. Still others, according to police, have turned to committing other crimes such as burglary and auto theft.

What is tagged varies by the age of the tagger. The younger taggers, ages 10 to 15, typically mark school grounds and property. Older teenagers, besides defacing the overhead freeway signs, target walls, public transportation such as buses and trains, and other public areas such as traffic signs, bridges, and street poles. In effect, anything that can be viewed by the public is fair game to these graffiti vandals. Less geographically bound to protecting a particular neighborhood turf than are the ethnic and inner-city gangs, the taggers spread their marks far and wide on their nightly runs.

Typically, taggers declare all public buildings and edifices as their "turf" to display their art, whereas ethnic gangs limit their gang graffiti to the neighborhood boundaries of the gang. Taggers are driven by a need to gain "instant fame" as their "work of art" is viewed by everyone. They "battle" with rival tagger crews to see who can damage as much property as possible in a given area in a set period of time—typically a week—with someone preselected as judge to declare the winner.

The Lexicon of Taggers

Along with the dress and behavior has come an entire lexicon of tagger terms including, but not limited to, the following, listed in a Southern California newspaper:

- *all city*—tagging all over, not just in one area
- *homies*—fellow members of your crew
- *kicking it*—to relax with your homies

- *toy*—a novice, amateurish tagger
- *ranker*—a person who chickens out, does not defend his tag
- *slipping*—being caught by rival taggers without homies to back you up
- *kill or kill a wall*—to completely cover with graffiti
- *seek and destroy*—to tag everything in sight
- *to be down*—to be a dedicated tagger, accepted by your crew
- *to get up*—to spread your tag in as many places as possible
- *to be rank*—to have the privilege of deciding who is in and out of your crew
- *hero*—an adult who would turn in a tagger
- *landmark*—a prime spot where a tag will not be erased
- *to be buffed*—to have a tag cleaned off by authorities
- *to be crossed out*—to have a tag erased by a rival tagger (5)

Still more terms were found in another newspaper:

- *bomb*—to put a series of large letters on a wall usually in more than one color
- *bombing run*—when a tagging crew comes together for the express purpose of putting up as many of their tag names and the name of their crew as they can
- *def*—a really good tagger who is considered to be "cool"
- *dis*—to disrespect someone by writing over or on another tagger's work
- *fresh*—pieces of tagging styles that are considered good
- *head*—the best tagger in a crew artwise
- *jack*—to steal a tagger's supplies, usually by robbery
- *jump-in/out*—like street gangs, several members will beat a person who wants to get into the crew or who wants to leave the crew
- *mob*—putting as much graffiti on an object as possible; usually in a short period of time
- *rack*—stealing, shoplifting paint, markers, etc.
- *rolled-up*—arrested
- *slash*—to cross out another tagger's/crew's name; meant as an insult or challenge
- *spot*—a store to shoplift from, which is kept a secret from other taggers

- *take-out*—to defeat another tagger/crew in battle
- *throw-ups*—put large bubble-style letters on an object
- *wild style*—unique style of tagging that exhibits overlapping letters (6)

Police Definition of Taggers

Because of the widespread, wanton destructive nature of taggers, police have had to come up with definitions and criteria for tagger identification. Four such criteria have been developed that assist authorities in arresting and charging graffiti vandals. These criteria include:

1. when an individual admits to being a tagger;
2. when a reliable informant identifies an individual as a tagger;
3. when an informant of previously untested reliability identifies an individual as a tagger and it is corroborated by independent information; and
4. when an individual has been arrested several times in the company of identified taggers for offenses consistent with usual tagger activity (7).

THE PROLIFERATION OF TAGGERS

With over 600 tagger crews identified by the police in Los Angeles County alone, the tribes have developed a variety of names or monikers. AAA, for instance, stands for Against All Authority. Some of the more prolific crews include: TIK, Think I Kare; KMT, Kings Making Trouble; CMF, Criminals Murdering Families; EWF, Every Woman's Fantasy; KNP, Knock Out Posse; and INF, Insane Family.

Other tagger names colorfully depict the nature of their activity: ABC, Artist By Choice; ACK, Artistic Criminal Kings; AIA, Artists in Action; APT, Ambushing Public Transit; BCA, Best Creative Artist; BLA, Bombing Los Angeles; CFK, Crazy Fucking Kids; CMC, Creating Mass Confusion; DFA, Defiest Boys Around; DCP, Destroying City Property; and ETC, Elite Tagger Crew, to name but a few.

Taggers are not just limited to white juvenile males. Several tagger crews reflect both ethnic and gender diversity: TWM, Tagging With

Mexicans; TUL, Three United Ladies; UMK, United Mexican Kings; and RSK, Rasta Social Kings.

To the critics of taggers and to the general public fed up with the mess these youngsters have caused, TWY—Totally Wasted Youth— seems to, unfortunately, aptly size up the situation.

What Brought About the Rise of Taggers?

The tagger scene appears to be behavior that started out as an innocent form of youth culture. Known initially as "party crews" or "housers," these were youths who organized underground parties and liked to invent new dance steps. A spinoff of "house parties" and the hip-hop dress of the early 1990s, they have come up with unusual sounding names for themselves. Like every type of clique, they travel in groups, make up T-shirt designs, and on weekends and after school gather for social occasions.

The popularity of becoming part of the tagger scene also seems to stem from suburban white youths' interest in gangsta rap, the currently popular music of some black urban youths. Enjoying hip-hop music and "getting down" becomes, for these white "home boys," their form of replicating inner-city, black ghetto "chic."

To one observer, tagger crews and posses are merely a new form of seeking a distinctive identity and gaining recognition.

> For kids, the hip lexicon of the day is to call your friends your posse. It's the influence of the street culture on kids who don't necessarily want anything to do with the street. You know, suburban kids who listen to rap and hip-hop music. They think they're Marky Mark and the Funky Bunch. Posses are the way kids seek recognition (8).

But others see taggers in the 1990s as not a new youth phenomenon at all, pointing to a group of people in the early 1970s in New York City who called themselves "TAG" for "Tough Artist Group." In fact, according to one police official, tagging crews in Southern California first appeared in the early 1980s when youngsters began writing graffiti in an exaggerated balloon-type style of writing referred to as "bombing." The most famous "graffiti artist" in the late 1980s was a youth who used the moniker "Chakka."

Another explanation given for the presence of tagger crews is the response by suburban youths—at least in the Southern California area where they have first emerged on a grand scale—to the increasing diffusion of traditional inner-city ethnic gangs outward into suburbia. Rather than merely mimicking the delinquencies and vandalism of these urban youths, suburban tagger crews are forming to compete with or oppose them. In effect, the taggers have reversed the direction of gang diffusion from inner-city outward. That is, the tagger's movement patterns—and night runs—frequently are from suburban areas along the freeways back toward the inner-city, leaving their marks or pieces (calling cards) to indicate their presence and influence along the way.

In this regard, tagging is to these blue- and white-collar suburban youths what traditional graffiti is to lower-income, traditional ethnic gangs. Tagging becomes a response to gang diffusion. As stated earlier, it is a rallying cry, claiming, "We will not be overlooked. We will not be trampled on."

According to this view, the actions of taggers are similar to that of racist skinheads, the topic of the next chapter, in that they have arisen in response to ethnic diffusion. Teenage racist skinheads emerged in suburbia in response to ethnic and minority families moving into formerly, generally all-white neighborhoods. Whereas taggers symbolically leave their mark, racist skinheads have resorted to different forms of recourse.

In some ways, tagging is more of a "passive-aggressive" act; one is not striking out against a particular person or group. Instead, one is attacking—through tagging—the symbols or mere edifices of society. Like juvenile firesetting (the focus of a previous study I conducted), a youngster who tags buildings is being less confrontational than overtly or personally attacking his or her enemy or antagonist. Defacing a street sign, moreover, is a less drastic form of "crying for help" than torching the local school.

Differences between Taggers and Traditional Gangs

Several differences have been noted between tagger crews and traditional inner-city ethnic gangs. For one, the name of an individual tagger as well as one's crew can often change. However, like the traditional gang, one's name, nickname, or moniker—which becomes one's personal tag—may reflect one's physical appearance or personality quirk. One youngster interviewed is named "Lurk" because he lurks or hides behind bushes.

Not all taggers belong to a tagging crew. Some prefer to work alone. By contrast, gang members—or "OG's" for "Original Gangsters" as they are now more commonly called—nearly always "hang with their homies," maintaining steady group interaction.

Interview with Members of a Tagger Crew

In an extensive interview I conducted with four members of one tagger crew, the KMTs: Kids Making Trouble (not their real name), the adolescents said there was no detailed organizational structure to their group. One 15-year-old, "Jerry," explained,

> The only organization we have is when we are in a battle. A battle is when two or more crews get together and pick an area to tag. When we do it, the battle lasts one week. Whichever crew has their name up the most is the winner.

These tagger members also contend that, unlike gangs, they do not have any special type of initiation process. None of them were "jumped in" as is the case with traditional gangs. (Police, however, claim that tagger crews are starting to use jump-ins to initiate new members.) One 16-year-old, "Travis," maintained,

> The only thing that matters is if the other members like your (art) work. You just give them a sample and they will tell you if they like your style. That's what's important to get you accepted.

Unlike traditional gangs, taggers are not territorial. There are rarely any boundaries for a tagger. Whereas traditional gangs build up and maintain their group, taggers drift in and out of crews, often changing their names whenever they tire of the old one. The number of taggers within a crew fluctuates since it is so easy to get in or out of these groups.

The taggers interviewed indicated that the members of these crews come from all socioeconomic backgrounds and races. As another teenage tagger, "Kevin," explained,

> Taggers want to get along with gangs. We are afraid of gangs in our community. All we want is to be able to write on walls. So long as we do not write over the gang names, we are safe. However, if a crew does write over a name of a gang, they must arm themselves. This is when taggers become violent. Some gangs now require "payoffs" for taggers to move through their areas.

In response to a question of what type of weapons taggers might use to defend themselves, this juvenile replied,

> Taggers will disguise chisels in pens. These are not only for pro-tection but to permanently write on windows. One of our greatest concerns is that at night, gangs will mistake us taggers for a rival gang member and shoot us.

Kevin maintained that at first they tagged because it was fun and exciting, but fame soon took over for the initial fear they experienced.

> Everyone knows who you are. They recognize your tag. My par-ents at first were angry and upset, particularly when the police arrested me. But after awhile they compensated for my behavior. They told the police, "Well, at least my kid's not shooting people. He's still alive."

In discussions with another teenager, "Fred," a self-proclaimed 18-year-old "former tagger," he indicated that tagging, for him, was just a fad.

> Tagging is associated with clothes and music which always changes. My friends and I quit tagging because after awhile, it became boring. Now we throw rave parties. This is much more profitable. (Taggers often overlap in membership to "dance crews," who attend rave parties.) We have mandatory searches for weapons on entering guests. No one is discriminated against. Anyone can attend these parties for a couple of bucks. The goal of these parties is to make money. The profits go toward throwing bigger and bigger parties."

The taggers interviewed for this study did not believe that what they do is a crime. They felt strongly that their tagging was art and an expression of themselves. "When confronted by the police," one tag-ger told me, "I felt insulted because he called my 'pieces' graffiti!"

PENALTIES FOR TAGGING

Unfortunately, taggers are driven by a desire to inflict increasing destruction in order to achieve notoriety among fellow crew members. In the past, taggers knew that, if caught, they would only be charged with a misdemeanor offense. However, this is changing. Community officials and the law, in order to develop some deterrent for these juve-niles, have submitted legislative proposals to make graffiti and "vandal-ism with priors" carry stiffer penalties.

In the past, depending on the jurisdiction, youths arrested for tagging were charged with the crime of vandalism and sentenced to 200 hours of community service or work. One new·proposal, the "Anti-Graffiti Ordinance," would if approved charge the first-time offender with a misdemeanor carrying a $500 fine or a six-month jail sentence.

Others have argued for a variety of different ways to deal with the problem. Some people have indicated a desire for the presence of a "Graffiti Court" to prosecute vandals apart from the traditional juvenile justice system and to offer different forms of community-diversion programs to assist these delinquents. Others want a civil lawsuit filed against the parents of taggers for not being more responsible in the upbringing of their children.

Ordinances in several cities now require parents to pay criminal fines or participate in the cleanup if their children are convicted of vandalism. First Offender programs, and ones such as Short-Stop in Orange County, mandate that parents and their delinquent offspring attend joint meetings and workshops to address the problem. Other communities have proposed fining parents up to $1,000 for tagging by their teenagers as well as denying the youth a driver's license until age 18 if convicted of vandalism. These are similar responses to those recommended by concerned citizens.

Other communities in Southern California have ordinances that require merchants to place spray-paint cans and large marking pens behind the counter or in locked shelves where they cannot be easily reached by the public. Varnish, paint thinner, and other materials that can be used as inhalants are now kept out of reach so that juveniles do not gain access to them to get high. In San Diego, for instance, the city has begun a program called "Responsible Retailers," which assists stores with ways to reduce the theft of graffiti tools.

Currently before the California state legislature is a bill to amend the state penal code on vandalism so that anyone so charged will be as an individual who "maliciously sprays, scratches, writes on, or otherwise defaces, damages, or destroys any real or personal property not his or her own." The amended bill distinguishes between types of punishment based on the amount of defacement, damage, or destruction. In general, a youth may not only be charged or fined for the amount of damage caused, up to $50,000, but may also face imprisonment for up to one year.

Also included in this pending legislation are several new laws restricting the sales and possession of aerosol containers of paint. Under the new ruling, for instance, it would be unlawful for any person under the age of 18 to purchase an aerosol container of paint that is capable of defacing property. Further, retailers that carry aerosol cans must post a sign informing potential customers that anyone maliciously defacing property with paint will be guilty of vandalism punishable by the new fine, imprisonment, or both.

Other communities make it illegal to allow graffiti to remain on private property. In San Diego that has become a law that is strictly enforced. According to an editorial in *The San Diego Union-Tribune*, "Tracking Taggers," there should be a law that extends to public property as well, along with one that would call for the expeditious removal of graffiti from freeway signs. To further crack down on these visual terrorists, city officials make presentations to community groups on how to prevent graffiti, how to organize paintouts, and how to tell if one's children are involved in tagging. The city also provides free, recycled paint for covering up unwanted markings (9).

There is every likelihood that the legislation previously mentioned will pass in California, if for no other reason than to serve as a deterrent and to cut dollar losses created by these graffiti vandals. The National Graffiti Information Network reports that tagging and other graffiti is a $4.5 billion problem nationwide. Locally, the city of Los Angeles spends $4 million per year on cleanup. According to Rapid Transit District Officials, removing graffiti from buses and RTD facilities costs $13 million per year or $1.1 million per month! The RTD made close to 1,000 arrests for vandalism on buses in 1992, a 101 percent increase over 1991 (10).

California is not the only locale in recent years where taggers have left their mark. On the East Coast as well, city councils have drafted new measures that would require buyers of spray paint to give their names and addresses to the salesperson. According to one report, more than 8,000 spray cans are used daily to deface property nationwide. New York City outright bans the sales of spray paint to minors (11).

Other Deterrents

New legislation is not the only line of attack to combat graffiti vandals and taggers. Police now use high-tech infrared equipment to spot taggers. Other departments not only set up stings to arrest taggers, they use a computer system to identify and track them by their tags and locations. Further, once a tagger is apprehended and provides police with information, it can be used to log and track other graffiti vandals.

The planting of more plants and shrubbery close to freeway walls also deters graffiti artists. And the placement of coils of razor wire—like that used to prevent inmates from escaping prisons—has been effective in keeping taggers off the freeway signs and overpasses.

Community watch groups are also on the lookout for taggers. According to one newspaper report:

> Others (citizens) have joined nighttime surveillance missions, some using infrared video cameras operated by remote control or peering from rooftops with binoculars, to help police arrest more of the region's thousands of taggers. Police also are asking residents to assist them by filing crime reports and taking photographs so that damage can be catalogued (12).

Other public officials say another way to combat tagging is to develop more art and recreation programs for youngsters. Other communities have developed anti-graffiti curricula for grade school students with a special emphasis on stressing kids' responsibilities to their community. Still other communities have set up 12-step recovery programs dubbed "Taggers Anonymous" for juveniles addicted to the rush of adrenaline they get from tagging. Youths on probation for tagging offenses are ordered by the courts to attend these group self-help meetings.

But the presence of tagger crews points to a general breakdown in society—a lack of respect for other people's property, and the increasing indifference and insensitivity that some youths have toward others and society in general.

The destruction of the public landscape by tagger crews and traditional gangs has increased the anger of the citizenry and sparked a desire for retribution. Fueled by a sense of duty to one's community, anti-graffiti activism now has a militant edge to it. "Enough is enough," people seem to be saying.

One newspaper account reported the following:

> At a recent San Pedro meeting to discuss the battle against graffiti, a member of the audience suggested cutting a tagger's hand off for a first offense. The comment drew cheers. In Encino, those at a meeting of a new anti-graffiti group spoke facetiously of hanging, shooting and castrating the vandals. The name of that group, Residents Against Graffiti Everywhere, or RAGE, emphasizes the emotions surrounding the issue (13).

These actions, of course, are not the answer. More appropriate social responses would be those previously mentioned in this chapter. But there is no doubt that the public is getting weary, warning their politicians to take action against these graffiti outlaws who, by their actions, are further breaking the spirit of neighborhood after neighborhood, suburb after suburb!

NOTES

1. Jaxon Van Derbeken, "Complex Dynamics Shape Local Graffiti Phenomenon," *The Daily News* (28 February 1993), p. A-1.

2. Shellee Nunley, "Life's an Exciting Game of 'Tag' for This Valley Youth," *The Desert Sun* (2 October 1993), p. A-3.

3. John M. Glionna, "Pals in the Posse: Teen Culture Has Seized the Word as a Hip Name for Groups; Not All Are Harmless," *The Los Angeles Times* (26 February 1993), p. B-3.

4. Van Derbeken, p. 14.

5. John M. Glionna, "Leaving Their Mark: Youths Risk Everything to Tag Walls, Buses and Traffic Signs with Graffiti," *The Los Angeles Times* (10 March 1993), p. B-1.

6. Van Derbeken, p. 14.

7. "Taggers" pamphlet, Los Angeles and Orange Counties LASD-Transit Services Bureau, February 9, 1993.

8. Glionna, "Pals in the Posse," p. 4.

9. "Tracking Taggers: Police Use New Methods to Combat Graffiti," *The San Diego Union-Tribune* (28 November 1993), p. G-2.

10. Hector Tobar, "County OKs New Graffiti Crackdown," *The Los Angeles Times* (3 March 1993), p. B-3.

11. Robert Hanley, "Jersey City Escalates Graffiti War: Proposed Law Would Take Names of Spray-Paint Buyers," *The New York Times* (11 June 1992), p. B-1.

12. Richard Lee Colvin, "Teaming Up on Taggers," *The Los Angeles Times* (13 April 1993), p. B-1.

13. Ibid., p. B-4.

7

▼

Skinheads: Teenagers
and Hate Crimes

"A Chilling Wave of Racism: From L.A. to Boston, the Skinheads Are on the March"

In San Jose they threatened to hang a black woman who was attempting to enter a public park. In another Bay Area community, a teenage boy was thrown through a plate-glass window when he tried to stop a group of them from pasting up an anti-Semitic poster. In Chicago one of their leaders was indicted after a spree of anti-Semitic vandalism. The bizarre force behind the wave of racist incidents: skinheads, loosely organized groups of violent youths who may be emerging as the kiddie corps of the neo-Nazi movement (1).

"Man Held in School Break-In: 'Skinhead' Painted Swastikas, Police Say"

An 18-year-old man who police said is a white-supremacist "skinhead" was arrested Thursday and charged with breaking into a second-grade classroom and spray-painting swastikas on the blackboard.

Detective Bob Farman said Derek James Smart, a transient, was linked to the break-in Sunday at Jamison Elementary School by instant photographs he took of himself and left in the classroom (2).

"Skinhead Convicted of Racial Killing"

A teen-age skinhead was convicted of manslaughter for killing a homeless black man during a drunken celebration of Adolf Hitler's birthday. Mark Lane, 19, of Liburn, Georgia, said he was extremely drunk when Benny Rembert was stabbed to death under a Birmingham bridge in April, 1992, during a skinhead celebration of Hitler's birthday. Lane, convicted Thursday, faces up to 20 years in prison when sentenced next month (3).

"Arrests of Teen Members of 'Skinhead' Faction Spell End to Spree of 'Hate Crimes,' Police Say"

When nine police officers burst through the door of Mark Covell's home 10 days ago, the 18-year-old Monrovia High School dropout was asleep in his bedroom, comfortably surrounded by the trappings of the youth gang he both founded and led.

Police said they found in Mark's room a gang photo album and newsletters, a 9-millimeter handgun and a .22-caliber rifle, a membership roster and a book that described gang rules, dress and tactics.

But the surroundings were not like those the officers had seen in connection with most youth gangs in the San Fernando Valley. Hung side by side on the wall of his bedroom were the flag of the Confederacy and the Federal Republic of Germany. On the nightstand next to the bed was a copy of Adolf Hitler's manifesto, "Mein Kampf." In the photo album, the pictures were of young men wearing Nazi arm bands, posing in sieg-heil salute, according to police.

Mark, known as "Peanut" by other members of the gang he named the Reich Skins, was taken in handcuffs after the raid at the two-bedroom Monrovia home he shared with his mother. In the days following, Los Angeles police arrested seven younger members of the gang. Police said the group, which had operated primarily in the western part of the Valley, was involved in racial terrorism activities—"hate" crimes—for the four to six months before the arrests. Now, they say it has been effectively stamped out.

Mark is being held in lieu of $100,000 bail at the Los Angeles County Jail on charges of attempted burglary and using unlawful, violent acts to effect political change. Under an obscure 1919 Criminal Syndicalism Act, he is charged with distributing the racist literature and painting the racist graffiti.

The complaint also alleges that on Oct. 7 he and a juvenile companion tried to break into the Granada Hills home of a Latino high school student. The complaint says that Mark carried a gun and yelled "white power," "down with Mexicans" and "down with blacks." Mark, who has pleaded innocent to the charges, was described by school officials as an average student who was a loner on the Monrovia High School campus before dropping out.

Police said Mark's mother was as astonished by what her son was accused of as the parents of other Reich Skins members and some school officials were. Some parents were surprised to find that their sons had swastika tattoos. What the parents, school officials and investigators still find puzzling was how and why youths from mostly middle-class Valley families became aligned with such extremist views (4).

Teenagers involved with the skinhead youth style have been present in the United States since the early 1980s. But not all youths who embrace the lifestyle share racist views. This chapter will attempt to understand both types of teenage youths: those who identify with the skinhead style in its traditional, racist form, as well as those who identify in nonracist ways as SHARPs (Skinheads Against Racial Prejudice) or SARs (Skinheads Against Racism).

The American skinhead youth movement appears to have been an outgrowth of English and other European patterns with some major differences, which this chapter explores. Besides a discussion and overview of skinhead teenagers in general, analysis of data collected from questionnaires given to several youths in Southern California who identify as either "hard-core" skinheads or as nonracist skins, along with interviews and case files of skins incarcerated for delinquent behavior, will also be presented.

CONTEMPORARY TEENAGE SKINHEADS

It was not until the second wave of the British skinhead movement that American youths picked up the skinhead lifestyle. By the mid-1980s, American skins had organized to the point where their racial views came to public notice. In 1985, for example, several dozen skinhead youth attended a three-day gathering of white supremacist organizations at the farm of a former Ku Klux Klan leader in the Midwest (5).

Although not all youths who favor skinhead dress styles support white supremacy, racist skinheads—as their name implies—express prejudice. They most typically identify with Nazi insignia and preach violence against blacks, Hispanics, Jews, Asians, and homosexuals.

Throughout the decade of the 1980s the skinhead movement also appeared to be growing. In 1985, the Center for Democratic Renewal of the Anti-Defamation League claimed that white power or racist skinheads (including teenagers) numbered only about 300 in the United States. By the end of the decade, however, their numbers were believed to have increased to over 3,000, peaking in 1989, and showing a decline in the early 1990s (6).

Early Roots to English Skinhead Movement

The development of the early skinhead movement in England can be traced to the late 1950s when distinctive youth styles first emerged. Basically composed of working-class males, these British youth wore "Edwardian" coats and tight pants. British society viewed these youths, known as "Teddy Boys," as threatening to everything the traditional family stood for.

The British media described these adolescents as "folk devils," harmful to society and the social order; and they created "moral panics" by heightening concern over their actual numbers and significance. The cult heroes of these "Teds" of the 1950s included such imported American heroes as Marlon Brando, James Dean, and Elvis Presley (7).

By the early 1960s, however, the Teddy Boys had evolved into "modernists" or "mods." The flashiness in dress of the mods imitated the styles of young blacks in America. The music of the British mods was "ska," songs with a popular West Indian beat. Toward the end of the decade, those mods who were more aggressive and shared a working-class dress, developed into skinheads.

Ironically, the original skinheads were black Jamaican immigrants to England, known as "Rude Boys," whose close-shaven hairstyle and music were quickly adopted by white working-class youths. Although the early British white skinheads were not necessarily racist, their values did revolve around recovering the traditional working class community from these new immigrants (8).

By the end of the 1960s, British skinheads were identified as a sep-arate youth culture because of their distinctive behavior, attitudes, and dress style. The new youth style was surprising in that the values the skinheads possessed seemed to be a reversal of the liberal trends com-mon to the 1960s. The skinheads, from the beginning, embraced an ultraconservative, working-class view.

In 1972, police harassment and increasing political pressures led to the decline of the London skinhead movement. But in 1976, with the emergence of punk, the skins resurfaced, possibly in reaction to the anarchical attitudes of the punks. The new skins revived the most extreme elements of the earlier skinhead styles in even more exagger-ated ways. The boots, jeans, and suspenders were revived and a new symbol was added—the swastika. The swastika had already been worn on the T-shirts of the punks, but the skinheads took this a step further by having the swastika tattooed in several different locations on their bodies, including the face. Their aggressive racial and working-class attitudes made them easy targets for recruitment by the adult-based, neo-Nazi National Front (9).

Today, skinheads in both England and America are characterized by a uniform appearance: Doc Martens or industrial boots, like those commonly worn by fire fighters, which can now be purchased in most large chain department stores; heavy jeans rolled up over the boots; suspenders; green flight jackets; and, most of all, short and manageable hair resembling servicemen in boot camp. All of these are an exagger-ation of a stereotyped, working-class image, reflective of traditional masculinity.

In America, skinhead gangs—like other youth gangs—initiate their members in a ritual act of "jumping in" which involves the potential member getting "jumped" (for example, attacked with fists) by four to twelve of the strongest members of the gang for a set period of time. If the potential members do not last that long, or are unable to "hold their own" by defending themselves, they will not be admitted to the group.

As in other traditional gangs, there are many symbols that relate to dress style in contemporary American teenage skinhead philosophy. If a skinhead has scuffed the steel tips on his boots, for instance, he is con-sidered to be tough. The more scuffed the boot tips, the more likely the skinhead has been involved with physical violence.

Likewise, if one sees a skinhead wearing his suspenders down, this may mean that he is ready to fight. If a skinhead wears white laces in his combat boots, it means that he embraces white pride. Red laces stand for a more aggressive white power. Yellow laces signal hatred for police or the claim that one has killed a police officer. Recently, graffiti drawn by skinheads in Southern California include a circle with a cross in the middle, with lines extending outside the circle (10).

Skinhead Violence

What links most skinheads is an embracement of violent acts. Skinheads use violence to dispel anger they have toward those they feel are different—including immigrants, homosexuals, and racial, ethnic, and religious minorities. As the media has noted, skins are responsible for a growing amount of violence around the country and around the world. In the early half of the 1980s, according to one source, the brutal tally of skinhead violence was 121 murders, 302 assaults, and 301 cross burnings (11).

This violence has continued, but the trend may have peaked in Southern California (although it continues to grow in European communities such as Germany and Italy). Incidents in the past several years, for example, have been recorded in such varied locales as Los Angeles and Santa Clara County, California; Las Vegas, Nevada; and Tampa, Florida, as the following summary accounts from newspaper stories demonstrate.

- In Los Angeles, "Kill the faggot!" was screamed as a homosexual man was repeatedly beaten with a metal pipe by two neo-Nazi skinheads. These particular skinheads went to the area to specifically harass homosexuals.
- In Los Angeles, three skinhead youths began shouting racial slurs and beat an Ethiopian immigrant with baseball bats for no apparent reason. A pair of teenage girls watched from a nearby car and shouted, "Kick him. Kill him," as encouragement to the attackers.
- In Los Angeles, a black security guard was stabbed to death when he tried to eject a large group of skins from a grocery store.
- In Santa Clara County, a 19-year-old skinhead was convicted of manslaughter after he fatally stabbed another white youth who had taken a black man to a party.
- In Las Vegas, five white supremacist skins were accused of attacking blacks and Hispanics, and of planning to exterminate Jews by placing cyanide in the air-conditioning units in a synagogue to remind them of the Holocaust where millions of Jews were gassed in Nazi concentration camps.

■ In Tampa, a 16-year-old skinhead was sentenced to life imprisonment for beating and stabbing to death a 41-year-old black transient (12).

As these news clippings indicate, a majority of the violent attacks displayed by skinheads are unprovoked and racially motivated. The usual victims are typically unarmed, outnumbered, and defenseless. Skins use baseball bats, steel-toed combat boots, brass knuckles, lead pipes, and knives in their violent acts.

From the beginnings of their roots in the late 1960s, skinhead youths have been violent. In England, much of this violence was directed initially toward immigrants such as Pakistanis, ("Paki-bashing") because of jealousy over their affluence. When the skinheads first appeared in America, their anger was expressed in similar ways, but took the form of hostility toward African-Americans ("black-bashing") and homosexuals ("gay-bashing"). As *Rolling Stone* magazine, in an extensive cover story in 1988 on skinheads, noted:

> It doesn't matter if you've done nothing wrong. If you're the wrong color, religion, sexual orientation, or you look at them the wrong way, they'll stomp on you (13).

Types of Skinheads

Though the appearance and dress of all skinheads tends to be similar, there are differences among them in thoughts and actions. Not all skinhead youths are racist and violent. In fact, distinctions can be drawn between them and three other types of skinheads: *nonracist, separatist,* and *political.*

The *nonracist* skins tend to exist in reaction to the racist skins, and their membership is racially mixed. Common names for these nonracist skins include both the previously mentioned SHARPs and SARs. Other similar nonracist youth groups include the "Two-Tones," gangs that comprise more than one race who share similar views; and "Straight-Edge," skinheads who do not carry weapons and are against racial violence and the use of drugs and alcohol.

Unfortunately, the anti-racist skins are often attacked by the Nazi skins for refusing to enter the racist fold. And these nonracist skins are often harassed and approached by the police and the general public who mistake them for racist skinhead youths. Few people in society realize that anti-racist skins actually exist. More often, the public assumes that all youths dressed in jeans, suspenders, combat boots, and who have shaved heads, are racist and violent.

Also typically nonracist are the separatist skinheads. These youths (and adults) consider themselves more as survivalists, concerned only with their own personal welfare and survival in the likelihood of a nuclear holocaust or natural disaster. Separatist skins do not care much about what is going on around them, and try to stay clear of overt racial violence. The separatist skins, who tend to be loners, tend also not to be gang affiliated.

More similar to the racist skinheads are the political skins. These youths often follow the orders of such groups as WAR (White Aryan Resistance) and the Aryan Brotherhood. Political skins are critical of the U.S. government, claiming that it supports minorities more so than the white race. These political, adult skinhead organizations often now recruit the more youthful teenage racist skins to be their "frontline" attack force in working toward a "whites-only" society.

Skinhead gangs are often found in America's prisons, where white convicts are frequently pressured to join up with the White Aryan Brotherhood, the Ku Klux Klan, and other such white supremacist groups. These white gangs are often formed in response to the presence of other ethnic groups who have formed their own gangs in adult prison (for example, Black Guerrilla Family and Nuestra Familia in California's prisons).

White gangs—so-called stoner gangs—are also present in institutions in California housing juveniles. Similar to the situation in adult prison, white youth join these gangs as a defense, or in opposition to, the presence of the wide variety of ethnic gangs in the various camps and institutions of the California Youth Authority (for example, the black Crip and Piru or Blood gangs; an array of both Northern and Southern California Hispanic gangs; and Asian gangs).

Apart from these specialized situations, teenage skinheads appear to be most frequently involved with the racist or nonracist skinhead groups, and less likely to be involved with either the separatist or political movements.

Skinheads' Racial Views

Much of the violence displayed by teenage racist skinheads originates from their racial views. Whereas black gangs are often motivated by power, money, and drugs, and Asian gangs are motivated by profit, skinhead gangs are motivated by racism. Racist skins, approximating the patterns of ethnic gangs, now are viewed by authorities as roaming the streets and doing whatever they feel is necessary to protect their own white race (14).

Although the actual numbers of teenage skinheads involved in gangs are small (250 to 300 in California, according to the State Department of Justice in 1990), skinhead juvenile street gangs maintain a presence, particularly in suburban areas in Southern California where there is continued ethnic movement out from the inner city of Los Angeles. The presence of such skinhead gangs is malleable as well. Neo-Nazi skinhead gangs nearly doubled in size in one year during the late 1980s (15).

Such individuals and groups are of special concern to authorities because of their propensity for violence and racist behavior. As one 17-year-old youth, "Bob," interviewed for this study recounted,

I used to frequent the punk clubs, drink heavily, and listen to heavy metal music. I also enjoyed surfing. I became attracted to the skinheads at about the age of 13 largely as a way to stand out from the other kids.

Sporting the standard look with a shaved haircut and the skinhead dress of military flight jackets, pants rolled above Doc Martens or combat steel-toed boots, and suspenders and boot laces whose color identified the specific skinhead gang he belonged to, this juvenile had carved a small swastika on his leg. Bob also indicated he had served time in the California Youth Authority for aggravated assault.

Racist American skinheads, like the earlier British skins, are against immigrants and nonwhites and view them as a threat, believing that they steal employment opportunities. Jealous of, and angry at, the affluence that many immigrants acquire—while they perceive many whites to be struggling, unemployed, and homeless—racist skinheads want to establish a nation only for whites. To accomplish this they plan to ban all other races, whom they refer to as "God's mistakes" (16). Tom Metzger, the founder of the White Aryan Resistance movement, who resides in Fallbrook, California, is quoted as saying, "White people are on the way out unless they do something. The worst invasion is the biological invasion. Third World immigrants come here, have children, and take over" (17).

In the past several years, the White Aryan Resistance (WAR), located in Southern California, has frequently been accused of encouraging and inciting teenage skinheads to commit violent acts against blacks and other minorities in order to promote white supremacy. Supplying the teenage skinheads with their WAR newspapers and comic books featuring the killings of blacks and Jews, the movement's main target has been to stop nonwhite immigration. In fact, many white racist skinhead gangs take the name WAR as part of their title— such as the Huntington Beach WAR Skins or the La Habra WARS.

Racist teenage skinheads follow the same line of thought as the Aryan Youth Movement (AYM) and the White Student Union (WSU). Unable to create their whites-only society, they express their frustration and anger by beating and harassing all minorities. As Bob told me, "I'm white and proud of it, and if that makes me racist, so be it."

Reasons explaining why some teenagers become part of the anti-racist skinhead movement seem less complex. According to one authority, youngsters become members of SHARP as a reaction against the racist views of their parents or other family members. In other words, according to this source, "Some SHARPs hate their parents because their parents are racists" (18).

Skinheads versus SHARPS

The teenage skinhead movement is varied. Because of its secrecy and its suspicion of authority, it also proved difficult to study. But to gain some understanding into both the teenage racist and nonracist skinheads, it was decided to interview several youths in Southern California who identified as one or the other of the two groups.

A questionnaire was developed, using seventy-four questions from the "Youth Survey" that had been distributed to punkers and metalers in Southern California and New Zealand. (See Appendix B, "Youth Survey 2.")

Attempts were made to distribute the questionnaires through various sources and contacts to self-identified skinheads in the Southern California area. Through these efforts, thirty-two youths were contacted, completed the questionnaire, and agreed to be interviewed in some detail. Twenty-three of these youths self-identified as hard-core, racist skinheads, and nine defined themselves as nonracist skinheads. Additionally, case files from the California Youth Authority elicited three more youths who maintained a racist skinhead philosophy while incarcerated. An analysis of the thirty-two questionnaires and the three case files served as the basis for the discussion that follows.

Results of the Youth Survey

In examining the statistical analysis of the thirty-two questionnaires, several key patterns emerged that differentiated the two groups of teenage skinheads (see Table 7.1). Because of the small number of respondents sampled, however, these findings should be viewed with some reservation.

Hard-core Racist Skinheads. Those youths who clearly identified themselves as racist skinheads, compared to those who self-identified as nonracist skinheads, differed in their responses to fourteen of the forty-six statements on the survey (or 30 percent of the items). These hard-core racist skins agreed, for instance, that it was good to be rebellious; that skinheads were a new form of gang; and that the drinking age should be lowered. They also were likely to say that they spent a lot of time away from home; feel that their peers viewed them as trouble-makers; and feel that both their teachers and fellow students treated them badly.

These hard-core skinheads disagreed with the statement that they were against racism in any form. They believed that kids should not be punished like adults; agreed that there were too many immigrants; and stated that they had been considered a bully while in grammar school. The racist teenage skinheads reported not liking their parents, having parents that disapproved of their lifestyle, and believing that minorities should be excluded.

Furthermore, those youths who identified as hard-core skinheads were also most likely to share these other characteristics: felt bored with their life; had been in trouble with the police; had family members who were themselves racists; had contemplated suicide; and admitted to spending a lot of money on drugs.

Nonracist Skinheads. By contrast, those youths who completed the questionnaire who identified themselves as nonracist skinheads, or members of SHARP, shared views that distinguished them from the racist skinheads in nine of the forty-six items (or 20 percent of the statements). The nonracist skinheads believed that there would not be a nuclear war in their lifetime. They disagreed with the statement that there were too many immigrants in America, and were less likely to want to exclude minorities.

The nonracist skinheads also indicated that they were less likely to view skinheads as delinquent (since as skins they were not necessarily

Table 7.1

Racist versus Nonracist Skinheads

Identify as a Skinhead

Believe it is good to be rebellious	<.001
Believe skinheads are a new form of gang	<.003
Believe the drinking age should be lowered	<.003
Spend a lot of time away from home	<.01
Peers see them as troublemakers	<.01
Teachers treat them poorly	<.01
Other students treat them poorly	<.01
Disagree they are against racism in any form	<.01
Feel kids should not be punished like adults	<.02
Was considered a bully in grammar school	<.03
Believe there are too many immigrants	<.03
Do not like their parents	<.04
Parents do not approve of their lifestyle	<.04
Feel minorities should be excluded	<.04

Identify as a Member of SHARP

Believe there will not be a nuclear war	<.0003
Believe there are not too many immigrants	<.001
Less likely to exclude minorities	<.01
Less likely to view skinheads as delinquents	<.02
Do not spend a lot of money on drugs	<.02
Affiliate with a religion	<.04
Believe blacks and Hispanics are equal to whites	<.04
Was not considered a bully in grammar school	<.04
Less likely to spend time away from home	<.04

Those Who Were Considered Bullies in Grammar School

Peers see them as troublemakers	<.001
Spend a lot of time away from home	<.01
Do not like school	<.01
Believe there will be a nuclear war	<.01
Been in trouble with the police	<.02
Less likely to like their mother	<.02
Parents do not approve of their lifestyle	<.03
Identify as a skinhead	<.03
Spend a lot of money on drugs	<.03
Peers treat them poorly at school	<.03
Believe music they listen to is violent	<.04
Hang out only with their own group	<.04
Believe drinking age should be lowered	<.04
Have tattoos	<.04
More likely not to be a SHARP	<.04

Table 7.1 (continued)

Music They Listen to Is Violent

Believe that life is boring	<.01
Abused by parents as a child	<.02
Participate in gay- or black-bashing	<.02
Spend a lot of money on drugs	<.03
Friends use drugs	<.03
Was considered a bully in grammar school	<.04
Less likely to be happy	<.04
Do not like their mothers	<.04

Have Friends Who Use Drugs

Parents do not approve of their lifestyle	<.01
Believe music they listen to is violent	<.03
Have considered suicide	<.03
Less likely to favor the death penalty	<.03
Was considered a bully in grammar school	<.04

delinquent). Furthermore, they did not spend a lot of money on drugs; they maintained a religious affiliation; and they viewed blacks as being equal to whites. They indicated they had not been considered bullies in grammar school. They also were less likely to spend time away from home compared to the hard–core racist skins.

The SHARPs also reported being happy with their lives, and sharing these additional characteristics: affiliated with their own group; agreed they would fight in a war to protect their country; felt that their parents were happy with their own lives; felt close to their families; and had parents who approved of their lifestyle.

These youngsters, however, were not totally nondiscriminatory in their views. These nonracist teenage skinheads agreed with the statement that society should discriminate against homosexuals or gays (a view which may have been influenced by their stronger religious affiliation); and they reported that they had family members who were themselves racists.

Cross–tab statistical analyses were also conducted on three other items from the Youth Survey which are germane to this study: being a bully in grammar school; listening to music that is violent; and having friends who use drugs.

Being a Bully in Grammar School. Those skinheads who agreed with the statement, "In grammar school I was considered to be a bully," compared to those who disagreed with the statement, were also more likely to have peers that now perceived them to be troublemakers; spend a lot of time away from home; not like school; and believe that there would be a nuclear war in their lifetime.

These youths who had been perceived as bullies in grade school were also more likely to have been in trouble with the police; not like their mothers; spend a lot of money on drugs; feel that their peers treated them poorly at school; and agree that their parents did not support their lifestyle. These teens also expressed the belief that the music they listened to was violent; reported hanging out only with their own group; felt that the drinking age should be lowered; and admitted to having tattoos.

In looking at these patterns, it appears that being anti-social is behavior that has been associated with these teenagers since early adolescence at least. It should not come as too much of a surprise that some juveniles who were bullies as youngsters, grew up to become racist skinheads as teenagers. The fact that delinquent teenagers (in this case, the hard-core racist skinhead), in general, were also likely to have been bullies in grammar school is borne out by behavioral science research on bullies.

Bullies—or "schoolyard menaces," as one psychologist terms them—are a subset of aggressive kids who seem to derive satisfaction from being psychologically or physically abusive with other youngsters. Harming others becomes a way of life for them, the means by which they gain power. Such behavior results from some combination of parental influence, aspects of the child's home environment, and an unruly temperament. Too little parental love and care, and too much freedom in childhood, contribute strongly, according to one researcher, to the development of these aggressive personalities (19).

Others have speculated that the defenseless child who ends up as victim reminds the bully of his or her own defenselessness against abuse at home, and the humiliation and shame it caused. Bullies, in other words, feel threatened by their victims' vulnerability. In the classic pattern of "the victim who becomes the victimizer," these bullies lash out at others in ways similar to what had been done to them (20).

In another study of what happens to bullies in later life, the researchers found that such children carry their aggression with them into a relatively unsuccessful adulthood. They are more likely than their less aggressive classmates to abuse their spouses and they tend to punish their own children more aggressively, thus raising a new generation of bullies (21).

Listening to Music That Is Violent. Besides having been considered a bully in grammar school, the racist teenage skinheads in this study also agreed with the statement that the music they listened to was violent. More importantly, those whose musical tastes were more violent were also significantly more likely to agree with the statement, "As a child I was abused by my parents." This raises an interesting question: might early exposure to violence in childhood (that is, being abused by one's parents) condition or socialize one to more readily embrace violence in one's musical preferences?

Six other characteristics were associated with those skinheads who listened to violence in their music. They reported having participated in minority bashing; spent a lot of money on drugs; had friends who used drugs; had been considered a bully in grammar school; were less likely to be happy; and did not get along with their mothers.

Having Friends Who Use Drugs. Finally, one other pattern was evident from an analysis of the thirty-two questionnaires. Those teenage skinheads in the sample who said their friends use drugs were more likely to have parents who did not approve of their lifestyle; to believe that their music was violent; and to have considered suicide. They were also less likely to favor the death penalty; and they, too, had been considered a bully in grammar school.

Results of the Interviews

Examples of Racist Skinheads. Very typical of the hard-core, racist skinhead youths that completed the questionnaire was "Paul," a 17-year-old ward of the court who was residing in a group home when contacted and interviewed. The youngest of three kids, Paul came from a working-class family.

Based on his responses to the interview and the questionnaire, Paul disliked school, and believed his teachers and peers at school mistreated him. He also did not get along with his parents. In response to the open-ended, "fill-in" questions (see survey), Paul contended that a skinhead was one who "stands up for what he believes," and that anyone who was not a skinhead was a "wimp." According to Paul, anyone who did not like his kind of music was either a "fag" or a "fairy."

Paul claimed that blacks and Hispanics were not equal to whites, and felt that there were too many immigrants in our society. To support his beliefs, Paul reported having participated in both gay- and black-bash-ing. Such violent behavior appeared to begin for Paul at an early age. Paul came from a family that definitely agreed with his strong racist views. He also indicated that he was a loner, only socializing with those in his own racial group.

A second youth, "Tom," further exemplified the typical racist skin-head that completed the survey. At age 18, Tom felt that his parents were too authoritative. Tom, also, did not like school, not caring what his teachers or peers thought about him, although he indicated they did consider him a troublemaker. Tom also believed that America has far too many immigrants; and he admitted to participating in gay- or black-bashing, claiming that our society should discriminate against homosexuals.

Tom believed that it was important to be rebellious, which may have something to do with his drug abuse and past problems with the police. He also indicated he had been considered a bully in grammar school. Politically, Tom was very conservative. He believed that our society should employ the death penalty. He also said that he would fight in a war to protect his country.

"Joe" exemplified the racist skinhead attitude as well. He is a 17-year-old who was brought up in a racist environment. He is an only child who came from a middle-class background. Joe shared, along with his parents, the view that blacks and Hispanics were not equal to whites, and that there were too many immigrants in our society. Joe also reported having participated in gay- and/or black-bashing in support of his beliefs. To Joe, a skinhead was someone who "believes in the white race."

Joe disliked school and felt his teachers and peers treated him poorly. At an early age Joe became violent. He reported that he was a bully in grammar school. Due to these factors, perhaps, Joe indicated he only socializes with those in his own racial group.

Another youth interviewed who affiliated with the violent White Aryan Resistance movement was "Rhonda," age 18. Rhonda was brought up in a racist environment and her answers conveyed this. She came from a large family, having seven siblings. Rhonda gets along with her parents, who both hail from working-class backgrounds. Her father's occupation was a factory worker and her mother was a house-wife or "domestic engineer" as she wrote on the form.

Rhonda defined non-skinheads as "gutless pinkos." She was against blacks and gays and had participated in "bashing them with a club."

Also, she felt that the country has too many immigrants, and that they should not be allowed to live in white communities. She strongly disagreed with the nonracist SHARP's views—crossing that group out on the survey form with a white power symbol.

Examples of Nonracist Skinheads. One female interviewed, "Julie," reflected the skinhead identity, but she identified with being a member of SHARP. As noted previously, some teenagers embrace the look and demeanor but reject the racist overtones of the skinhead subculture. Other nonracist skins reject the drugs and alcohol that seem part of the outlaw stance. Julie sported a shaved head with long bangs and dressed, according to her, "alternatively." Julie reported getting along with her mother but not with her father because she was abused by him as a child. Julie currently enjoyed school and was happy with her life, though at one time she had felt like committing suicide.

Julie did not consider herself to be aggressive nor a troublemaker, and she reported never having been in trouble with the police. She believed that blacks and Hispanics were equal to whites, was against racism in any form, and did not think that society should discriminate against homosexuals.

One youth, "Rod," also reflected the nonsupremacist attitude. Rod viewed racist skinheads as violent and too publicized for his liking. He believed in the Two-Tone doctrine of "black and white unite," and he freely associated with people outside of his own racial group. He appeared to be positive about life and comfortable with his views.

Rod enjoyed school and got along with his parents who were both teachers. He also indicated that he got along well with his two sisters. Rod was a part of the Straight-Edge scene, commenting, "It's our little way of trying to set examples for the younger kids and even the older ones. Drugs are a bad scene and we should stay away from them."

"Greg," a 17-year-old American Indian, also followed the Straight-Edge view. He, however, seemed more ambivalent than most. He spent a lot of time at home, and reported that he got along with his parents, teachers, and peers. Greg believed, however, that there were too many immigrants in the country, and that society should discriminate against homosexuals. On the other hand, he believed that blacks and Hispanics were equal to whites. Greg also expressed the view that everyone was responsible for their own actions, and that they should be punished accordingly—including minors who break the law.

Another nonracist skinhead, "Steve," also identified with the Straight-Edge movement. This was emphasized with a "Drug-Free" tattoo on his arm. Steve, age 16, saw himself as an individualist, and encouraged people to be themselves. He reported getting along well with both parents and enjoying school. He was happy with his life and has never contemplated suicide. Although not a member of SHARP, he felt that all races were equal. He, too, however, felt that society should discriminate against homosexuals.

Teenage Skinheads in the Youth Authority

Extensive case files of three youths, currently incarcerated in the California Youth Authority, who identified themselves as skinheads, were also examined.

One young man, "Simon," first joined the skinhead movement in San Diego at age 13. From his file it was noted that he was attracted to the San Diego skinhead gang even though he was not from the area. As a young teenager, Simon participated in gang activities that included partying, going to shows, and having their "own community" in Balboa Park.

According to Simon, the enemies of the San Diego Skin Heads were the Choir Boys. The two gangs had been at war for a long time, and approximately nine people from the San Diego Skin Heads had been killed in shootings during a four-year period. Simon could give no reason when asked why he would want to continue to affiliate with a gang that had such a high mortality rate.

Simon left this gang when his family moved to Los Angeles. But he soon began associating with the Hollywood Skins, which included some members who had also relocated from San Diego. According to Simon, the enemies of the Hollywood Skins included the Lads, Sacred Right, Suicidal Boys, HRP (Hollywood Rat Patrol), and Circle One.

In the three months that Simon was involved with the Hollywood Skins, he reported he had fought with his fists in two gang fights. He stated that he had many friends but no current girl-friend. Simon, now age 18, was incarcerated for driving under the influence of alcohol, causing a great bodily injury accident. At the time of his arrest he was attending a local high school, residing with his mother, and living in an area he described as "middle class, mellow, and having low crime."

Simon stated that he first began smoking marijuana at age 14, smoking on a daily basis between ages 14 and 16. He began drinking beer and hard liquor at age 14 as well, and that continued until his recent incarceration. He also had experimented with cocaine, PCP, and crystal meth. Within the California Youth Authority, Simon associated with the Nazi Low Riders (NLR).

A second CYA ward, "Robert," age 16, also affiliated with the Nazi Low Riders, along with the Supreme White Power (SWP) movement. Coming from a substance-abusing family, Robert's natural parents had divorced as a result of his father's heavy drinking. The ward continued to live with this father, however, because he could not get along with his mother's boyfriend. Upon release, Robert's plans were to resume living with his mother. According to his probation officer, there was some concern about this since the ward would be residing in the area where all of his prior delinquent friends lived. According to the report, Robert, when drinking, was easily led by these peers.

Since incarceration, Robert had experienced many behavioral problems, including peer conflict, fighting, horseplaying, and using marijuana. The probation report concluded that Robert was a rather undisciplined, incorrigible youth who did not handle alcohol or drugs well.

The third skinhead ward, "Warren," age 16, appeared to have learning disabilities and tested far below grade level. His difficulties stemmed from being influenced by an older Nazi party sympathizer. The probation material also pointed out that Warren had become a member of the Aryan Prisoners' Association once he entered the juvenile justice system.

Because of Warren's continued Nazi group activity inside the youth authority, he had received severe sanctions from the authorities. He was also having difficulty getting an early parole. Like the others, Warren suffered from an alcohol abuse problem. He had also experimented in the past with marijuana and LSD, and had been attending a mandatory alcohol and drug abuse program while in CYA.

Warren reported that he dropped out of the eighth grade at age 15 due to a lack of interest. According to his file, he had experienced learning difficulties in the early grades, and had been identified as hyperactive. Warren also suffered from severe health and allergy problems that disrupted his progress in school for a significant period of time.

Prior to incarceration, Warren had only limited employment. He helped out in the family cleaning business, worked for several months as a carpet layer, and was employed for five months as a mechanic in his uncle's tire service. During his three years in CYA, Warren showed no improvement. He had made no significant progress toward rehabilitation. Although, according to his file, he had mainly kept a low profile, had not been a behavioral problem, and had not been involved in any known gang activities, it was apparent to the staff that his attitude and extreme racist philosophy had changed very little. When Warren first arrived at CYA, items of Nazi paraphernalia were found in his personal property, including a calendar noting Adolf Hitler's birthday. Warren appeared to still support the messages of Nazism, white supremacy, and racial hatred.

In summary, Warren—although coming from a more stable family background—appeared to have difficulty adjusting to school, and was negatively influenced (like the others) by substance abuse. As he experienced learning problems in public schools, he began to form doubts about his own adequacy as a person. Whether due to a dissatisfaction with the existing social order, a need to belong to something, or for some other reason, Warren chose to affiliate with a fascist ideology.

SKINHEADS' "RULES OF CONDUCT"

In 1990 law enforcement officials in the Orange County area of Southern California reported teenage skinhead gangs to be one of four new gangs to set up operation in the region. (The other three gangs included new Hispanic, Vietnamese, and multiracial gangs.) According to the report, skinhead gang members in Orange County were sometimes difficult to document because they frequently held jobs, finished school, and blended in with regular life.

The report also noted their hang outs, such as video arcades and malls; their most common tattoos, such as lightning bolts, swastikas, and white power mottoes; and their mode of dress which is similar to that of skinheads in other parts of the country, including shaved heads (in part, so that their hair does not get pulled in a fight), heavy steel-toed boots, suspenders (often worn hanging), and military-style jackets.

According to the report:

In the past year, skinheads have kept a relatively low profile in Orange County. Motivated by hate, racism, and power, their criminal activity here, to date, has included hate crimes, such as bashing gays; burning crosses or defacing synagogues; and drugs. Many have become more mainstream, covered-up their tattoos, and grown-out their hair, although still retaining their racist philosophy. Their gang names include Death Squads, and Huntington Beach Skins (22).

Included in this 1990 report was an example, confiscated by authorities, of rules used by one white youth gang in the county.

Rules of the Nazi Low Riders

Don't smoke after a black. Don't drink after a black. Don't talk and associate with a black. If anything goes down like a fight and the person who's getting his butt beat is a Nazi Low Rider (NLR), you are supposed to jump in to protect that person.

Whatever the President says, goes. No doubt about it or you'll be put on a shine (suspended). You are supposed to be cool with the Chicano's because they are with the whites in a way of protection. If something big comes down, and either race needs help, you are supposed to "go down" with them and help fight, etc.

Everything a NLR has—like a "canteen," they are to share with all of their gang. Nothing should be refused to another member. When you give somebody a light off your cigarette, don't let them touch it or hold it, because you don't want to catch their germs.

Don't talk to "Kacks," people that are on a shine. For violating the rules, the penalties are either to go behind the wall and fight or get put on a shine. In some cases, both (23).

A pamphlet circulated by members of WAR Skins gives an intriguing glimpse into the group's ideology. The flier, written by two teenagers—one, the head of WAR Skins, and the other, the Vice President of the Aryan Youth Movement—was covered with Nazi swastikas and the logos "Young Nazis" and "Skinheads." (All grammatical errors and mistakes are as they appear in the leaflet.)

The attitude of a skinhead is generally ready to fight and on guard all the time. Skins do not usually go around and start trouble. Its only when people start to make the jump on skins. When that happens, the skins end up winning! Skinheads are mad and tired of the system screwing them over.

Skinheads are the All American white youth. They love mom and love their flag. The dress of the skin is rough, smart and clean. All in all, the skinhead uniform is working class, ready to fight because our heads are shaved for battle.

Skinheads are against non-white immigration because, these people take our jobs and land and give nothing in return. Skinheads are Anti-Semitic, because we know the Jews have extorted us for there personnel means. Skinheads are anti-abortion, we all know that abortion is another form of genocide, the non-white races and the jews sit and laugh at our self-annihilation (24).

The pamphlet also recommended the standard skinhead uniform for both men and women. Women, however, were also allowed to wear miniskirts and fishnet stockings, wool kilt skirts, and a fringed skinhead hair style. Finally, the flier stated that skinheads should be "pro-American, pro-family and pro-work, but should violently oppose communism and homosexuals" (25).

In Northern California, a skinhead organization called the "American Front" espoused the typical message of hate aimed at Jews, blacks, homosexuals, communists, government, the media, and just about everyone or everything else. Their telephone hotline carried this message:

We in the American Front feel it's high time to slay the hook-nosed, bagel-stuffing, penny-pinching, gentile-sacrificing, holy-hoax-preaching beast. The fact still remains that white revolution is the only solution . . . . If you don't want to fight, then prepare yourself to be hung on the day of the rope with the faggots that you feel so equal to. Hail victory (26).

SOCIETY REACTS TO SKINHEADS

Explanations for the Rise of Such Gangs

In explaining the rise of teenage racist skinhead gangs across the country, one observer notes two factors. For one, black drug gangs from the Los Angeles area, including both the Crips and the Bloods, have extended their marketplace for selling and distributing their drugs (for example, crack cocaine). As these black gangs have moved into suburban white neighborhoods, their presence has fueled racist fears. Like the rise of tagger crews (see Chapter 6), white racist skinhead gangs have emerged, in part, as a challenge to these former inner-city ethnic gangs who have moved into white suburban neighborhoods and public schools.

Others might disagree with this view. In general, racist skinheads appear to vent their rage and aggression by attacking (and killing) unarmed, law-abiding citizens. Often, they are not battling other gangs (that is, defending their turf or neighborhood). Inner-city gangs can hardly be blamed for these skins' cowardly, unruly, and delinquent actions.

The second factor, according to this authority, has been the media. The tendency has been for the press and television news to give these new skinhead gangs media coverage. By engaging in violence on television (for example, the skinhead's disruption of a "Geraldo Rivera Show" on the subject of teenagers and hate crimes), racist skinheads gain more recruits. "When they see Geraldo beaten," he noted, "membership goes up."

This observer further contends that skinheads are basically undisciplined bullies or social misfits, engaging in drug abuse, and quick to fight other gangs. When asked what law enforcement should do, he replied that skinheads should have mandated, as their sentence, the need to complete a high school education.

Although skinheads' views should be protected under the rights of the First Amendment which guarantees freedom of speech, their racist views need to be countered with minority group sensitivity training. This, he feels, can best be accomplished within the school setting. Part of the judicial sentencing, furthermore, should involve the family in some type of sensitivity sessions since many of the racist views are learned at home (27).

"Protesters Attack White Supremacists: 'Skinheads' Are Chased, Beaten in Glendale"

A mob of protesters shouting "Nazi scum" chased and beat a small group of teenage white supremacist "skinheads" Sunday before a speech by a white supremacist leader. Two of the youths suffered minor facial cuts but injuries to the other three victims couldn't be determined because they fled. About 40 or 50 people in the crowd of some 300 took part in the attack outside the Holiday Inn about 2:30 p.m., said police Sgt. Dean Durand. Three people were arrested and two were held for questioning (28).

Whether rationally or irrationally, society has reacted each time that a new youth culture has emerged. Many people and organizations become concerned with these youth groups, viewing them as deviant or delinquent, and act to discourage their proliferation. When the skinheads first emerged in the United States in the early 1980s, such reactions and countermovements quickly developed.

One political movement, formed to combat racist skinheads, both adult and juvenile, and their violence, was the Northwest Coalition against Malicious Harassment in the state of Washington. This organization had two stated purposes: first, to address and combat all forms of religious and racial harassment and violence which many of the skinheads in the region often had displayed; and, second, to assist communities, groups, and individuals in establishing effective, peaceful means to eliminate these acts of harassment and violence (29).

Besides the emergence of such organized groups to politically challenge the skinhead movement, individuals have personally taken a stand against skinhead racism and violence. For instance, one lawyer in California recently sued WAR for inciting young neo-Nazi skinheads into killing a black man. Many gay and lesbian organizations have worked with police and elected officials to bring attention to harassment from racist skinheads and to report and prosecute overt acts of hate crimes.

Organized protesters and the mass media have also acted and spoken out against skinheads and their beliefs. In March 1989, for example, protesters outnumbered skinheads 4 to 1 at what was supposed to be an "Aryan Woodstock" concert with white-power rock groups. Although thousands of skinheads were expected to show up for the two-day concert in the Bay Area, most present were protesters who were against the skins' racist views. And the media was in support of these protesters' actions (30).

Many white power rallies across the country end before they can begin. Often, mobs of protesters, shouting slogans, disrupt the speeches of white supremacists (in ways similar to the preceding news clipping item). In May 1990, one such "white power" rally was ended when American Front Skins (AFS) were hit by a barrage of sticks and bottles hurled by anti-fascists who outnumbered the skins at least 20 to 1. Anti-racists, marching behind a banner that read "Fight Racism," and chanting "No Nazi, No KKK," caused the police to take the racist skinheads—many, 18- and 19-year-old teenagers—away for their own protection (31).

Some groups quietly protest skinhead youths by counseling them and by working with their parents. Others, as has been noted, are louder and choose to protest by fighting and rallying against the philosophy and violence that the teenage racist skinheads embrace.

NOTES

1. John Leo, "A Chilling Wave of Racism: From L.A. to Boston, the Skinheads Are on the March," *Time* (25 January 1988), p. 57.

2. Jonathan Volzke, "Man Held in School Break-in," *The Orange County Register* (9 June 1989), p. B-3.

3. "Skinhead Convicted of Racial Killing," *The Desert Sun* (23 October 1993), p. A-4.

4. Michael Connelly, "Arrests of Teen Members of 'Skinhead' Faction Spell End to Spree of 'Hate Crimes,' Police Say," *The Los Angeles Times* (1 November 1987), p. B-1.

5. Bill Wallace, "Skinhead Crimes a Growing Threat," *The San Francisco Chronicle* (3 December 1988), p. A-1.

6. "Young and Violent: The Growing Menace of America's Neo-Nazi Skinheads," (New York: Anti-Defamation League of B'nai B'rith/Civil Rights Division, 1989).

7. Nick Knight, *Skinhead* (London: Omnibus Press, 1982).

8. Ibid., p. 8.

9. Ibid., p. 23.

10. "Skinheads," *Propaganda* 6, pp. 9–14.

11. Leo, p. 57.

12. Barry Came, "A Growing Menace," *Macleans* (23 January 1989), pp. 43–44.

13. Jeff Coplon, "Skinhead Nation," *Rolling Stone* (1 December 1988), pp. 54–65.

14. Ibid.

15. "Shaved for Battle: Skinheads Target America's Youth," (New York: Anti-Defamation League of B'nai B'rith/Civil Rights Division, 1988).

16. Richard E. Meyer, "The Long Crusade," *Los Angeles Times Magazine* (3 December 1989), pp. 14–31.

17. Came, p. 43.

18. Ibid.

19. Marjorie Roberts, "Schoolyard Menace," *Psychology Today* (February 1988), pp. 53–56.

20. N. M. Floyd, "Pick on Somebody Your Own Size!: ControllingVictimization," *The Pointer* 29 (2) pp. 9–17.

21. Leonard Eron et al., *Learning of Aggression in Children* (Boston: Little, Brown and Company, 1971).

22. "Gangs in Orange County," *The Orange County Register* (21 January 1990), p. M-2.

23. Ibid.

24. Bill Wallace, "Skinhead Crimes a Growing Threat," *The San Francisco Chronicle* (3 December 1988), p. A-2.

25. Ibid.

26. Tamara Jones, "Violence by Skinheads Spreads across Nation," *The Los Angeles Times* (19 December 1988), p. A-1.

27. Susan Manuel, "Former UH Professor Battling Roots of Racism," *Honolulu Star Bulletin* (21 March 1989), p. B-l.

28. Robert Jablon, "Protesters Attack White Supremacists: 'Skinheads' Are Chased, Beaten in Glendale," *The Los Angeles Times* (13 July 1989), p. B-1.

29. Manuel.

30. Jennifer McNulty, "Skinheads, Demonstrators Clash at Rally," *The Orange County Register* (5 March 1989), p. A-3.

31. "'White Power' Rally Over Before It Starts," *Daily Bulletin* (6 May 1990), p. A-3.

8

▼

Stoner Gang Members in the Youth Authority

Diary of a Teenage Stoner

We arrived in San Diego on Monday morning about 4:00 a.m. We woke up some time in the morning about 9:00 a.m. and went to some campground and took some showers, and, guess what? We got fucked with by some dick head, whiteboy cop who started talking shit about how we can't just go in a camping ground and take showers. He asked me if I wanted to go to San Diego juvenile hall. He was going to give us all tickets, but Dingy paid $3.00 for each of us. So about 11:30 a.m. we went to the beach and had raw potatoes, uncooked bacon, and cold burritos, with no fuck'en drink (hard times).

After our bitch'en breakfast it started to liv'en up a little bit. We scored a case of Schaffer and headed up to Yuma, Arizona. We cruised around for a little looking for some weed. Finally, we saw some whiteboys about 6:00 p.m. at some arcade. So we asked them for some weed and Dingy pitched in $15.00 and they pitched in $10.00 so we bought a quarter. Crazy ended up dividing it and fucked them over. He gave them about three joints. Fucked up those posers' whole day. So after that we went to the store and I got a case on credit at 7:30 p.m. Bud bottles. After that Crazy took

us on a little adventure to the orange fields in Yuma. We ended up
turning around and found a Motel 6. After that we were kicking
back, drinking beer and smoking some weed. Me and Crazy got
bored, so Dingy took us to 7-11 and got a case and a half of Bud
cans on credit. These people are cool about credit. But some van
was chasing us for about four blocks. Finally he turned around. So
about 10:30 p.m. we got back to the motel and partied some more,
and passed out. We woke up in the morning at 8:30 a.m. and
started drinking some more and smoking some more weed. We
were all pretty hungry so Dinky took Chuck ("Loner") to the store
to get some lunch meat and bread on credit. We munched down
and drank till about 1:00 p.m. and left the fuck'en food.

We then went to a gas station to get a map, and the nice people
gave us a case-and-a-half on credit, but I guess they changed their
mind and some bitch ran after us. So we jumped in the car and
bailed to a free camping ground in the middle of the desert about
2:30 p.m. We were cruising around in the desert, then went into a
little town to get some shit on credit. Me and Loner got two car-
tons. Loner was taking a long time so I went in to see what happened and ended up getting a carton too. Then we bailed back to
the desert. We ended up almost getting busted around 4:30 p.m.
The fuck'en pigs found a case of beer and a half a bottle of
whiskey. The license plates were covered with a red "Suicidal" (a
punk band) rag. Finally, they let us go about an hour later, but
they gave Dingy and homeboy Loner a ticket. They're supposed
to go to court out here on March 5th. But they said, "Fuck the
court." So we found a spot to camp about 6:00 p.m. Later that
night about 9:00 p.m. we all went hiking but ended up getting
fuck'en lost, and were fuck'en thirsty. So we seen a camper truck
and asked them for some water. They gave us all water. Then we
asked them how to get back to our campground, and they told us
and we got back about 10:30 p.m. I ended up falling asleep and
Dingy, Crazy, and homeboy Chuck kicked back in the tent listening to the radio and playing cards.

We woke up about 7:00 a.m. and Dingy, Lisa, and Chuck went
to the store and got some more stuff on credit. They got some
lunch meat, bread, and paid for some water and soda. After we
munched out, Crazy, Chuck, Lisa and me went hiking again. We
fucked around, leaving our graffiti on some rocks.

We left the camping place at 1:45 p.m. Now we headed toward
that little town again for some more shit on credit. We arrived at

the store. Me and Crazy kicked back in the car checking out some old ladies. There's nothing else to look at. There's not one good bitch in this whole fuck'en state. There's nothing but old people here. Dingy got some cookies and punch, and Chuck scored some beer. He ended up buying a case and a box of matches on credit. We were ready to jam, listening to "Slayer," and headed toward the Colorado River. We arrived at the river about 3:00 p.m., and just kicked back, drinking some beer. Later we all jammed to the store to get more beer. Chuck had a case in his hands but ended up tripping on the way out and fucked up his arm. We went back to the river where we were camped and started drinking again.

We woke up at 8:00 a.m. Me, Crazy, and homeboy Chuck went and walked around for a while and then went and tipped the tent over that the girls, Dingy and Lisa, were sleeping in. After that we went swimming in the river and threw Dingy and Lisa in the cold ice water.

Later we went to Alpha Beta in Blythe, California, to get some more shit on credit. Dingy got some steaks and Loner got some hot dogs and candy bars. I got a knife from Thrifty's drugstore and a frisbee to fuck around with. Chuck got some lighter fluid from Thrifty's and salami from Albertson's. These people are cool about credit out here. There's a few nice bitches out here—blondes.

When we got back to the river me, Crazy, and Chuck jumped in. That was a couple of hours ago. But since then it's been pretty fuck'en boring. I want to get a case on credit but fuck'en Dingy don't want to take me until later, so fuck it. It's 5:45 p.m. and it's deader than heaven. I'm just kicking back writing this journal. Crazy is playing the guitar. Dingy's making some sandwiches. Lisa's kicking back, and Chuck's cleaning some shit that he threw on the window of the car. There's no more fuck'en beer, and we haven't had weed for about two and a half fuck'en days. That's pretty fuck'en long.

RUNNING WITH THE HOME BOYS

This account was written by a 17-year-old juvenile who was a member of a white, teenage stoner gang from Northern California. Currently incarcerated in the California Youth Authority for grand theft, this home boy, "Stray," wrote in his journal, which was confiscated by

authorities, about activities that seem aimless, but sadly are representative of the daily lives of so many of these suburban outlaws who have no
direction or purpose in life.

The juvenile justice system has been quite concerned about the
proliferation of teenage stoner gang members since the early 1980s.
Although the term *stoner* seems to have been first attributed to the long-
haired youth of the counterculture and hard-rock music era of the late
1960s and early 1970s, it was not until the advent of the heavy-metal
music scene in the 1980s that youth groups collectively identified
themselves as being stoner gang members.

According to one official, "stoner" used to refer to juveniles who
used marijuana and were "stoned" all of the time; who were involved
in the anti-Vietnam war movement; and who were part of the "tune
in, turn on, and drop out generation." The stoner groups of that period
presented only marginal problems for law enforcement officials through
their truancy, anti-social behavior, and delinquent activities (1).

Such groups, however, have undergone a metamorphosis in the past
two decades and have been increasingly implicated in violent street
crimes and numerous homicides. Instead of being merely retreatist
gangs noted for their drug-using, kicks-oriented subculture, these
stoner gangs have become criminal gangs noted for extremely violent
activity. Some stoner gangs also appear to have a strong interest in the
occult and satanism (see Chapter 9).

According to this same official, stoner groups vary in size from
approximately ten to forty members, and range in age from 13 to 20.
Their members tend to congregate in specific locations during and after
school such as video arcades and shopping malls. Their locations, however, are not treated by them as "turf." Nor are these areas defended in
the traditional sense as other ethnic, inter-city gangs mark and protect
their areas.

The youths involved in such stoner group gangs adopt a specific
style of dress, including T-shirts depicting their favorite heavy metal
group. They frequently attach drug and other paraphernalia to their
clothing such as upside-down crosses, pentagrams, hexagons, swastikas,
coke spoons, and roach clips. Their hair is frequently worn shoulder
length.

Satanic hard-core stoners, furthermore, favor Converse tennis shoes
because of the five-pointed star embossed on the shoe. This they equate
with the pentagram, an evil or magic symbol. Other distinctions
include their having satanic and other forms of occult graffiti written on

their clothing such as "666" (the mark of the devil or the beast), "All Religion Sucks," "Death to the Pigs," "LSD," and "Satan is Lord."

The stoners tend to be followers of specific heavy metal groups such as Motley Crue, Black Sabbath, KISS, Twisted Sister, and many others. The deeper the juveniles become involved with the stoner group and heavy metal music, the more rebellious and hostile they become.

WHITE YOUTH GANGS AS CULTS

Some criminologists view these youngsters as belonging to new youth cults, which are both hard to identify and which differ greatly from the more traditional ethnic gangs. One management consultant firm recently hired by the state of California to look into the new phenomenon of "Youth Gangs as Cults" raised several relevant questions including: Who is involved in these youth cults and how do these individuals identify themselves? What role does heavy metal music play in youth cult identification? What criminal and other problem activities are youth cult members responsible for? How widespread is the problem of youth cults and why is their membership increasing? And what is being done in an attempt to reduce cult membership (2)?

The report argues that membership in such youth cults appears to be growing at epidemic proportions, but that the number is difficult to measure because group affiliation is both secretive and hard to identify. Although heavy metal music appears to the most common denominator linking these youths, membership is not a direct result of identifying with this music. The report further states that cult members can identify one another readily through their common dress: metal-spiked wrist cuffs, collars and belts, sacrilegious or anti-Christ items, and T-shirts denoting their heavy metal heroes or bands.

The report also notes several patterns that distinguish these youths from the more traditional street gangs: Most of their cult activities are secretive and more difficult to identify. The group often holds an ideological linkage (such as satanic music), and engages in more ritualistic than territorial protection. The group follows few codes with nothing considered sacred. The group's goal is not to protect, but to destroy. Cult membership is predominately white and of higher economic status than that of the more common ethnic street gang members. And these groups are located in suburban rather than urban areas (3).

The report concludes that the stoner gangs' anti-social and criminal activities include using illegal drugs, abusing girls, assaulting parents, and drawing graffiti. In its most extreme form, grave robbing and the desecration of human remains and churches are some of their more bizarre activities.

The Gang Information Services Unit for the state of California distinguishes between four types of stoner gang members. Similar to the distinctions drawn between other more traditional gangs, the first type is the *wannabe* gang member who is trying to get into the gang and may dress and act the part to impress the actual gang members.

A second, also less serious, type is the *peripheral* gang member who gets involved when time warrants, but who is also attending school or holding down a job and so has other responsibilities and priorities. He may "get down" with the gang if a serious altercation warrants his presence.

Of more serious concern is the *hard-core* gang member who lives entirely for the gang, is frequently an officer, and is responsible for planning and carrying out the gang's activities. This third type of stoner "gang banger" is the focus of this chapter.

A similar threat is the *satanic hard-core* gang member, who is involved in more ritualistic activities. This last type will be the focus of the following chapter.

Similar to classification systems previously discussed, The Gang Information Services Unit (GISU) also utilizes the following criteria for classifying a minor as a stoner gang member:

> The minor is a self-admitted stoner. The minor has tattoos (e.g., a pentagram, "666"), and/or satanic-type graffiti, or markings of known stoner groups on his person, clothing, or in his possession. The minor is in the company of known stoners when he is taken into custody, and, when interviewed, the minor does not deny being a stoner. Finally, the minor's name or moniker frequently appears in stoner graffiti (4).

Stoner Gangs at CYA

According to a spokesperson for the California Youth Authority (CYA) who was assigned to specifically work with and monitor juvenile gangs, stoner youth gangs compose only 5 percent of the total 1,200 gangs in the state. Their membership, however, appears to be growing and is of increasing concern to authorities.

Furthermore, according to this same authority, skinheads are just one faction of the stoner gangs, a term or category the CYA uses to include those "Caucasian-based youth gangs which affiliate with both heavy metal and punk identities and music, and which include youth involved with satanic cults as well."

According to one report, stoner gangs are structured similarly to other inter-city, ethnic gangs characterized by criminal behavior. That is, they have a common dress, display colors, claim a name, and sport tattoos. Stoner gangs in suburban America, including skinheads, are more likely to hail from the middle class, but in other respects they are typical gang members as they come from broken homes with high instances of drug abuse and where many had been abused as children. According to this same report, the state of California has the highest level of juvenile stoner gang membership as well as the most criminally violent activity (5).

Because of this unsettling fact, it was decided to study all of the so-labeled—or so-identified by authorities—stoner gang members incarcerated within the CYA as of January 1990. Included in this group were all of those youths imprisoned for either skinhead or satanic behavior, as well as those who identified with the punk rocker or heavy metal scene, since the stoner gang category established by the CYA incorporated all of these youth styles.

Because of clearance restrictions, only those youths so identified as stoners by the youth authority were analyzed. There was no way to know whether all such stoner gang youths housed at that time in one of the many juvenile institutions in California were included in the sample group. Further, there was the possibility that some youths identified as stoners were not, in fact, stoners. For purposes of analysis, however, the study had to rely on the identification protocol setup by the CYA.

There is some danger in using institutionalized youths in a study of this sort because not only is one not guaranteed that all cases provided fit the specific category one is analyzing, but there is no guarantee of consistency from one case file to the next. So, information gathered by various people and agencies on the different wards may not be uniform. The researcher, in other words, may be left to draw conclusions based on insufficient and uncollaborated reports.

Then, too, there is the problem of generalizing about stoner youth from juvenile institutional settings to stoner youths found in the broader society. For these reasons and obvious limitations, the results reported in this chapter should be viewed as preliminary and investigative.

On the positive side, however, using case files from sources such as the CYA is valuable because each file on these youths was extensive. Most of the files numbered over one hundred pages, each with detailed notes of every commitment offense; every encounter with police; and meetings with institutional psychiatrists, psychologists, intake evaluators, probation officers, and the like. Every nuance of the juveniles' prior police records, court-ordered visitations and family evaluations, as well as behavior records within the various institutions where the wards had been housed, were systematically and chronologically logged in these files.

As part of the study, case files were obtained on the fifty-two male youths who were categorized by the CYA as stoner gang members. Further, the CYA also provided a comparative printout of these stoners' patterns, along with the overall patterns of the entire youth authority population, so that parallels could be drawn between the two groups.

As mentioned, not all information was available in the files. As the summary table, "Profile of Stoner Gang Members in the California Youth Authority," in Appendix B notes, only percentages and actual numbers for specific patterns that were included in the files were tabulated. Further, a separate column notes the number of wards' files that did not discuss a particular item.

Besides the overall patterns provided by the CYA on both the stoners and the general ward population, some forty items were gleaned from a detailed analysis of the fifty-two stoner gang members' files.

Per the institution's use, a stoner gang member was defined for the analysis as a "long-haired, unkempt youth who got into trouble with the law for drug or alcohol-related activities, and who fit one or more of the four criteria established by the Gang Information Services Unit" as outlined previously.

For most of these juvenile delinquents, the name of their gang clearly indicated that they were stoners, and made their identification simple. Several California stoner gangs adopt the term "stoner" within their title or affiliation, such as the Heavy Metal Hangout Stoners of Newport Beach. Other stoner gangs take such clearly identifiable names as WAR Skins; La Habra Skinheads; Los Angeles Death Squads or LADS; Suicidals, whose members are followers of the Suicidal Tendencies rock group; Hitler's Youth; True Sons of Liberty, which stands for "Lost" spelled backwards; and the Sacramento Express Stoners.

Sacramento Express Stoners

One case file from the CYA discussed the arrest of three youths, ranging in age from 16 to 19, apprehended for burglary. All three were members of the Sacramento Express Stoners, and their behavior was fairly typical of stoner gang members in general.

Included within their case files was a summary of the police interviews conducted at the time of their arrest. One of the three wards, "William," admitted to being involved in heavy metal gangs and satanic worship. Formerly affiliated with a stoner gang in San Francisco named the "0Is," William had a "zero" and an "I" tattooed on his forearm. This insignia, he said, stood for the "Brotherhood of Endless Working-Class Punks." He told the officers that this skinhead gang originated in London and had chapters throughout the world.

According to his file, William had joined the Sacramento Express Stoners when he first moved to Sacramento. This gang included both punkers and skinheads. A majority of their members were white males, and they believed in the Nazi movement. Referring to the Third Reich, William claimed, "The power that was, will be ours again." The ward claimed that they had seventeen members in their Sacramento-based gang, and were actively recruiting more teenagers. William described the following as common attire for the Sacramento Express Stoners:

> Either a shaved head or hair cut short; clothing consisting of a white T-shirt, suspenders, 501 bleached-white Levi's, commonly referred to as "snow caps"; large biker-type boots or Doc Martens with the pants rolled up to the top of the boot; and a leather jacket which depicted a low rider and a Playboy bunny.

William further maintained that their enemy, the Deathheads, was the largest, most feared and hated gang in the Northern California area. This rival gang had been involved in numerous assaults at dances, and their Deathhead graffiti, consisting of a Doc Martens boot with banners painted around it, was visible in certain parts of Sacramento. William claimed that the Deathheads were serious about gaining power. Currently numbering thirty, these Deathheads called themselves the "Pride and Glory Warriors." The normal hangouts for both stoner gangs was in the downtown mall, several neighborhood parks, and a local dance hall.

According to William, the Sacramento Express Stoners received their "backup" for any major activity from a San Francisco group known as "Bash," which stood for Bay Area Skin Heads. Their usual weapon of combat was mace.

The other two Sacramento Express Stoners youth apprehended, "Michael" and "George," also agreed that their common enemy was the Deathheads. Michael, at the time of this arrest, was on CYA parole, having served one year in a juvenile facility for an armed robbery offense. Both juveniles also contended that they were involved in hustling homosexuals, saying that they made money off the gays in the downtown area. Michael and George told the arresting officers that they made as much as $100 a day for sexual favors.

The boys also admitted to being involved with slam dancing at the gigs, sadomasochistic practices, and satanic worship. Both explained that to gain admittance to their gang, one had to be "jumped in," beaten up by at least three persons, and pay $20.

PROFILES OF STONERS

According to information provided by the Research Division of the California Youth Authority, stoner gang members represent only a small fraction (3 percent) of all the white males in their juvenile justice institutions.

Stoner Gang Members Compared to Other CYA Wards

A review of the printout on the fifty-two stoners showed that their most common commitment offense was burglary, with 70 percent incarcerated for this offense, followed by aggravated assault, auto theft, and armed robbery. Reflecting California's overall demographics, a high percentage of the stoner gang wards resided in Southern California (81 percent). Likewise, they more typically came from urban or suburban backgrounds, compared to rural areas.

In over three-fifths of the cases (62 percent), the income level of the homes of these wards had been evaluated as either "adequate" or "more than adequate," based on the standard intake information completed on all wards. Stoner gang members appeared to come from slightly higher socioeconomic backgrounds than the general ward population. Further, nearly three-quarters of the stoners tested at average or above average intelligence (72 percent). Nearly all of the stoners had a work history prior to incarceration (88 percent). And all but two were Caucasian.

These patterns contrasted sharply to the "typical" CYA ward, based on the information for the entire population. Generally, incarcerated wards come from lower socioeconomic backgrounds. They test at below average intelligence (based on standard IQ tests which have been criticized for failing to account for ethnic and racial diversity). Furthermore, typical wards have had a sporadic work history prior to incarceration, if they have had a history of employment at all. And they are disproportionately non-Caucasian.

Even with an average or better than average IQ, these stoner gang wards were still evaluated as low or nonachievers. None of the wards, for instance, had yet graduated from high school. Two-thirds had been previously placed in special education classes while in the public schools prior to incarceration. Over two-fifths had dropped out of school (43 percent) with most leaving high school in the tenth or eleventh grade (68 percent). And three-fourths (76 percent) had overall poor school achievement which, as prior research has noted, has been demonstrated to be one of the strongest predictors of subsequent juvenile delinquency (6).

Nearly all of the wards (96 percent) had "priors," meaning that they had been arrested for some previous offense and possibly had been incarcerated in some other facility or correctional program prior to their current placement within the CYA. Further, these wards were comparatively young to be housed in the more secure, higher-custody-level institutions. Two-fifths (42 percent) were 16 or under at the time of initial admittance.

By contrast, the "typical" CYA ward was more often an older teenager or young adult. (Delinquents charged in juvenile court and incarcerated for an offense serve time mandated by the length of their sentence and by their rehabilitation and behavior while in custody. The maximum time such juveniles serve is until they reach the age of 25 when, according to law, if sentenced as juveniles they must be discharged from the youth authority back into society.)

Most of the stoner gang members came from small families. Half of the wards, for instance, had only one other sibling. No specific birth order differentiated the group. For those youths from larger families, however, nearly half of the stoners were middle siblings. One of the fifty-two wards had a physical handicap. Two of the wards had been adopted, according to their files. By contrast, in my earlier study of juvenile firesetters, a larger number had been adopted as young children (14 percent), and adopted children have been viewed as being at greater risk to engage in delinquent acts (7).

FORMS OF ABUSE

The data clearly indicated that both alcohol and drug abuse were these stoner gang members' major problem. For example, as the stoner profile in Appendix B shows, two-thirds of these youths (69 percent) began taking (often multiple) drugs before the age of 13. These youths were drug abusers before they were even teenagers!

The Problem of Substance Abuse

All fifty-two of the wards studied had a history of abusing drugs and/or alcohol. In fact, the commitment offenses that brought them to the attention of authorities, and which sentenced them to the CYA, overwhelmingly centered around their possessing illegal drugs, selling illegal drugs, or committing crimes against property such as burglary and theft which were conducted to get money to purchase drugs or alcohol.

Furthermore, these youth frequently come from multigenerational substance-abusing families. With regard to the parents of wards, where information had been gathered at least one parent was noted to be a substance abuser in some 89 percent of the cases. In fact, in one-fourth of the cases (25 percent) the wards had parents who *both* abused drugs. Where just one parent was noted as a substance abuser, it was more often the father (57 percent for the father versus 7 percent for the mother).

Drug abuse was not just a family activity. A careful reading of their files indicated that nearly all of the stoner gang members were reported to have been strongly influenced by their peers (98 percent). And nearly all of the peers that these wards socialized with were also known by authorities to be involved with drugs.

These wards, it tragically appears, had been socialized both at home and among their peer group into a pattern of substance abuse. No wonder they are called "stoners"! And the fact that the wards began abusing drugs at an early age, and they are considered to be both heavy and multiple-drug users (94 percent), indicates the severity of their substance abuse problem.

John. The psychiatric evaluation of one ward, "John," was fairly typical of the drug dependencies of these stoner gang members. John, age 16, had a long involvement with the law prior to his commitment offense of trespassing, stealing a gun, and receiving stolen property. According to his file, during the five years preceding incarceration, he had several counts of burglary and running away from placement. He associated primarily with other delinquent individuals involved in substance abuse. He had some limited work experience as a landscaper.

His history of alcohol and drug abuse indicated that John had abused alcohol since the age of 9. Prior to that age he had been on ritalin for his hyperactivity. As a teenager he had also abused marijuana. He reported that he used both alcohol and marijuana in order to make himself feel good. He denied that he was feeling depressed at any time but he simply wanted to make himself feel better. He also reported having tried cocaine, crank, and speed. He did not like these drugs as well and found them to be too expensive for chronic use. He had never shot up.

Academically, the ward did well in grammar school, according to information in his file. Subsequently, however, he was identified as learning disabled, and was enrolled in special education classes. It was also felt, at the time, that John used the disability as an excuse to avoid responsibility for his behavior. John reported that, currently, in high school, he was getting "C" grades. According to the case report, the juvenile got along "okay" with his teachers and found it easy to ask for help when he needed it. His test scores indicated he performed at the ninth grade level in English and fifth grade level in mathematics. He indicated that he did not think that the drug program in prison was helping him, and felt that the group therapy sessions were "more or less a game," and that people were "kissing up to the staff" in order to get privileges.

John was the younger of two children. His parents separated and divorced while he was an infant. Contact with his biological father had been very sporadic. His mother raised him and his older sister as a single parent. According to his file, there was a long history of chaotic family environment. Even though there were behavior problems on the ward's part, repeated attempts to involve the family in counseling had all failed. John's family situation had changed recently. His mother had remarried and although John had not met the current husband, he had seen pictures of him, and planned to work in his stepfather's restaurant once he was released from the youth authority.

John voiced many mixed feelings about his incarceration. As he told his caseworker,

> If I were on the outs right now, I would probably be doing other drugs and getting into bigger kinds of trouble. This time I have to do all the school stuff here and that helps me.

Lawson. A second stoner ward, "Lawson," also came from a disruptive family life where drug taking was common, as his psychiatric report indicated.

Lawson's background indicated a chaotic history of living with his mother, who had a series of liaisons with men who abused drugs and alcohol. Since the ward was 11, he had been involved in petty theft, and had been placed at several homes with unsuccessful results. When he was 13 he became involved in burglary and was again placed unsuccessfully. At 15 he violated probation, was placed in juvenile hall, and, after assaulting a supervisor there, was transferred to the Youth Training School (YTS), the most secure of the CYA institutions.

Lawson, it appeared, had a reasonably good education, received "Bs" and "As" in his coursework, and, according to his teachers, was at least at grade level.

A moderately tall, handsome, youthful-appearing, 16-year-old Caucasian adolescent, Lawson had abused nearly every drug obtainable. The list included crank, coke, speed, weed, gasoline, paint, acid, and typewriter whitener. His favorite drugs were weed and typewriter whitener. The ward described in detail the effects of these various agents.

> Crank for example, made me hyper, a good feeling. Coke mellowed me out. Speed provided hallucinations. Weed made me paranoid. Gas made me hallucinate and lose control and occasionally black out. Paint was the same as gas, with an additional feature of having an echo chamber phenomenon. That is, I heard sounds as if there was an echo. Acid provided hallucinations.

Lawson never knew his natural father. He was the product of an extramarital affair. The ward's stepfather, and legal husband of his mother, died of a heroin overdose when Lawson was a young child. His second stepfather was an active alcoholic, and that relationship terminated due to alcohol and physical abuse. Lawson was the oldest of seven children.

Lawson's juvenile rap sheet involved charges of petty theft, second-degree burglary, violation of probation, and battery. Reported in his thick file were numerous incidents addressing the delinquent's explosively violent behavior toward not only family members and friends, but also institutional staff.

Even with this background, Lawson was currently being considered for parole. If granted, he would live with his aunt rather than his mother, because his mother had a recent history of cocaine abuse. His mother was also getting married again, and Lawson did not know his future stepfather.

As these two case studies sadly indicate, these wards have typically had a history of dysfunctional home life. Other studies of delinquent youths have noted similar patterns. In one study, preadolescents who reported that they did not get along with their family, and did not feel cared for, had less affectional relationships; identified less with their parents; and were more likely to initiate substance use (8).

The stoner gang members in this present study followed a similar and, unfortunately, too common path. Like youth in the other studies, the wards discussed here imitated their parents' drug taking, and tried to impress their peers by engaging in "adult behavior."

Like the delinquent youth in the other studies, the stoner gang members incarcerated in the CYA did not get along with their parents. Where information was available, nearly all (93 percent) stated they did not get along with their fathers, and most (86 percent) were found not to get along with their mothers. Furthermore, indicative of dysfunctional families in general, the wards shared these disturbing patterns: the parents of these wards were frequently divorced (53 percent); a stepparent was often present in the household (43 percent); and the families of these delinquents often had moved when the ward was quite young (72 percent), creating a disruption in the early years of the child's life.

Physical and Sexual Abuse

Many of these wards had experienced physical abuse within the home. Where information was available, it appeared that nearly half (47 percent) had experienced some form of physical abuse. Information on whether the wards had been sexually abused as youngsters was less frequently indicated in their files. In only twelve of the fifty-two cases was the topic of sexual abuse even mentioned. For these wards, however, it

appears that for some, sexual abuse had likely been a contributing factor in their anti-social behavior.

Edward. One ward that experienced physical abuse as a youngster was
"Edward." The following account was taken from his psychiatric case
report. Edward's commitment offense at the age of 16 was for armed robbery. He claimed he committed his offense as a means of survival since
his relationship with his parents was poor and he wanted to be independent. He claimed his parents had "too many petty rules" for him.

While institutionalized, Edward had had several rule infractions
such as not following instructions, showing disrespect, talking during
silence, being out of bounds, and possessing contraband. Edward was
the third of four children of an intact marriage. According to his case
file, he grew up in a household that was fairly strict. Punishment was
usually meted out by taking away personal property when it conflicted
with the family's moral values.

According to his mother, the ward had been a happy child until two
years before his arrest when he suddenly changed, becoming more defiant and noncompliant. It was at that time that he gave up his relationship with his parents' church, and began to ingest alcohol, marijuana,
and other drugs.

Edward, a tall, thin, 16-year-old Caucasian adolescent, tested as
above average in intelligence. Reports in his case files indicated that he
expressed anger at being at CYA, blaming his parents for his incarceration. He attributed most of his problems to the authoritarian nature of
his family, and their overly strict attitudes and behavior which resulted
in his receiving many humiliating punishments as a child and young
adolescent.

His parents' use of physical punishment was administered inconsis-
tently. He believed that this accounted, in part, for the circumstances of
his three brothers. His eldest male sibling currently was in
Leavenworth, a federal prison, for having transported drugs while in the
military. His second oldest brother had just been released from jail for
burglary. Edward was in the youth authority. And his youngest brother
was hyperactive and had been under psychiatric care for many years.

Edward's mother and father were strict, religious individuals. The
father had served his entire career in the military. They ruled the family
with strict guidelines, according to Edward. With all four of their sons
having serious behavioral problems, the parents' "strict guidelines" had
not seemed to work.

Edward, besides having an extensive drug history, also was involved with a neo-Nazi stoner gang in prison. Membership in the Nazi Low Riders (NLR), he claimed, provided him with a social group he could belong to. And while he did admit to having a sense of white dominance, he felt that it was "under control" and that it did not mean "putting down other races." He believed he got along well with all ethnic groups on the hall, but he was not sure how the staff responded to his NLR affiliation.

Edward's treatment psychiatrist interpreted the teenage ward's antisocial behavior in this way:

> Edward is an angry young man who clearly is defiant of all authority, probably stemming from relationships with his family. Dynamically, he has incorporated authoritarian figures and this identification with them leads to his current behavior. He defends himself by joining hostile groups, attenuating somewhat the intense rage he feels within himself, but at the same time getting into difficulty. Basically, however, he is not a violent individual, but uses it to act out especially in relationship to events occurring within the family.

According to Edward's parents, prior to his arrest for armed robbery at a food and liquor store, he had been steadily influenced by a neighbor boy who gave him drugs. Within the year prior to his incarceration, Edward had begun to run away and refused to accept any direction or guidance from them. He also began to express opinions that they (his parents) were too strict, and that he could not abide by their religious expectations.

Located within his case file was this written report that Edward had given the authorities upon his arrest, recounting the circumstances that led up to his commitment offense.

> I was really fed up with my parents. I felt boxed in. I planned on running away. I needed the money to live on. I found an old shotgun that might not have worked. It was rusty. I thought I could get some food money if I robbed the store. I picked one (a convenience store) I thought would be used to robbers. I went in by myself and threatened the man at the counter verbally in a way so as to cover for the unloaded gun. I grabbed the first fist full of cash I saw because I was really scared and ran. I threw the gun in a dumpster and hid until the cops quit searching. I only got $30.

Edward was apprehended later at a continuation high school because witnesses recognized him running from the store. At the time of Edward's arrest his father was employed as a law clerk in the local county jail. Edward's case, unfortunately, was representative of many of the stoner gang members incarcerated by the youth authority.

Many of the stoner gang members in the CYA were bullies. By their late teens, they had already exhibited a history of physically and/or sexually abusing other youths either inside or outside the institution (52 percent). Having also been the recipients of parental abuse themselves when they were youngsters, these wards had shifted roles from being the victim to becoming the victimizer.

Such anti-social and self-destructive behaviors—which are unfortunately learned at home—are all too common. Our nation's juvenile justice institutions and adult correctional facilities are filled with individuals who were abused as children and who, unfortunately, grow up in turn to abuse others.

Furthermore, both the juvenile and adult facilities seem to perpetuate these patterns of abuse as well. In one of my earlier studies on a men's medium-security, adult prison in California, I documented the pattern whereby men who had been sexually exploited and victimized or "turned out" in one institution had frequently, upon transfer, become the victimizers or aggressors on other younger, vulnerable men in the institution under study (9).

Ted. One stoner gang ward, "Ted," fit this profile of the physically and sexually exploited youth who, in turn, became the exploitive youth. According to his prison psychiatrist, Ted, age 17, had been both physically abused by his parents and sexually molested by an adult male. Ted described a chaotic and confusing family history involving multiple moves, family conflicts, and school problems.

In Ted's case file, his psychiatrist noted that the ward was quite open about being raped by an older man who had picked him up after he ran away from home. Likewise, he readily described an incident of excessive physical punishment he received at the hands of his mother and stepfather, leading to his being removed from the home. The psychiatrist concluded that Ted had a strong tendency to strike back, or get even one way or another, for wrongs done to him. It appeared he had experienced several incidents of physical abuse from his parents.

Ted's commitment offense was for molesting his younger 10-year old half-sister. She claimed that Ted had fondled her vagina and breasts. He denied the charges, attributing her lying to jealousy.

Stoner gang members, as has been noted, are of increasing alarm to authorities in California and throughout the country. Only since late 1986 have personnel who detail juvenile gangs in California begun to track these youth involved with white youth gangs. As this investigative analysis of stoner wards illustrates, these youths, besides being abused, are serious substance abusers themselves. Further, they have come from dysfunctional families where substance abuse has been the pattern. Their primary peer group comprises juveniles who are also substance abusers.

In conclusion, any attempt at rehabilitating these delinquents must address their alcohol and/or drug-related problems and dependencies, as well as the dysfunctional family and social conditions that have accounted for their rage.

NOTES

1. Dennis McLellan, "Spikes and Studs: Tipping the Scales against Heavy Metal, Punk," *The Los Angeles Times* (21 February 1985), p. V-1.

2. Lynne P. Cannady, "Youth Gangs as Cults," (Sacramento, CA: Evaluation, Management and Training, 1989).

3. Ibid.

4. "Stoners and the Occult," pamphlet (Los Angeles County Sheriff's Department, East Los Angeles Gang Unit "Operation Safe Streets"; Los Angeles, CA, 1986).

5. Esteban P. Castaneda, "Report on Youth Gangs," (Sacramento, CA: State Task Force on Youth Gang Violence, 1988).

6. Martin Gold, "School Experiences, Self-Esteem, and Delinquent Behavior: A Theory for Alternative Schools," *Crime and Delinquency* 24 (1978), pp. 29–45.

7. Wayne S. Wooden and Martha Lou Berkey, *Children and Arson: America's Middle Class Nightmare* (New York: Plenum Press, 1984).

8. Jonathan Shedler and Jack Block, "Adolescent Drug Use and Psychological Health," *American Psychologist* 45 (May 1990), pp. 612–630.

9. Wayne S. Wooden and Jay Parker, *Men Behind Bars: Sexual Exploitation in Prison* (New York: Plenum Press, 1982).

9

▼

Satanists: Devil's Children?

"No Satan Worship at This School"

This year's handbook for students at suburban Homewood-Flossmoor High School makes the rules clear: No running in the halls, no tardiness and no worshipping Satan.

School officials said the rule was included in this year's handbook to protect the students. Officials were told by neighboring districts and Chicago police at a recent seminar that interest in the occult is growing.

Last spring, school officials found two markings on lockers and one scuffed on a floor that resembled "an upside-down A in a circle," a symbol of Satan worship.

According to the new policy, students may be suspended for "occult or occult-related activities," placing such actions in the same category as "defiance of faculty authority" or "violation of school smoking rules" (1).

"Police Respond to Satanic Behavior on Gatos High School Campus"

Police went to Gatos High School before the football game Friday night. They found a goat that had been sacrificed and hung from the crossbars. Off to the side was a pentagram symbol.

Other satanic-appearing related activities have also recently surfaced. Two weeks ago a dairy cow was reported stolen and later found sacrificed with the pentagram symbol next to it. It had been discarded in an open field near the high school campus where students congregate on weekends.

Police have also found a number of satanic temples in the foothills north of the high school campus lately (2).

"Authorities Probe Satanic Link in Teen Murder-Suicide Case"

In November, Thomas Manning's Catholic school teacher assigned students to research other religions. The studious 14-year-old did his paper on Hinduism but police say he became more interested in the subject that earned friends an A: satanism.

Within weeks, the All-American neighborhood paper boy became a defiant, hostile teen buried in library books on the occult and listening to heavy metal rock music. His teachers noticed the transformation and warned his mother on Thursday. By Saturday night, mother and son were dead.

Police said Manning was entranced by the occult as he stabbed his mother at least 12 times and tried to kill his father and 10-year-old brother by setting fire to their Jefferson Township house. Then he slit his throat and wrists with a Boy Scout knife, slumping dead on bloody snow in a neighbor's back yard (3).

The Gang Information Services Unit for the state of California distinguishes between the hard-core stoner gang member (see Chapter 8) and the satanic stoner gang member, the focus of this chapter. The main difference between the two groups is that the satanist is involved in more ritualistic activities. Because of this distinction, it was decided to look more closely at this special group of satanic stoners.

One-fifth of the stoner gang members in the California Youth Authority group of fifty-two wards had been, or continued to be, active satanists. None of their commitment offenses, however, were tied to crimes involving satanic rituals. Similar to the stoners previously discussed, all of these teenage satanists had engaged in burglaries or robberies as their commitment offense. And all had, like the others, a history of drug and alcohol abuse.

All the stoner wards, regardless of category, had a socialized delinquent aspect of their lives. For both the satanic cult members and the hard-core stoner gang members, the juveniles had obviously found a subculture that accepted them, and often encouraged and reinforced their drug-taking and delinquent identities.

Over half the wards in the sample proudly admitted to their treatment personnel that they were still gang affiliated (57 percent). Two-thirds (67 percent) admitted listening to heavy metal music. This behavior was noted in their case files by the treatment personnel since the authorities felt such music had been a negative influence on their lives. Several of the treatment personnel specifically noted in their evaluations of these wards that a destructive link appeared to exist between these youths listening to heavy metal music and identifying with a racist skinhead or satanic lifestyle.

PROFILES OF SATANISTS

As best as could be determined based on the reading of the case files, one-fifth of the stoner wards strongly identified with satanism. One such ward, "Greg," fit the typical profile in that he both participated in satanic activity and claimed to have been part of a satanic cult. Several incidents were described in his probation report that exemplified the typical "progression" for those youngsters who become involved with satanism (a pattern that will be discussed at greater length later).

In his early teens, Greg had, according to his parents, become interested in playing the game "Dungeons and Dragons." His parents destroyed the game after they interpreted it to be an evil influence. The more the minor rebelled in the home setting, the more his parents destroyed his personal belongings. According to his parents, they confiscated what they perceived to be "all evil influences" such as his Iron Maiden, AC/DC, Judas Priest, and Ozzie Osbourne records, his evil drawings, and his *Satanic Bible*.

When questioned about his involvement with satanism, Greg told his probation officer that his ties were limited to self-gratification and identification. He indicated he did not concern himself with satanic rituals. He studied religions and felt satanism met his needs. He further expressed some resentment because his parents forced him to go to the

Nazarene church against his wishes. Satanism was his way of rebelling and getting back at them.

Greg told this officer that he had only been involved with satanism since the beginning of his sophomore year in school. Although he knew other youths who were interested in satanism, his involvement, he claimed, was more of an individual activity and those other people were not really knowledgeable. Greg did admit drawing graffiti and other drawings using satanic symbols such as "666," an inverted penta-gram with a goat's head in it, and upside-down crosses. The minor reported that he associated these symbols with rock bands.

Even so, the following document was written by 16-year-old Greg while he was incarcerated. It was confiscated during a room search, and indicated his continued, strong involvement in the satanic youth cult. This rather bizarre account was included in his case file.

> The P.S.S. (Piedmont Satanic Stoners) (not its real name) is an organization within the Satanic Church and has been planned and will be started by me and P. Jay. All who enter this organization will be given names symbolic such as these.
>
> The P.S.S. is an organization made for spreading Satan's word and the use of drugs throughout the area. Weed will be grown on land owned by the P.S.S. and coke and horse (hard drugs) will be imported on our smuggling ships. We will also have organized robbery and burglary. All these funds will go to support ourselves and our church.
>
> On our smuggling ships will also be smuggled guns to sell to street gangs in other areas. We ourselves will not be a street gang. We will be an organization within a church. When we are released from the youth authority, P. Jay and I are going to learn the ways of the sorcerer under Anton Le Vey, the High Priest. You are also welcome to join us and to become a leader of the P.S.S.
>
> In a huge house we the priests will all live with our women and drugs. The house will be a hot partying house, with secret tunnels and rooms behind the walls to escape from the pigs in case of a large raid. But for the most part we will have nothing to fear of the law, for our chief warriors will be a lion. Our others will be dobies (dobermans) and pit bulls trained to kill trespassers. We will also have 20 armed men and a large arsenal of guns and explosives.
>
> Our main ceremonies will be held in the basements and hidden cellars beneath the house. The lowest cellar will be a dungeon with torturing devices and a stone altar where we shall slay our

enemies in blood sacrifice. In town we will have a stone church where we will hold services. At ceremonies we shall wear the necessary items: black hooded robes, red inside for worshippers, purple and silver pentagram medallions. But on the streets our uniform shall be: a black leather jacket, black 501's, our P.S.S. bandanna on the head or around the right leg, and a black T-shirt with P.S.S. on the front.

The shirt is not necessary, and neither is the jacket in hot weather, but the 501's and bandanna should be worn most of the time. Our women will wear tight black 501's, black spandex, a tight black leather mini-skirt, a black dress cut high on the hip and low at the breast, or some other black, revealing clothing.

Everyone should always wear the stoner pentagram, and all the men in our organization will always carry a weapon. Our colors are these: black for our evil; white for our skin (as the demons said, only whites shall be in our organization); and red for the fire in our hearts and the blood on our hands. Our numbers shall be 666, for the beast we salute, and 13, for the marijuana we smoke.

REBELLION AGAINST ORGANIZED RELIGION

Only three of the fifty-two incarcerated stoner gang members appeared to embrace any traditional religious affiliation. Such affiliation, however, might not have been a topic that was asked of them by their intake counselors.

If a pattern emerged at all based on a reading of their files, it was that several of the wards (such as Greg) embraced satanism as a means of embarrassing their parents. By affiliating with such a controversial religious sect as satanism, these misguided youth seemed to get back at what they considered to be the very rigid moral code and traditional religious values established at home by their parents. Believing in, and following, Satan was their ultimate act of defiance.

By affiliating with satanic cults, these teenagers were undoubtedly engaging in behavior they knew would deliberately upset and provoke their families. What better way to get back at one's father who might serve as an elder in a more mainstream church than by closely identifying with a belief and a lifestyle that was antithetical to everything one's father embraced?

A similar pattern was observed in another study I previously conducted on juvenile firesetters. In one part of that research I found that
an unusually high number of children of fire fighters (10 percent) had
deliberately set fires. This behavior was explained, in part, as a means
by which the youngsters retaliated against their fathers in a decidedly
symbolic way. Their arsonist behavior was also viewed as a "cry for
help" on the part of the youngsters to get their fathers to pay greater
attention to them (4). Thus, in a comparable way, rejecting the traditional religious values of ones' parents and embracing satanism was a
typical pattern for several of these CYA wards, including one ward
named "Ken."

Ken. According to the prison files, Ken was a thin, 15-year-old youth,
with long, stringy, recently dyed hair, who showed little use for personal hygiene. To his caseworker he appeared antagonistic and hostile,
and seemed to care little for authority in any shape or form.

Ken expressed interests in music, playing the guitar, partying, and
witchcraft. He claimed that satanism was a belief, not a religion. He had
a special fondness for spells calling for destruction. His career objective
was to play the guitar and become a musician in a heavy metal band.

Ken grew up in Southern California. His natural parents divorced
when he was 2 years old, and he was reared primarily thereafter by his
mother. He claimed to have never had any contact with his natural
father, a Colombian. Ken's mother remarried when he was 12. In Ken's
estimation,

> My stepdad didn't like me or my sister. He'd slap me around. He
> would yell at me. He was consistently abusive. My stepdad was
> crazy. He had to go get psychiatric help. He was a Vietnam guy.
> I've always hated him and I always will. He forces all of that
> Seventh Day Adventist church school shit on us.

Ken told his counselor that his mother was currently in the process
of divorcing this man and that she had a new boyfriend. He said that
he was happy to see his stepdad go. Ken said, "He'd come down on
me for any little thing. My mom stayed with him because he was
feeding us."

Ken claimed that the relationship with his stepfather progressively
deteriorated to the point that Ken decided to move out of the house
when he was 14. He moved into the home of a friend who was 16. Ken
stayed with this family for six months. When asked why he left at that
point, he responded, "I got kicked out when I brought home a girl
who stayed for the night."

Ken moved back home. At that time, his mother was living with her new boyfriend, or with a man whom Ken described as her "boss." Ken was asked about his relationship with this new man. He replied, "Bill's kind of cool, but he starts to play God and stuff. He ain't my dad so I don't have to listen to him." The therapist interpreted this reaction as Ken's bitterness about never having had a father to really look up to. Ken made it quite clear that he was not accepting that authority from just anyone.

It was also clear, according to the therapist, that Ken had a problem with his mother's authority as well. Commenting on his mother, Ken said,

> I've never really gotten along with my mom. She's always been irrational, screaming and yelling all of the time, especially if she doesn't get her way.

Ken viewed his mother as rather unstable, and, by implication, he had not respected the kind of relationships that she had had. It was also clear to him that her male friends had been far more interested in her than they had been in fathering Ken. To this point he seemed, according to the therapist, to have rejected all forms of authority.

Ken also had a younger sister, Michelle, who was 14. In his opinion, "She is the only one normal enough to talk to. We argue but I can get along with her." He described himself as a "metalist stoner" and as a "lowlifer."

When asked about his partying lifestyle, Ken related it to his satanic religious philosophy, which he had studied one year prior to his incarceration when he was 14. He said that he became particularly interested after reading the *Satanic Bible*, by Anton Le Vey. Ken noted,

> What I liked most was not having the moral restrictions. Morals hold you down. The satanist philosophy takes the guilt off you when you do stuff.

Ken admitted that most of his friends in high school were into drugs. He also admitted being into drugs quite heavily himself. He said, without hesitation, "I've been into everything except heroin and PCP. But I like crank the best."

As far as Ken was concerned, this was an acceptable way of life. He was critical of his use of marijuana, however. He said, "I want to give up weed because of my lungs. I want to be a lead vocalist." His ambition was to be a rock star. To him, these people symbolized the ultimate in human achievement. Ken also told his therapist that he was not afraid of dying, claiming,

Because when I die I think that I'll be "a pit beast" in hell. A pit beast is a creature who had served Satan on earth and was therefore used by Satan in hell.

I'll be one of those torturing the preppies and the hypocrites. Satan won't destroy those who help him. Hypocrites are the ones who'll burn.

The therapist interpreted Ken's responses as feelings of bitterness and resentment toward those others such as "preppies and hypocrites" whom Ken saw as conforming to societal norms. Although Ken derided these people, he also felt sadness at not being accepted by them.

Ken was arrested for stolen property. Four days prior to his arrest, police had been called to his home where he was apprehended for brandishing a broken beer bottle at his parents. The police report on this incident noted that Ken was "totally out of control," and that his behavior would lead one to suspect that he may have been on drugs. The police, however, did not take action at this initial disturbance.

In conversations with Ken's mother, she said that her son had recently told her that he was "really the son of Satan and the son of the devil." He also apparently had told his mother that she simply had him "for the devil's purposes." There was no question, according to the therapist, that some of these recent incidences were of great concern to Ken's mother and her boyfriend.

With regard to Ken's behavior inside the institution, his case file noted that he had not been a behavior problem as far as acting out. However, he had been violating hall policies such as talking on silence and being out of bounds. Of greater concern to authorities was his recent involvement in gang activity, including both the Nazi Low Riders (NLR) and the Supreme White Power (SWP) groups. These two factors had played a major role in preventing him from progressing in the treatment program.

Skip. Other wards in the youth authority who had been involved with satanic behavior were queried about their activities. One ward, "Skip," described what would typically take place at a satanic sacrifice.

The most common animal used was a goat which would be hogtied, and have its throat slashed with the blood drained into a pan. The blood would then be chilled in a refrigerator for approximately three hours. Once the blood had chilled, numerous tabs of LSD would be diluted into the blood and the concoction would then be consumed by numerous people in attendance at the ritual. They said you could then "really get to see and meet the devil." The goat was then discarded after the ceremony.

Rob. Another 17-year-old ward, "Rob," who resided in a rural area in Northern California, claimed that besides animal sacrifices, he had also been involved with burning crosses in front yards. He claimed that this signified the devil. He also admitted to placing the decapitated heads of animals such as cows and goats that had been sacrificed during satanic rituals on neighbors' front yards. He stated that this was a common practice with satanic groups.

Rob had also been involved in sadomasochism. According to the police report, he had numerous healed scars on both arms and hands. These, he said, had been caused by razors during an S&M session.

According to the police, satanic cults have been active throughout the nation for many years. These groups have been reputed to be involved in ritualistic homicides, child abuse and/or molestations, kidnapping and animal mutilations, as well as many other forms of deviant and criminal behavior.

According to these authorities, satanism, which started out as a casual fad practiced by juveniles, has now ended up as a new delinquent subculture. In recent years, youths in the Southern California area have been apprehended for mortuary vandalism and graveyard burglary. In one instance, satanic graffiti were painted on the interior walls of mortuaries, and urns containing human ashes were stolen and never recovered. In another incident, members of a stoner gang entered a mausoleum and removed marble slab covers to crypts and painted satanic graffiti on the walls. And in yet a third incident, urns containing human ashes were stolen and used by stoners in satanic rituals, according to police reports.

The self-admitted stoners who were apprehended said they broke into the mausoleum, broke open several crypts, and removed and opened caskets. Body parts were removed and thrown all over the interior of the location. Body parts were also intentionally mixed together (5).

Other youths have been involved with animal mutilations. Close to where I reside, remains of goats, cats, chickens, and pigeons have been found in cemeteries. All had been decapitated and drained of their blood. Several cats were found nailed to trees. Even on the Cal Poly campus, half the young goat herd one recent year, according to campus police, had been sacrificed in ritualistic fashion. Their carcasses were left at the grisly scene but the blood had been drained from their bodies. This past spring, several baby pigs were also killed with their remains placed in a ceremonial manner.

THE PASSAGE INTO SATANIC BEHAVIOR

One sociologist, Martin Sanchez-Jankowski, extensively studied three satanic gangs in California in the late 1980s. He was initially approached by a member of one of the satanic gangs to study their new gang. He was able to chronicle events of the gang though he did ask that the gang members wear masks at their rituals so that he would not know their individual identities.

Each of the three gangs Sanchez-Jankowski studied numbered about thirty. All were similar in activities but had no contact with each other. All were composed evenly of both males and females. All of the members had first become involved with the satanic gangs in their late teens. All of the members had come from white, middle-class backgrounds. And all were Christian, from "high Protestant" backgrounds such as Methodist, Lutheran, or Episcopalian faiths.

All of the youths developed into satanism in a "natural way," according to Sanchez-Jankowski. They had known each other before they became involved. None were strangers nor had any been recruited. The members of each of the three satanic gangs had attended the same high schools. They had shared similar musical tastes, clothing styles, and the like.

They had initially formed as social cliques, to have private parties where drugs were present and sex took place. Symbols of the devil were used to counteract Christian morality, almost as a rationalization for their behavior. What started out as a fad soon developed, however, into something more serious. As parties continued, the group wanted to learn more about satanism. The private parties shifted to "rituals" and the meetings became a "Black Mass." At this point, according to Sanchez-Jankowski, the groups shifted into more institutionalized behavior. The groups developed an ideology; they met, read, and discussed the *Satanic Bible*. A theology emerged with Satan as the pinnacle.

Activities now involved more ritualistic drug taking—usually hallucinogenic drugs taken three to four times an evening—and the group began at that point to sacrifice animals. Frequently, one of the members would submit to sexual activity, abuse, and pain. There was blood letting within the ritual.

According to Sanchez-Jankowski, such activities created a bonding among the members. Everyone knew everyone else including knowing each others' parents. Pictures were taken of their events for "historical records"—but this served as a social control measure as well.

Sanchez-Jankowski noted that without the historical tradition of satanism throughout the world, these cults would not have continued. But since these members had been reading published material, and were tapping into the cultural tradition, they were able to form more long-lasting institutions (for example, Church of Satan).

Sanchez-Jankowski concluded that these patterns suggest that cult formation can occur in quite natural ways. People do not have to exhibit psychopathological tendencies before embracing satanism. All in all, according to his observations, it took approximately two years for the teenage group to shift from a fad into a full-fledged cult (6).

TYPES OF TEENAGE SATANISTS

Not all youths involved in the satanic scene are equally committed to witchcraft and pagan rituals. For points of comparison (based on material provided by a student who, though not a satanist, had numerous job-based interactions with them while she was in college), three distinct types of teenage satanists can be delineated (7). These include the *soft-core* satanists, the *noncriminal hard-core* satanists, and the *criminal hardcore* satanists.

Soft-core Satanists

The soft-core satanists are usually younger than the other two types, ranging in age from 12 to 16. Although typically male, groups also sometimes include a few females. Generally, they are from the same social backgrounds as members of the other two groups. The soft-core satanists frequently are underachievers although above average in intelligence. They are generally sociable but easily angered, and suffer from low self-esteem.

Soft-core satanists get involved in satanism as a means to upset, provoke, and embarrass their parents. Their anger, which is rooted in frustration, often is directed toward their family. These young people—who are often the product of "religious" homes—begin to feel they are living in a world full of hypocrites. This feeling usually begins as the teen matures and begins to think for himself or herself. As this happens, two things occur almost simultaneously. First, the anger and frustration build. Second, the child begins asking questions about Christianity that are not supposed to be asked because they usually have no answers since many religious teachings are accepted on faith.

As the questions mount and the intensity of the anger builds, this young person with enough intelligence to get into trouble, and not enough to get out of it, begins looking for trouble. About the time these people begin to experiment with drugs, they also try to find the antithesis of Christianity. They find it in satanism.

These soft-core satanists usually "practice" magic or satanism with a small group of friends who also want to do what will anger their parents. For the most part, they only know what they have read in Le Vey's book, or in H. P. Lovecraft's *Necronomicon*. As such, they do not have access to what sets the stage for the hard core.

These people, in many ways, are crying for help. Unfortunately, help is not what they get. Their actions, accompanied by heavy metal, marijuana, and alienation, are usually dealt with far too harshly by their parents and persons in authority, such as teachers. Such reactions and labels further alienate these juveniles who retaliate by moving more deeply into the lifestyle, in a pattern known by sociologists as *labeling theory* whereby the youth progresses from primary into secondary deviance.

Satanism, heavy metal, and drugs are merely symptoms of underlying family issues. However, they are usually thought of as the causes. More often than not this is not so. Alienation sets in way before the teen seeks out any satanic behavior.

The parents of these children deny the trouble their teens are facing and do not address the issue until it reaches the boiling point. Faced with a child who is dabbling in satanism, the parents' responses seem to determine whether or not that youngster will progress into one or the other of the next two types.

If the parents kick their child out of the house at the first sign of satanic-related behavior, for instance, that action may force the child into even greater involvement. It is critical that the family address the other issues and concerns that the family as a unit is experiencing. In other words, involvement in satanic behavior by a youngster is not the only concern facing these often dysfunctional families. Most families, however, seem to deal with the symptoms and not the problem. This merely accentuates the pattern, pushing some children even further into the satanic realm. The kids have typically gotten behind in school and this compounds the issue as well.

It is at this point that family therapy is essential, with honest, open communication and with each family member listening to what the other has to say. There is a need to set up programs like Parents of Punkers to assist these families whose children are involved in soft-core satanism.

Noncriminal Hard-core Satanists

As with the first type, these people begin soft core. However, they usually make some sort of "adjustment," embracing more of a satanic identity while still continuing to successfully function within society. They are typically older adolescents to young adults, ranging in age from 15 to 24.

This group, composed equally of males and females, are average in scholastic work. Their satanic involvement may be done for some attention seeking, as they are typically flamboyant. They do not commit criminal acts, however. These are the satanists who follow Le Vey to the letter. They seem to believe in satanism for its valuing of the profane; but they generally do not believe in Satan as a deity per se. For them, satanism is a religion (or cult) based upon worldly pleasures.

Criminal Hard-core Satanists

The third group, examples of which are the several CYA wards discussed earlier, come from all types of backgrounds, socioeconomic classes, and statuses. They are both underachievers, youngsters who are quite bright, and overachievers, those who have scholastic difficulty.

Some of these juveniles have severe sociopathic characteristics. They are manipulative, suffering from low-impulse control. Typically, these are the ones that receive the media coverage. They commit human and animal sacrifices; assault; kidnapping; and sexual, physical, and mental abuse; among other atrocities.

These are the people who begin in soft core, but because of psychological and social dysfunctioning, become criminal. The acts this group commits go beyond a cry for help because they lose touch with what is appropriate. Sometimes these people come from abusive backgrounds themselves.

Unlike the soft core who practice alone or in small groups, this criminal hard-core type practices in "Covens of 13." The covens are characteristically secretive, ritualistic, manipulative, and controlling. Initiates are typically "required" to prove themselves through acting as slaves to the coven and the rites, allowing themselves to be used sexually and physically abused. Members are required to participate through coercion and blackmail.

The covens take the *Satanic Bible* and the *Necronomicon* and carry the rites to an extreme. In the case of Le Vey's book, they often distort what he has written. Hard-core satanists also use other forms of "high" magic from Norse or Egyptian mythos.

Signs of Satanic Activity

In the last several years numerous seminars have been given throughout the country by law enforcement officials alerting authorities to the dangers of satanic cults, and instructing them on how to look for signs that such groups have developed or are present in their respective areas. Pat Metoyer, of the Los Angeles Police Department, in a presentation, "Witchcraft, Devil Worship, Satanism, and Satanic Cults," distinguished between the *self-styled satanists* and the *satanic cults*.

The *self-styled satanists* were frequently young people between the ages of 12 and 24 who became involved by buying the *Satanic Bible*; by renting movies such as "Rosemary's Baby," "Damien," and "The Exorcist"; by listening to heavy metal music by such groups as Ozzy Osbourne, AC/DC, and Black Sabbath; and by consuming drugs. On the other hand, the *satanic cults* were secret groups of young people who engaged in criminal activity including animal sacrifices, grave robbery, church desecration, cannibalism, drug taking, and forced sexual activity (8).

According to Metoyer, the profile of the satanic cult member was one between the ages of 12 and 24; a Caucasian, who had a high IQ;

who was typically defiant, angry, a loner, and isolated; and who was a multiple-drug user—similar to those I examined in the CYA. Frequently, these youngsters were overly involved with their music. They came from broken homes, and were highly impressionistic, according to Metoyer. Their parents typically had problems with their children being isolated. The boys, for instance, retreated to the privacy of their own bedrooms to set up their own world.

Members of satanic cults, in contrast to the typical juvenile delinquent, come from higher socioeconomic backgrounds, in part because of the expenses involved. Dabbling in satanism and the occult involves making purchases and obtaining implements. The activity is therefore often restricted to those youngsters who have access to funds to buy drugs and the satanic paraphernalia (9).

Other police officials have studied the rise of juvenile satanic cults as well. Sandi Gallant, of the San Francisco Police Department, calls teenagers' interest in satanism "a way to get everything they want right now." Teenagers involved with satanism also express the view that they do not have a future because of the violent nature of our society. Gallant contends that involvement of the young with satanism began to mushroom in the early 1980s, and that there may now be upwards of 2,000 satanic groups in the United States with as many as 2 million members (10).

One spokesperson for the conservative Christian Research Center in Tustin, California, argues that there are at least 5,000 hard-core satanists in Los Angeles County alone, and that they have engaged in mock human sacrifices, drug abuse, kidnapping, sexual violence, and animal mutilations. Dr. Walter Miller, director of the center, is quoted as saying that there were at least 15,000 recorded cases of animal mutilations during the decade of the 1980s (11).

Not all public officials view such delinquency as satanic-cult-related, however. Many law enforcement officials believe that there remains little credence to satanic-motivated delinquency, and argue that each delinquent act should be handled on a case-by-case basis. Furthermore, these officials contend, the satanic-related acts of some juveniles are oversensationalized by the media and distorted out of context. As one official explained,

> Much of the interest in satanism remains a mere fad, a trendy spin-off from the culturewide interest in the occult. And some of it is sheer fantasy produced by drug-induced paranoia (12).

The Influence of Heavy Metal

One common element that satanists share is their interest in heavy metal music. One observer noted that the emergence of heavy metal music in the late 1960s corresponded with the formation by Anton Le Vey of the Church of Satan in 1968 (13).

This observer also argued that heavy metal music contains satanic messages that are very important to juveniles since these youngsters often have "poor self-images." Teenagers who succumb to these influences typically are social outcasts, and are frequently "the type of kids who aren't in step with their peers."

Heavy metal groups, this observer believes, are frequently linked to satanism. For instance, AC/DC stands for Anti-Christ/Devil's Children. The heavy-metal musical group KISS stands for Kids (or Knights) in Satan's Service. And the popular musical group Black Sabbath refers to the day of Satan worship (14).

Furthermore, the satanic sign made with the index and little finger extended can frequently be seen in many heavy metal rock videos and stoner gang member graffiti. Kids at concerts shout, "NATAS" (Satan spelled backwards). Others contend that there are messages on records dealing with Satan, and that when the records are played backward—a technique known as backward masking—the messages can be heard. This backward writing appears to be an important aspect of satanic cults, and serves as part of the mystique many stoners find attractive. The concept of backward writing is reputed to have originated with the Church of Satan (15).

Satanists and Traditional Gangs

Lawrence C. Trostle, who has extensively studied one stoner gang in the Los Angeles area, contends that stoner gangs—though known to congregate in specific areas—have no extended claim to specific land or turf. In this regard they tend not to feud or engage in gang wars with other gangs. Because of this pattern of being nonterritorial, stoner gangs are viewed as the "gypsies" of the gang subculture (16).

This is particularly true for the stoner gangs that are also satanic cults. Frequently, the more traditional ethnic and neighborhood gangs stay clear of the satanists, viewing them as being "loco" or crazy. Also, more traditional, ethnic gang members do not see stoners as "real men," but as "wimps" and "sissies." Consequently, these stoner gangs do not pose a threat to them.

Typically, the stoners and satanists frequent one particular location one week, and move on to another the next. In this sense, stoner gangs are location-oriented and not territorial. Such locations in the Southern California area include specific shopping malls, arcades, video games, record shops, fast food restaurants, cemeteries, freeway underpasses, and abandoned rock quarries.

Thus, when they encroach upon a traditional gang's turf, stoners or satanists are not perceived as invaders or trespassers. In this sense, satanic cults have been pretty much left alone by the other types of gangs that may be also located in the area.

Some probation officers working gang detail have noted that some juveniles become stoner gang members so that they will not be required to join the more traditional ethnic street gangs of their neighborhoods. And other juveniles, upon parole, join stoner gangs to avoid breaking their parole restriction against affiliating with their own ethnic gangs (17).

Other observers, however, have argued that stoners, including satanists, do fit the profile of a bona fide gang. For one, stoners claim certain areas as their own. Territorial boundaries, however, are used in a slightly different context by these stoners. Whereas street gang members claim certain geographical locations or portions of the community as their territory, the stoner groups will claim certain musical groups or types of music as their territory.

Second, in terms of distinctive dress, the heavy metal accessories and T-shirts cater to the stoners' ego just as the specialized dress of African-American and Hispanic gang members set them apart. Third, the usage of graffiti is another characteristic both groups share in common. Both types of gangs use graffiti to mark their presence, with the satanists often marking their areas with a "666" (18).

Conversations with a Gang Specialist

As part of the larger study of renegade kids and suburban outlaws, it was decided to interview a parole agent who specializes in gang detail. At the time of the interview he was assigned to the Gang Information Services Unit (GISU) of the California Youth Authority. The primary activities of this unit included identifying and monitoring the movement of individuals involved in all youth gangs and gang activities within the youth authority jurisdiction. This is accomplished by collecting, collating, analyzing, and evaluating gang-related information involving CYA wards and disseminating this information to affected agencies throughout the state.

The GISU also serves as the chief liaison with law enforcement agencies throughout California. The unit provides technical assistance to law enforcement agencies with gang-related cases where CYA wards are involved. It provides guidance and assistance in establishing gang intelligence units, files, and/or training.

The interview that follows covers a wide range of issues on the groups that have been touched upon in this book. The comments by this administrator provide us with some insight into how the public officials at the state level who are charged with stemming gang violence view these white delinquent youths, compared to other types of gangs and forms of juvenile delinquency also found in the youth authority. His comments also serve to bring to conclusion our analysis of the various forms of *suburban outlaws* discussed in the last three chapters of this second section of the book.

Q: How do these stoner gangs define their turf?
A: They fight with whatever is handy, but usually they do not use guns. They are more street fighters and brawlers.
Q: How large are these gangs usually?
A: Several are big gangs with twenty-five members or more. In Northern California there are two fairly large gangs: the ERSS (Enterprise Redding Satanic Stoners) and the BASH (Bay Area Skin Heads). Recently in the San Francisco area, two groups took the same name and went to war over who could claim the name.
Q: As musical tastes change, will these stoner gangs die out?
A: It will likely diminish except for those who are deeply into it. One notes a big difference when you compare these punk rockers and stoners gangs with ethnic gangs like Chicano gangs. Chicano gangs, and black gangs like Crips and Bloods, for that matter, have a structured society. These stoners are more individualistic. So they have nothing concrete to sustain them.
Q: Why does the public not see these heavy metalers and stoners as gangs?

A: When you talk to their parents about their teenage youngsters' activities, they don't admit to involvement because the parents don't want to admit they are failures.

Q: Does treatment in the youth authority help them?

A: They eventually outgrow it. But they engage in a lot of vandalism and wreak havoc along the way.

Q: Do these juveniles fit the profile of the "career criminal"?

A: Punk rockers are more like the old category of "incorrigible." They are more concerned about lifestyle. Generally, they do not intend to hurt other people. With other types of gang members like stoners, there are career criminals.

Q: Why have not blacks and Chicanos been more involved in the punk rock, heavy metal, and stoner-type gangs?

A: Punk rockers are against everything and stand for anarchy whereas blacks and Chicanos have structure and organizations. Punks break away from the establishment. Blacks want structure and to be part of it.

Q: What are some of the stoner gangs that you are most concerned about?

A: Actually there is a pattern in the Los Angeles area for some of the Chicanos to get involved in the stoner gangs. For instance, there are now stoner Chicano gangs in East LA such as the Oiler Stoners, LOTT Stoners (stoners who like vacant lots), and FTW Stoners (Fuck the World Stoners). These youngsters identify as white and not with their Hispanic background.

Q: Why is this so?

A: Many of the heavy Chicano gang members were arrested in the late 1970s. In the early 1980s, to fill the void, punk rockers and heavy metalers took over. In Stockton, California, the same pattern happened. Drive-by shootings took out the early Chicano gang leaders. Once they were removed, white metalers became the role models for the younger Chicano kids.

Q: Do you see any difference between punk rockers and stoners?

A: Yes. Stoners will fight with punkers. They will fight anywhere—at concerts, in the mall, on the streets. Bay Area Skin Heads are taking on the punkers at Sunrise Mall in Sacramento.

Q: What about satanism?

A: Right now there is a grievance being filed by a student at a high school in Southern California. The youth claims that satanic worship is part of his religion. The grievance was filed over a year ago and has now gone to arbitration. The kid had been caught drawing upside-down crosses. The majority of the stoner gangs involved in satanism have tried to commit suicide, and have practiced extortion.

Q: Where did the term stoners come from?

A: In the 1960s, stoners meant white groups that were stoned all of the time. Some used the term *surfers* or *hippies*. *Stoners* at the time was a national term tied in to the sixties drug culture. In the seventies the term stoners started to change. By the eighties there was an increased tie-in to satanic worship. Now the term refers to individuals who are involved in satanic dabbling and satanic worship with distinct dress styles and ideas. Stoners and heavy metalists are interchangeable although there is an intermediate transition before they become satanists.

Q: Do you predict stoners will proliferate?

A: No, it's a phase for our young people. But it will leave a lasting effect on those that get involved. Only two juveniles currently in the California Youth Authority have been linked to human sacrifices although they did not actually do the killing. These two came from Modesto but they were involved with an adult group.

Q: Do you see other ethnic groups moving into the stoner gangs?

A: Only a few since most ethnic youths grow up in areas where there are established street gangs. The few Hispanics involved that I mentioned are there because of a lack of ethnic gangs in their neighborhoods.

Q: These so-called stoners, can they be rehabilitated?

A: They are no different from anybody else. We haven't had them around that long to see the change. They do hang out with white supremacists in the institutions, however. They go their own way on the street since there is an absence of white supremacist groups in their neighborhoods. In the institutions they join in the actual white supremacist gang dynamics because they have to align themselves with someone. These supremacists will accept them because the stoners will "get down and fight."

The punk rockers, on the other hand, get treated like a "punk" (effeminate homosexual). They are viewed as a disgrace by others and will get "punked out" (forced into sexually submissive roles).

Q: Why so much drug abuse by the stoners?

A: Unfortunately, it is just reflective of the larger society. Only stoners use drugs more so. The occult devil worshippers use a lot of drugs, chemicals, and sex involvement.

Q: Is there much unity among various stoner gang members throughout the state?

A: The stoners in one juvenile institution will come together. They develop monikers, symbols like a hand signal or a particular way of wearing a piece of their clothing, and the correctional staff are on the lookout for those. Most of the stoners are sent to the camps because the majority of their offenses are lightweight, and they are serving less time.

On the opposite hand, punk rockers do share a common dress style and look in the institution. Like the stoners and heavy metalers, the punk rockers' styles caught on right away because all of the symbols were readily available such as the musical styles and their popular cultural musical heroes.

Q: Why the involvement with satanism?

A: Satanic worship has always been there. It is not just tied to the popularity of the movie "Rosemary's Baby." Satanic cults have always been around. It's just that they have become more commercial with the bands picking it up. That's what made it more popular.

Q: Do you share the de-programming concept of "de-punking" and "de-metaling," or the "Tough Love" approach to dealing with these kids?

A: My opinion is a reality-type therapy. I think confrontational therapy works best with them. In the institution there are no distinctive ways to deal with satanic youngsters and punk rockers. No specific programs have yet been established for them. No program in any of the CYA's institutions is issue-oriented with the punk rockers and stoners.

Q: Do you see any distinctions among any of these youths involved in the white youth cults?

A: Stoners actually are totally different from punk rockers. The majority of the stoners will likely end up in white supremacy groups. Skinheads, in particular, will follow this pattern.

Currently, there are about twenty skinheads in the youth authority that are being used by the clan, whereas there are only two punk rockers currently being held in YTS (Youth Training School). Punk rockers are more of a fad or phase whereas skinheads and stoners will maintain a white identity and be part of the juvenile justice institutions for a long time.

Q: How come these stoner gang member wards have not been involved in any sensationalistic crimes in California? We read about such crimes committed by youths in other states.

A: There was one incident in the late 1970s in Orange County where a body was discovered underneath a bridge. Nearby there was a dead animal that had been sacrificed in a ritualistic way.

In the late 1970s all the "heavies" in the street gangs were arrested and imprisoned and taken off the scene. With the absence of leaders it led to a void. This was filled by video and rock music which gave youngsters a new role model and a new scene to become involved with. With punk rock bands, many of the singers killed themselves. Heavy metalers did not. Heavy metal seldom professes suicide whereas that is more common in punk band lyrics.

It seems that Asian youngsters who get involved in gangs now use heavy metal or punk dress more so than in the past. It seems that because of their street gang activity they would be rejected by their families and kicked out on the street. They would then congregate where other kids were, such as in video arcades, and so would pick up the dress style of the other white youth groups.

Q: Any other thoughts on this topic?

A: A couple of years ago the authorities were observing some of the kids playing "Dungeons and Dragons" in the camps. Once they understood what the games meant, they decided not to allow the juveniles to play those games.

As I mentioned, some kids have filed formal grievances so that they can conduct their own satanic services while in the youth authority. This has not been allowed even though Code #4027 on "Religious Freedom in Local Detention Facilities" states that "all prisoners confined in local detention facilities shall be afforded reasonable opportunities to exercise religious freedom."

NOTES

1. "No Satan Worship at This School," *The Los Angeles Times* (9 September 1987), Part V, p. 10.

2. Frederick M. Muir, "Police Respond to Satanic Behavior on Gatos High School Campus," *The Los Angeles Times* (16 August 1992), p. A-1.

3. "Authorities Probe Satanic Link in Teen Murder-Suicide Case," *The Los Angeles Times* (11 March 1989), p. A-1.

4. Wayne S. Wooden and Martha Lou Berkey, *Children and Arson: America's Middle-Class Nightmare* (New York: Plenum Press, 1984).

5. Lawrence C. Trostle, "Stoners Emerge as Demonic Delinquents," *California Peace Officer* 5 (October 1985), pp. 20–21.

6. Martin Sanchez-Jankowski, "Youth Culture and Satanic Cult Formation," paper presented at the Western Society of Criminology meetings, February 1988; Las Vegas, NV.

7. The typology of satanists and some of the discussion that follows, which is presented in edited form, was provided by Lisa Collins.

8. Pat Metoyer, "Witchcraft, Devil Worship, Satanism, and Satanic Cults," paper presented at the We-Tip National Conference, April 1988; Ontario, CA.

9. Esteban P. Castaneda, "Report on Youth Gangs," (Sacramento, CA: State Task Force on Youth Gang Violence, 1988).

10. Lawrence C. Trostle, "The Stoners: Drugs, Demons and Delinquency," graduate dissertation (Claremont Graduate School, Claremont, CA, 1986), p. 139.

11. Ibid., p. 140.

12. Ibid., p. 144.

13. Metoyer.

14. Richard Valdemar, "Stoners, Satanism, and the Occult," paper presented at a conference sponsored by the California Youth Authority, 7 May 1986; San Luis Obispo, CA.

15. Ibid.

16. Trostle.

17. Castaneda.

18. Valdemar.

▼

PART III

Parental and Societal Responses

10

▼

Reactions to Youthful Offenders

"The Rise in Kids Who Kill"

Dwayne Wright was 17 when he spotted Saba Tekle on a highway in northern Virginia, decided he wanted to have sex with her and pumped a bullet into her back when she tried to run away. Wright, now 19, awaits execution on Virginia's Death Row.

Five New Jersey teen-agers, two of them 14, allegedly strangled a pesky classmate with an electrical cord as he recited the prayer Hail Mary in his car. Three of the boys admitted to the murder in April and will testify against the others.

Two Pasadena juries Friday found teen-agers David Adkins and Vincent Hebrock guilty of murder in the shotgun slayings of three girls—including Adkins' girlfriend—during a party at one of the girls' homes. A witness says Hebrock, who was 17 at the time, boasted to Adkins, who was 16: "Yeah, dude, we smoked 'em all" (1).

"Another Day in Court for Rock Music"

Rock music is back in the courtroom—on death charges. Six weeks after the British rock group Judas Priest was absolved of causing the suicide-related deaths of two Sparks, Nevada, youths, fellow British rocker Ozzy Osbourne faces similar charges in Macon, Georgia.

In two separate product-liability cases that are being considered jointly in a deposition session this week in a Macon federal court, subliminal messages allegedly hidden in Osbourne albums are blamed for the suicide shootings of two teenagers (2).

As *Renegade Kids, Suburban Outlaws* has noted, America's youths are faced with a multitude of choices in terms of adolescent identities. Many of the problems these youngsters face stem from our society's push to make children grow up quickly. The portrait of today's child, in the words of one observer—"dressed from birth to look like a miniature adult, pressured to read before kindergarten and left unsupervised after school"—is causing great alarm among psychologists and sociologists who suggest this trend is symptomatic of an underlying societal disregard for their well-being (3).

David Elkind, for one, contends that the hurried child sometimes develops into the hurried teen, expected not only to achieve at school but to fill in for the absent parents at home (who are forced to work). Elkind writes,

> Many parents, schools and much of the media have been hurrying children to grow up fast, but they also have been abandoning teenagers (4).

Other observers contend that children today are getting the short end of the stick. An ever-growing number of children living in poverty, increases in infant mortality, childhood obesity and lack of fitness, delinquency and teenage pregnancy, and deteriorating public education are all thought to account for the increased problems facing this generation of youngsters, the post-baby boomers.

Furthermore, today's young children are bombarded with adult experiences and violence on television and in the movies, making them less sensitive and more sexually precocious than earlier generations of young people. As one expert notes, "Given the high divorce rate, children often have a front-row seat while watching one or both parents date" (5).

Forced to grow up "too fast" has also meant, according to the experts, that teenagers do not have the proper adult guidance, direction, and support they need to make a healthy transition to adulthood. Many are being pushed to act like adults long before they are ready. One Southern California study found that 80 percent of high school seniors held jobs. Although much public focus has dealt with the obvious return of mothers to the work force in the past twenty-five years, little attention has been given to the effects of the teenage entrance into the work force in the same period (6).

Other observers note that in addition to being rushed into adulthood, this generation seems increasingly intolerant of others. In Southern California, for instance, residents, young and old, of multiethnic Los Angeles County are finding it increasingly difficult to cope with one another's racial and cultural differences. The Human Rights Commission has found a marked increase in hate crimes since the beginning of this decade. In its report to the County Board of Supervisors, the commission noted that hate crimes, motivated by racism, religious bigotry, and intolerance of homosexuality, have been steadily rising across the county since 1986.

In 1989, 378 hate crimes were reported for the county. For the first six months of 1992, however, the figure was 272. The commission attributed the increased intergroup tension to demographic changes across the county as well as to a rise in the general level of violent crime across the nation. Blacks are victims in more than half of all racial crimes, Jews in 9 of 10 religious hate crimes. Violence against homosexuals and Asians is also rising, according to the report (7).

Such behavior is not limited to Southern California. In an excellent new book on the subject, *Hate Crimes: America's New Menace,* the authors argue that such behavior has spread across America in epidemic proportions (8). And Europe, from Germany to Bosnia, has been racked with a rampage of "ethnic cleansing" and violence against ethnic minorities. Election results in Russia have brought to power leaders of a right-wing nationalistic movement. Ethnic cleansing may tragically sweep beyond the borders of Bosnia.

In America, meanwhile, equally alarming news has been the sad statistic of the rise in the number of kids who kill. Juveniles, it appears, are arming themselves more than ever. According to recent FBI crime statistics, the number of juveniles arrested for homicide between 1981 and 1990 increased 60 percent nationwide. This far outpaced the 5.2 percent increase among adults (9).

Furthermore, an unprecedented 2,003 youths were arrested for murder and non-negligent manslaughter in 1990. And though juveniles are still far less likely to kill than adults, 1 in every 6 people arrested in the United States for murder in 1990 was under 18 (10).

How has society attempted to address some of these trends? And what have been some societal responses from the *school system,* the *mental health agencies,* the *juvenile justice network,* as well as *concerned citizen groups* to the varied youth styles discussed in this book? These various societal responses will be the concerns of this concluding chapter.

THE SCHOOL SYSTEM RESPONDS

On a typical day each month, nearly 1 of every 3 high school students in some areas of the country deliberately missed one or more academic classes. According to experts, soaring truancy rates reflect breakdowns in families and schools, leading to more school dropouts and more neighborhood crime. Educators echo the concern, saying they are faced with more broken families, more poverty, more joblessness, more homelessness these days. Schoolwork takes a back seat when a kid is fighting to survive, they say.

To combat truancy some school districts have resorted to "bribing" the students. One school, for instance, makes students with perfect attendance records for each month eligible for a drawing with cash prizes. However, only 79 of the 1,600 students qualified in the month of May during a recent year (11).

Some teachers contact parents when a student starts missing class, but just contacting the parents does not always do the trick. As one counselor noted,

> Parents of these students frequently respond by blaming the
> school, stating, "Why aren't you doing something? My kid's
> are not going to class, so why don't you do something? It's
> your responsibility."

Truancy is not the only problem. More often schools are bombarded by acts of crime. According to the California Department of Education, during one academic year in the late 1980s, 1,005 out of 1,028 school districts in the entire state reported a total of 157,597 incidents of crime on the school grounds. These crimes varied from assault, robbery, and burglary, to murder. Notably, 71,351 of these incidents were against property, resulting in a total dollar loss of $22,878,540.00 (12).

To combat such high crime rates on school campuses, the state has developed a program, "Operation Safe Schools." This program sets up early intervention, prevention, and education programs tailored to assist school districts in maintaining safe, secure, and peaceful school environments.

According to the program's preliminary evaluation, there have been considerable benefits for students in those school districts that

have participated in Operation Safe Schools. Benefits included: attendance improved; academic achievement level improved, test scores
and grades were raised; the number of students going on to higher
education increased; discipline problems decreased; violence and vandalism lessened; drug and alcohol abuse decreased; negative peer pressure was reduced; the morale level of students and faculty increased;
student self-image improved, decision-making abilities were
enhanced; and goals were set and achieved.

"Project Safe" at "Raging High"

One of the high schools analyzed in an earlier chapter ("Kicking Back
at 'Raging High'") was selected to participate in this innovative program. Identified as "Project Safe" on this particular campus, the success
of the program serves as a model for other school districts looking for
ways to improve their school environment.

In the eighteen months prior to funding for "Project Safe," the city
in which Raging High School is located had experienced numerous
incidents of drug and alcohol offenses. In fact, the police department
reported over 1,000 drug arrests resulting in the seizure of drugs valued
at almost $1.5 million.

During this same time period, juvenile felony arrests for this suburban community had risen by more than 60 percent. Most of these
offenses were for possession of drugs or were drug-related such as
assaults, auto thefts, burglaries, and possession of weapons. Furthermore,
according to police officials working gang detail, there had also been an
alarming and frightening 300 percent increase in gang activity within
the city in that same time period. Since there was only the one high
school within the city, almost all of the juveniles arrested were students
in the target area.

These delinquent activities in the community obviously had an impact
upon the school system. In 1988, the school district reported 176 assaults,
56 arrests for substance abuse, and criminal damage of property totaling
over $21,000. Furthermore, the high school suspended 339 students for
violations of the California Education Code. With a total student enroll-
ment of 2,757, this represented 12 percent of the student body (13)!

Included in the reasons for school suspension were possession of drugs
or alcohol, selling drugs, possession of weapons, robbery, extortion, and
damage to property. The work of an undercover police officer on campus had led to the arrest of nineteen students in one crackdown. All of

the student arrests were drug-related. In fact, in the academic year 1987–1988, 56 students were apprehended at school for use or possession of alcohol; 52 for use or possession of marijuana; 15 for use or possession of other drugs; 36 for drug sales; and 4 for driving under the influence.

Results of a Student Survey. A survey of the students at Raging High School, conducted by the counseling staff in 1988, indicated that 68 percent of the student body reported consuming alcohol periodically; 31 percent smoked marijuana; and 26 percent reported using cocaine or amphetamines.

The survey data also revealed that the majority of students agreed with the statement that drugs were readily available on campus. Further, students who participated on a panel set up to discuss the findings revealed they had used cocaine in class; reported that marijuana was regularly smoked in the bathrooms; and stated that virtually any drug could be purchased on campus.

The students also indicated that they did not know of resources within the larger community to assist them in dealing with their drug- or alcohol-related problems. A majority of students also indicated that they did not feel comfortable going to their teachers or other staff members to discuss such problems.

Student drug abuse was also noted by the faculty. A similar survey given to faculty and staff noted their opinion that 53 percent of their students used alcohol and drugs from two to three times a week. An overwhelming majority of the faculty (80 percent) felt that more school resources, personnel, and time should be devoted to solving this problem.

Like the other suburban high schools discussed earlier, Raging High comprised students from fairly affluent family backgrounds. Only 5 percent of the student body, for instance, came from families that received financial aid (AFDC or Aid for Dependent Children). The ethnic population of the school district was predominantly Caucasian (73 percent), followed by Hispanic (13 percent), Asian (8 percent), African American (5 percent), and other ethnic groups (1 percent).

Besides the problems with student drug and alcohol abuse, and even with a predominantly middle- to upper-middle-class student body, the school district had seen an alarming increase in the number of gangs. In one year alone, the number of gangs identified on the campus had increased from three to twelve, according to a police official assigned to gang detail at the high school.

Half of the twelve gangs composed of students on campus were Hispanic (with names like 9th Street Pimps, Raging Ghost Town,

Playboy Z, Calle Nueve Raging, Raging Los Olivos, and Empire Villains) (some names have been changed). Two Raging High School gangs were black gangs (Raging High Crips and Cyco Block Gangsters). Three of the suburban high school gangs were white gangs (Team Mad Dog; Raging Local Stoners, a satanic cult gang; and Master Race Youth, a racist skinhead gang). And one gang was an ethnically mixed street gang (Tough City Boys).

Implementation. With major drug problems as well as the proliferation of gangs, Raging High was one of the school districts funded by California in 1989 to develop strategies to address these critical concerns. A licensed school clinical psychologist (a former student at Cal Poly, Pomona, and my contact with this school) was hired as project crisis coordinator for Project Safe. The team included a police officer assigned to gang detail who also served as liaison officer with the school and the police department, and one other psychologist; these three professionals developed a series of workshops aimed at concerned parents.

Under the auspices of the local PTA chapter, the three discussed such topics as warning signs (for example, student dress, behaviors, attitudes, self-esteem); interventions (for example, discipline, parental supervision, outpatient counseling, hospital programs, and probation); and successful parenting skills.

The crisis coordinator also assisted the regular school counseling staff and instructional faculty by revising the "Student Referral Form" so that early signs of student problems could be more readily identifiable. All faculty were encouraged to take a critical look at their students, and to report to the counseling center or for private referral to the crisis coordinator any student who exhibited four to five symptoms from the problem areas listed on the form.

Student Referral Form

Grades. Drop in grades, decline in quality of work, obvious failure, lack of motivation (apathy);

School Attendance. Excessive absences, excessive tardies, excessive class cuts, suspension(s);

Extracurricular Activities. Loss of eligibility, lack of involvement, student drops out of activity;

Physical Appearance. Glassy or bloodshot eyes, loss of coordination, slurred speech, bad hygiene, sleeps in class, physical complaints, physical injuries, staggering or stumbling, smells of alcohol or pot, lethargic;

Disruptive Behavior. Defies rules, needs constant discipline, irresponsible, denies responsibility, blames others, fights, cheats, smokes, obscene language or gestures, gets attention dramatically, cries in class, often in unauthorized areas, hostile attitude toward authority, hyper or nervous;

Other On-campus Observable Behavior. Sits in parking lot, drug or alcohol conversations, talks freely about drug or alcohol use, avoids contact with others, erratic behavior day-to-day, drug-related doodling, changes friends or has negative relationships, acts defensively, sudden popularity, belongs to older social group, hypertension, refuses touching, uncommunicative, drug-related clothing or jewelry, sexual looseness or intimacy in public, withdrawal or becoming a loner, time disorientation, unrealistic goals, inappropriate responses, possible depression, seeks adult advice about "hypothetical" situations, draws satanic/death/gang symbols; and

Off-campus Behavior. Family relationships, runaway, job problems, law enforcement involvement, other (14).

To implement the Project Safe program, all district staff members participated in an eight-hour in-service training program on adolescent chemical dependency in the fall semester of 1989. The staff was instructed on the policies and procedures for intervention and referral of high-risk students to the Project Safe staff. Parents were also educated on youth substance abuse and informed about the referral and intervention process. Even the students were instructed on how to identify those fellow students who were chemically dependent in new drug education classes set up in the school. Students were encouraged to refer themselves, their friends, and even their parents to Project Safe for counseling and assistance.

Once a student was referred, the Project Safe crisis coordinator performed assessments and interventions. After evaluating the severity of the problem, appropriate treatment was determined and referral made—often to an outside agency, physician, or therapist. The two-year funded project also served as a resource center, and monitored services available in the community to make effective referrals.

In summary, the Project Safe crisis coordinator filled the gaps needed in combatting student substance abuse. The crisis coordinator did not handle discipline, class scheduling, career counseling, or other day-to-day functions of the existing counseling staff. Instead, by working in conjunction with the counselors and teachers, the crisis coordinator and the Project Safe program were set up to combat student drug abuse, drug-related crimes, and gang activity.

Other Programs

Other innovative programs have also been set up on high school campuses to address social concerns. One such program, "Hands Across the Campus," was developed by the Los Angeles Unified School District and the American Jewish Committee with the stated goal of "learning respect for diversity."

Hands Across the Campus develops awareness of the roles and contributions of people of various cultural, racial, and ethnic backgrounds, and awareness of the dangers posed by organized hate groups. One component of the program was to develop a social science elective class that helps students relate course content to their personal experience and the pluralistic society of which they are a part.

It also includes planned activities outside the classroom. Among the many successful programs are symposia designed to improve racial harmony; plays and assemblies focusing on intercultural and interethnic themes; international fairs; and essay, speech, and poster contests to foster community sensitivity and tolerance.

THE MENTAL HEALTH SYSTEM RESPONDS

Overall, inpatient hospitalization for children under age 18 increased from 82,000 to more than 112,000 in the decade of the 1980s. Some of these adolescents are seriously disturbed and suffer from severe or acute mental disorders, or they have drug or alcohol problems. But in other cases, according to some critics, they may be simply rebellious teenagers struggling with their parents over issues such as dating, what music they can listen to, and other issues once thought of as typical "growing pains" (15).

Some of these youngsters have been held behind locked doors, virtually without civil rights. In the late 1980s the American Psychiatric Association condemned unnecessary hospitalization, calling for a wider range of affordable outpatient services.

Adolescent treatment hospitals have become big business. Large corporate chains such as Charter Medical Corporation, the Hospital Corporation of American, and National Medical Enterprises have expanded their facilities throughout the country as local laws allow. According to the National Institute of Mental Health, in 1980 there were only 184 private psychiatric hospitals with specialized programs for minors; in 1988 there were 450 (16).

Since insurance companies usually do not reimburse for less restrictive treatment such as outpatient therapy, private hospitals have found it lucrative to provide inpatient treatment. Typically such programs, covered by the parents' insurance policy, charge up to $900 per day for adolescents who might otherwise be treated as well or better through outpatient therapy. Some policies cover up to 100 percent of inpatient costs. By contrast, insurance generally reimburses a much smaller percentage of the expenses of outpatient care. Therefore, it is often more convenient, and less of a financial burden, for parents to commit their children than to get them effective counseling. Most communities do not offer intensive home-based services. Parents are forced to choose between once-a-week outpatient counseling at best and full hospitalization.

Furthermore, as one critic notes, evidence suggests a correlation between the length of time a minor stays confined in such a facility and the number of days health insurance provides for inpatient care, suggesting that many facilities only keep the minor as long as the insurance policy can cover the expenses.

Marketing has played a part in the business of treating these adolescents. As another critic notes, hospital advertising often implies easy answers and gives the worried parent the impression that the program can "fix" anything. One local program in Southern California even set up employee-incentive programs to gather new business, offering Caribbean cruises for staff members who generated the largest number of hospital admissions. The contest was referred to by its critics as "bounty hunting" (17).

Newsweek magazine, in a comprehensive article—"Committed Youth: Why Are So Many Teens Being Locked Up in Private Mental Hospitals?"—noted that the "illness" for which many teenagers are committed is usually not the kind commonly associated with institutionalization. Instead, the teenagers are admitted for behavioral problems, "conduct disorders," or "adolescent adjustment reaction." These confined youths, according to the article, are frequently those engaged in some form of anti-social behavior and do not suffer from delusional psychosis.

The article also cites the American Academy of Child and Adolescent Psychiatry's advice to parents in deciding whether or not to hospitalize a son or daughter. Eleven suggestions for parents are offered, including raising such issues as the treatment alternatives other than hospitalization; the responsibilities of the psychiatrist and other people on the treatment team; how decisions will be made about when to discharge your child from the hospital; and once discharged, what the plans are for continuing or follow-up treatment with the youngster (18).

Rosenbaum and Prinsky in 1991 reported the results of their study of adolescent care programs in Southern California. When these hospitals were given a hypothetical situation in which the parents' main concern with their 15-year-old son's behavior was the music he listened to, the clothes he wore, and the type of posters he displayed in his bedroom, 83 percent of the facilities believed the youth needed hospitalization. The researchers concluded that for these psychiatric treatment hospitals, the assumption that musical preference and appearance are strongly related to drug use and other mental health problems may be widespread (19).

Many patients' advocate groups believe that all teenage psychiatric admissions should be subject to stricter criteria. They urge parents to get second opinions if hospitalization is recommended for their offspring.

Despite these concerns and reservations, many adolescent treatment hospital programs have had great success in working with troubled youths. Generally, the treatment approach involves behavioral modification, group therapy, one-on-one counseling, peer counseling where appropriate, and education—including sex education as well as drug and alcohol abuse programs.

Most of the adolescent treatment hospital programs also provide concerned parents with lists of warning signs that encourage the parents to seek help if their children exhibit any one of the signs for several weeks. One such program in Southern California lists "10 Ways Your Teenager May Be Begging for Help!" in their newspaper advertisement. Included in their list of "frequent signs of adolescent emotional distress" are the following:

fallen or lowered grades
change in eating and sleeping habits
lashing out at people or objects
putting themselves down
changed sexual attitudes
secretive and suspicious behavior

running away

withdrawal

loss of interest in personal appearance and hygiene

preoccupation with death (20).

Other community mental health programs have been developed to assist parents with keeping their children alive and out of youth or street gangs. One program in Southern California emphasizes a parent-support group approach and even prints a brochure, "Don't Hang with a Gang," to inform other parents in the community. Parents are encouraged to:

know their children's whereabouts

be fair and consistent in their discipline

keep an open line of communication

hold their child responsible and accountable for his or her actions

monitor the way their child dresses for school

try to meet their child's friends and their parents

Other suggestions include:

1. Confront your child whenever you suspect something is not right.
2. Chaperone parties attended by your children, and make certain you know and trust the parents who host parties your children attend.
3. Be cognizant of the use of slang terms or hand gestures by your child to communicate with his or her peers (21).

THE JUVENILE JUSTICE SYSTEM RESPONDS

Depending on their offenses, delinquents under the age of 18 may be handled by the juvenile justice system as opposed to mental health programs. If specific crimes have been committed, as we have seen with the stoner gang members for instance, the juvenile is often sentenced by the courts to the California Youth Authority and incarcerated in one of several different levels of security, ranging from camplike to more secure, lock-down facilities. Depending upon the offense committed, some juveniles may instead be mandated to adult court.

The highest level of security in California is the Youth Training School (YTS) located in the southern part of the state. Here juveniles may go through a drug-rehabilitation program. They are also required to participate in group therapy and either continue toward a high school diploma or learn a trade in one of the many technical programs provided in the institution.

Those youth not deemed as serious offenders are often mandated by the courts to participate in some type of probation program, and, depending on the nature of their offense, may be required to pay restitution or complete community service as part of their sentence. Such programs may be either publicly or privately funded.

Back in Control. A program begun in the 1980s by two ex-probation officers works specifically with juvenile delinquents who have been involved with either the punk rock or heavy metal scene. The "Back in Control" program follows a "Tough Love" approach to working with these youngsters and their parents to establish strict guidelines of behavior that the youths must follow. If they do not adhere to the parents' rules, they may then be sentenced to stiffer lockdown type facilities.

The central aim of Back in Control is to de-punk and de-metal the juveniles. The program works to reprogram these juveniles, contending that they have been brainwashed into a youth subculture in much the same way as others have been processed into other cults (such as religious cults or communes). In order to rescue these youngsters from the control of their youth styles (including the negative influence of friends, music, and all the trappings of their deviant identities—for example, rock band T-shirts, posters, albums, and so on), the parents are encouraged to rid their homes of all such paraphernalia.

The youths are told to disassociate themselves from their former friends who still are involved in the respective youth styles. Strict curfews are established by the parents, and the youngsters are informed that if they break any of the rules established by their parents (with the assistance of Back in Control), there will be dire consequences (such as being grounded, kicked out of the house, or sent to reform school or jail).

In effect, by de-punking and de-metaling these juveniles, and by implementing a rule-based system of behavior, the organization assists parents in regaining control over their offspring's behavior—thus, the name, "Back in Control." As the organization's brochure advocates, adults must clearly state the rules, consistently and effectively following through to ensure their rules are obeyed. Parents must remove all of the influences associated with their youngster's objectionable lifestyle and replace them with "family values, time, and love."

Parents are encouraged by Back in Control to abide by the five guidelines of education, involvement, supervision, enforcement, and removal. Through education, parents are to become aware of bands, lyrics, and the messages they portray. With involvement in such programs as "Parent Watch," adults are encouraged to work together in a coordinated effort to look out for suspicious activity, unfamiliar individuals, and mutilated animals. Parents are advised to supervise and chaperon their offspring at concerts, and to listen to their music and monitor the literature they purchase and read.

A strict enforcement of current laws against alcohol consumption by minors, drug usage, and loitering is also to be followed. Finally, every effort should be made to remove any traces of graffiti since it perpetuates gang violence, revenge, and relays messages (22).

The organizers of Back in Control, along with representatives from other law enforcement agencies, have also developed seminar programs to alert other officials and concerned citizens about the dangers of the various white youth culture scenes including the negative aspects of punk rock, heavy metal, skinheads, and satanism. These one- or two-day seminars are given each year in a variety of locations throughout the nation. At these seminars—which attract overflow crowds—various experts present videotapes, display confiscated youth graffiti and paraphernalia, and play record albums to demonstrate their concern with the negative influences that are affecting today's youths.

Although these experts caution that not all youths involved with one or more of the youth styles are equally vulnerable, these police and juvenile justice officials claim that many youngsters do get caught up in the youth culture and become anti-social, if not delinquent. At these workshops and conferences, police departments, and those who work gang detail in their respective communities, are urged to become aware of the danger signs in their locales such as the presence of music-related graffiti, mutilated animals, and groups of teenagers sporting unique dress and hairstyles. The presenters also recommend both mental health treatment programs or Tough Love-approach programs for parents whose children are defiant, uncommunicative, and involved.

Program Effectiveness. How effective are these Tough Love-type programs? According to officials and parents, they are quite successful.

But some youths take issue with this view. One juvenile, who was interviewed for this study, felt that he had not been helped by such a program.

> For a few years me and my family went to Back in Control. That didn't work. My folks knew there was no way they could change me. Maybe they can take your clothes, your albums, and your posters and all but they can't take away your state of thinking. Unless they send you into electro-shock.
>
> They can't do it. They tried with me and my brother, and they could not do it. "De-punking" is what they called it. They took away everything that I had. I came home one day and they took away everything I had that was punk. My walls were stripped. My whole room was rummaged through. They threw it all away. And I had some real old shit in there—fliers from 1977. Old books that explained things about bands and stuff. Real old albums that you can't find anymore. All gone.

Other youths that were interviewed also expressed concern that the police used excessive force in dealing with them. As Skidd Marx (interviewed in Chapter 2) noted, punkers and metalers are suspicious of police because of how these youths are typically treated.

> There were trillions of cops at a youth riot in Huntington Beach at an "Exploited" gig. Cops were getting fucked up. Punks were getting fucked up. A pregnant girl got her stomach kicked in by a cop on purpose. A friend of mine was walking down a flight of stairs and a cop pushed him down the stairs and he was on crutches with a broken leg.
>
> About two months ago we were driving along the road and all of a sudden I see this dude running and I see this cop car speeding up. The guy is running from the cop car. The cop goes "bam" and hits him. He hit the dude! 'Cause he was drunk, he hit him. The cop took his door and went "bam" on his head. Smashed him in the head. The cop got out and sat on his stomach. He then picked him up by the hair and went "bam, bam, bam"—pounding him a number of times, smashing his head on the ground. We all saw it. He was just beating the fucking shit out of him. The cop handcuffed him, picked him up by the chain, and started dragging him all over the parking lot. The cop picked him up and started throwing him against the car. Put him in the car. Didn't duck his head down and he hit his head.

Several of the youths interviewed for this study discussed other incidents where, in their opinion, the police had acted inappropriately and used excessive force. Such incidents served to make these juveniles distrustful of police and to reinforce their disrespect for authority.

Several police departments, however, have consciously made attempts to sensitize their officers into working more constructively with these alienated youths. Often these activities have involved developing manuals or programs alerting youths about the risks of being heavily involved in one of these youth styles.

Other Programs. One law enforcement agency, for instance, developed a "Primer on Cults," which they distribute to both parents and their children. Included in this primer is advice such as knowing which cults operate in a given area; keeping lines of communication open between parents and their children; emphasizing love and respect for one another; and offering suggestions about how to disengage from a cult if conversion has taken place.

Another organization, Turning Point, established by probation officers working gang detail in the Huntington Beach area of Southern California, assists school districts that have problems on their campuses keeping their school environment safe. By working together, police departments and schools develop programs to increase adolescents' self-esteem and help them protect themselves against violence and crime (23).

Another recent program in Southern California, organized by law enforcement officials of the CYA, reunites groups of teens from rival gangs in a camplike mountain setting. Although initially instituted to work with inner-city ethnic gangs, the program has been successful and is used with white stoner gang members as well. In these highly structured settings, teens are encouraged to shed their gang labels and develop a shared unity of purpose. The camp offers rigorous outdoor activities such as hiking, canoeing, and backpacking. The teens attend mandatory group counseling and explore alternatives to gang activities. They learn they can be accepted outside of their gang.

The three primary goals of these mountain camp programs are: (1) to help teens take responsibility for effective decision making; (2) to clarify facts versus myths among gangs; and (3) to expand each youth's vision of the opportunities available to him or her (24).

REACTIONS OF CONCERNED CITIZENS

"Video Mimicry Backfires;
Hollywood Boy Burns"

A 12-year-old boy who stayed home from school set himself on fire imitating a rock music video by Motley Crue, one of his favorite bands. He set his legs on fire and suffered second degree burns because he doused his jeans with rubbing alcohol and touched a match to them. Motley Crue's video features a band member who lights his boots and then jumps into a pond.

"I thought it was going to happen just like it happened in the video. He just set his legs on fire and nothing happens to him" (25).

In recent years much attention has been given by the media to the question of whether youths are being strongly influenced by the music and videos they listen to. In court case after court case, parents of youths who have taken their own lives have sued recording artists for subliminal messages that the parents allege are included in the controversial artists' songs.

In one of the more famous cases, the lyrics of the heavy metal group, Judas Priest, were scrutinized. In the trial, the suit brought by the parents of two youngsters alleged that Judas Priest had "mesmerized" their sons "into believing the answer to life is death." The parents claimed the band's music had provoked their sons' actions by the subliminal recording of the words *do it* on the record.

When the Judas Priest case came to trial in August 1990, CBS and the band denied the existence of subliminal messages on any Judas Priest album. Opponents, however, denounced the group's music, saying they promoted violent, suicidal, and satanic themes. One witness for the prosecution, a medical director at a hospital for troubled adolescents, testified in court that he banned the group's music from his treatment facility because he believed it induced violent behavior in his patients. Another witness for the prosecution testified that the group's music glorifies Satan, causing youth to become self-destructive: "Putting a Judas Priest album on the turntable is like putting a loaded gun in a kid's hand" (26).

The case was decided against the plaintiffs. Judas Priest was absolved of the charges brought against them. The jury, in effect, ruled that the plaintiffs failed to prove that the defendants intentionally placed subliminal messages on the album, and that those messages were a cause of the suicide and attempted suicide of the two teenage boys. Even with this verdict, however, the prosecutors hoped that rock bands would get the message that they need to be more socially responsible.

Such public backlash has not been restricted to concern over the lyrics and songs of heavy metal bands. Rap music, including gangsta rap, has come under greater scrutiny. The lyrics of 2 Live Crew, for instance, were judged to be obscene and in violation of community standards. Pressures were lodged and law suits were filed against record stores that carried the albums as well as communities that hosted the rap band (27).

Lawsuits have been filed against other rap artists as well for alleged inflammatory messages in their lyrics. In 1992, a controversy arose over the Ice-T album that featured the "Cop Killer" rap song. Public uproar and pressure caused the removal of the song and subsequent reissues of the album.

Public outcry has not been restricted to musical lyrics and videos. In October 1993, a popular television show on MTV, "Beavis and Butt-head," came under attack for promoting unsavory behavior by its two teenage, heavy metal misfits. Due to the negative publicity and concern over the incident(s) discussed in the following news clipping, the network, at the urging of the cartoon artist, rescheduled the show to air later in the evening at a time when it was less likely to be seen by impressionable youngsters.

"Fatal Fire Blamed On 'Beavis and Butt-head'"

The mother of a 5-year-old who started a fire that killed his younger sister blames the MTV cartoon "Beavis and Butt-head" for promoting burning as fun, a fire official said Friday.

Fire Chief Harold Sigler said he wants the cable network to eliminate shows that might encourage playing with fire and would like to see violence on the show reduced.

"The mother is attributing the fact that he was fascinated with fire to the 'Beavis and Butt-head' segment where they are setting things on fire," he said.

The show features two teen-agers who comment on rock videos and spend time burning and destroying things.

In western Ohio, Sidney Fire Chief Stan Crosley blamed the cartoon for an August fire that three girls started after watching the program (28).

Media Watchdogs

Public officials and elected politicians note that the increase in violence in American society stems from several factors. Some cite child abuse. Others see the danger in the images of violence portrayed in television and movies as well as pop youth culture in general, including musical videos, video games, and toys. Still others argue that the prevalence of handguns has made violence a staple in the diet of many young Americans (29).

In late 1993 the nation's attorney general expressed concern about the degree of violence shown on television. The attorney general's comments appeared to support the efforts by others that have long called for some kind of control, or rating system, over various forms of popular culture. Of particular concern to these media watchdogs are those television shows, musical videos, and video games that depict gratuitous sex and violence aimed at the youth market.

Other politicians and citizen groups alike, while agreeing with the sentiments expressed, are concerned that setting guidelines for questionable media presentations might compromise the First Amendment rights that protect and guarantee freedom of speech.

Some citizen groups, however, have banded together to take immediate action. The Parents Music Resource Center, for instance, alarmed by the content found in many rock songs—specifically heavy metal which they refer to as the "bastard child of rock and roll"—suggests that record companies develop a rating system for albums, modeled after the rating system used by the motion picture industry (G, PG, PG-13, R, R-17) (30).

Others have voiced concern about the impact of explicit lyrics on American youths. Media watchdog organizations such as Focus on the Family and The American Family Association, two conservative groups, have attempted to sponsor legislation regulating the music industry. As a result, mandatory labeling legislation has been introduced (and defeated) in more than a dozen states.

According to a report by the American Academy of Pediatrics, rock videos contain too much sexism, violence, substance abuse, suicide, and sexual behavior. Urging parents to exercise control over teen's video viewing and to discuss the videos with their children, the academy cites these statistics: 75 percent of videos contain high incidences of sexually suggestive material; and 56 percent contain violence (31).

In response to pending legislation and further pressures from special interest groups, the Recording Industry Association of America recently created a standardized warning sticker to help parents identify albums containing allegedly explicit lyrics.

Research

Even with these expressed public concerns, very little scholarly research has been done into the effects of lyrics on adolescents. And those studies that have been undertaken have reported somewhat contradictory findings regarding whether or not listening to some forms of contemporary music affects adolescent behavior.

In one study, "Sex, Violence, and Rock 'n' Roll: Youths Perception of Popular Music," Prinsky and Rosenbaum surveyed nearly 300 Southern California junior high and high school students. Their conclusions were that the song lyrics—even when they included themes of sex, drugs, violence, and satanism—had little impact on the vast majority of teens. They found that most teens could not accurately describe their favorite songs. Of 662 songs students listed as their favorites, only 7 percent were perceived by those students as being about objectionable themes. The most popular single topic in song lyrics was love (32).

Students, in fact, were unable to explain 37 percent of the songs they named as their favorites. Most, according to the researchers, used rock 'n' roll as "background noise." The study concluded that musical beat or overall sound of a recording is of greater interest to teens, and that specific lyrics seem to be of little consequence to most kids.

In another study, conducted in 1985 by Vokey and Read, "Subliminal Messages: Between the Devil and the Media," the psychologists concluded that they were unable to find any evidence, based on a variety of tasks administered to participants in their experiments, to support the claim that the alleged presence of messages in the media influenced behavior by the listeners. The researchers also presented evidence to suggest that the presence of backward messages in popular music lies more in the imagination of the listener than in any actual messages (33).

Other academic research, however, has found that music fans do pay attention to the lyrics. In one survey, Wass, Miller, and Stevenson found that 87 percent of the metal fans reported knowing all or most of the words in the songs they listened to. The researchers also found a significantly higher degree of attitudes among the heavy metalers supportive of reckless and life-risking behavior (34).

Weinstein, in yet another study, observes that while heavy metal music carries on the tradition of cross-cultural concern with social problems first depicted in youth music in the mid-1960s, heavy metal differs from such sixties views of optimism about changing the future. Instead, heavy metal is concerned about problems but offers few solutions. Further, the music depicts the future as getting much worse, leaving the listener with a sense of despair (35).

In a 1993 study, "The Effect of the Heavy Metal Subculture on Violence: An Analysis of Aggravated Assault," Stack contends that while the cultural symbols of heavy metal often typify violence, this symbolism does not translate to a higher aggregate level of externalized violence, or violence by the listener toward others.

Although Stack notes that the album covers of heavy metal groups often symbolize a theme of violence using such symbols as skulls, monsters, violent-looking biker types, and gothic horror scenes—exacerbated by the visual dimensions of their videos and stage shows—he concurs with the views of other researchers that heavy metal's theme of "chaos" can be linked with greater internalized violence, such as depression and suicide (36).

This sense of pessimism and despair was present in the punk rockers and heavy metal youths I studied as well. However, I would make this distinction. As I have depicted in this book, there are different forms of behavior that disillusioned youths manifest. The *renegade kids* would be examples of youths, including punkers and metalers, who have turned their frustration, for the most part, inward. The *suburban outlaws*, on the other hand, particularly the stoner gang members, would be examples of youths who have taken similar feelings of depression and alienation and acted upon their frustration in more externalized ways.

Recall that in our discussion of the results of the cross-cultural study of punk rockers and heavy metalers in Southern California and New Zealand, over half the youths sampled stated that they did listen to messages in their songs. Furthermore, both California punk rockers (44 percent) and New Zealand heavy metalers (45 percent) agreed with the statement that their music was violent compared to the other groups studied. As a whole, punk rockers and heavy metalers in both countries, compared to the control groups, viewed the music they listened to as violent.

Summary. Societal reactions to youthful offenders have been varied. In summary, parents are encouraged to be more fully involved in all facets of their children's lives. Parents should play an active role in the quality of education their children are receiving. They should work to maintain open lines of communication—to assist with their offspring's selection of friends, musical interests, and leisure activities. If they have youngsters who are involved with one of the youth styles discussed in this book, parents should seek counsel and assistance from school counselors, clergy, and community mental health and social service agencies, as well as the local police department. Programs are available to help these youths. Parents should be cautioned to examine the methods used or claims made before selecting a specific service.

Final Thoughts

In closing, one wonders what identities youths will assume as society moves through this decade toward the twenty-first century. In addition to the continuation of the core youth styles discussed in this book, new youth styles will undoubtedly emerge. Those slightly older Americans now in their twenties (some of whom, after all, as teenagers in the 1980s embraced the youth styles examined in this book) have already been dubbed "Generation X" because of their indefinability. Others have referred to the current twenty-something generation as "slackers" or the "13th Generation."

But for those youths still in their teens, one observer writing in 1990 labeled them the "post–baby boom generation" or "posties," for short. Posties, in his opinion, were distinguished from earlier generations, including the now "over the hill" twenty-somethings, by being:

> Post-Yuppie, post-punk, post-AIDS and post-war. Upset by
> the rapid social changes going on in the world around them,
> they feel helpless, confused. They tread a narrow path between
> the fast trackers and the hippies of an earlier generation. Posties
> will want financial security, but not luxury. They will be satis-
> fied with less (37).

One such postie teenager I interviewed generally concurred with that view.

> We have so much possibility and no rules. There are no guide-
> lines, no rules like they had in the fifties. The eighties were

like the fifties, and the nineties are going to be like the sixties. It's all coming around again.

It will be interesting to see if, in fact, the decade of the 1990s creates a youth culture reminiscent of the 1960s. Already there are signs that such may be occurring. Dropping acid and taking other psychedelic drugs at rave parties, tie-dyed T-shirts, and bell bottom trousers are once again in fashion. Even platform shoes, a fixture in the late sixties and early seventies, have stepped back into style.

As was noted in Chapter 1, sociologists and historians have written extensively about the cyclic nature of American society, with a shift from liberal to conservative back to liberal periods occurring every thirty years or so. The 1960s were the decade of liberalism, and the rise of youth cultures of the political left such as student activists, ethnic militancy, and, subsequently, the women's, gay and lesbian, and men's movements. The 1970s saw a bridge between the decade preceding it and the one to follow in terms of the proliferation of youth styles, such as punk rockers. The 1980s ushered in the return to conservatism, and the rise of youth cultures of the political right such as heavy metalers and skinheads. Perhaps this decade of the 1990s, with a turn toward individual commitment and social change, will usher in a new period of democratic reform and youth movements on the left. Perhaps youth will become happier about their future, optimistic about their world around them.

Whatever happens, it is quite likely that the varied youth styles examined in this book—*mall rats*, *punkers*, *metalers*, *taggers*, *skinheads*, *stoners*, and *satanists*—will continue to be present in society in one form or another as we approach the millennium.

This book has focused, in some detail, on the lives of youths involved with society's more questionable and controversial youth styles. Hopefully, some insight into the conditions that cause so many of our young to embrace these identities has been gained. It is critical that the destructive aspects of some of these *renegade kids* and *suburban outlaws* be rectified. If not, many more teenagers will continue to see with sharp and terrible eyes.

NOTES

1. Dean E. Murphy, "The Rise in Kids Who Kill," *The Los Angeles Times* (16 August 1992), p. A-1.

2. Chuck Philips, "Another Day in Court for Rock Music," *The Los Angeles Times* (4 October 1990), p. E-1.

3. Joan Libman, "Growing up Too Fast: Experts Warn That Children Are Being Pushed to Act Like Adults Long Before They Are Ready," *The Los Angeles Times* (9 August 1988), p. V-1.

4. Ibid.

5. Ibid.

6. Ibid.

7. Marita Hernandez, "Hate Crimes Rise Sharply, Panel Reports," *The Los Angeles Times* (7 September 1990), p. B-2.

8. Jack Levin, *Hate Crimes: America's Growing Menace* (New York: Plenum Press, 1993).

9. Murphy, p. 26.

10. Ibid.

11. Jim Sanders and Patrick Hoge, "Truancy Soaring: Why Go to Class When Mall Beckons?" *The Sacramento Bee* (11 June 1989), p. A-1.

12. Ibid.

13. Michelle Proner, "Project Safe" (Sacramento, CA: Office of Criminal Justice Planning, 1989).

14. Ibid.

15. Richard Polanco, "Bad Medicine for 'Troubled Teens': Forced Private Hospitalization Is Abuse of Process," *The Los Angeles Times* (7 May 1989), p. V-5.

16. Ibid.

17. Nina Darnton, "Committed Youth: Why Are So Many Teens Being Locked up in Private Mental Hospitals?" *Newsweek* (31 July 1989), pp. 66–72.

18. Ibid.

19. Jill Leslie Rosenbaum and Lorraine Prinsky, "The Presumption of Influence: Recent Responses to Popular Music Subcultures" *Crime & Delinquency* 37 (4) (October 1991), pp. 528–535.

20. "10 Ways Your Teenager May Be Begging for Help!" *The Long Beach Press Telegram* (2 October 1988), p. A-8.

21. Coy D. Estes, "Don't Hang with a Gang," (Upland, CA: Upland Police Department).

22. Darlyne R. Pettinicchio, "The Punk Rock and Heavy Metal Handbook" (Orange, CA: The Back in Control Center), p. 29.

23. "Gang Prevention and Intervention Project" (Garden Grove, CA: Turning Point).

24. Ibid.

25. Ann Bradley and Richard Hart, "Video Mimicry Backfires; Hollywood Boy Burned," *The Miami Herald* (18 February 1988), p. A-1.

26. Chuck Philips, "The Music Didn't Make Them Do It," *The Los Angeles Times* (25 August 1990), p. F-1.

27. Chuck Philips, "Trial to Focus on Issue of Subliminal Messages in Rock," *The Los Angeles Times* (16 July 1990), p. F-1.

28. "Fatal Fire Blamed on 'Beavis and Butt-head,'" *The Desert Sun* (9 October 1993), p. A-6.

29. Murphy, p. 26.

30. David Winkel, "Rock & Raunch," *The Long Beach Press-Telegram* (22 December 1985), p. H-1.

31. "Music Videos May Be Hazardous to Your Health," *The Los Angeles Times* (14 November 1988), p. VI-2.

32. Lorraine E. Prinsky and Jill L. Rosenbaum, "'LEER-ICS' OR LYRICS: Teenage Impressions of Rock 'n' Roll," *Youth & Society* 18 (4) (June 1987), pp. 384–397.

33. John R. Vokey and J. Don Read, "Subliminal Messages: Between the Devil and the Media," *American Psychologist* 40 (14) (November 1985), pp. 1231–1239.

34. Hannelore Wass, M. David Miller, and Robert G. Stevenson, "Factors Affecting Adolescents' Behavior and Attitudes toward Destructive Rock Lyrics," *Death Studies* 13, pp. 287–303.

35. Deena Weinstein, *Heavy Metal: A Cultural Sociology* (New York: Macmillan, 1991).

36. Steven Stack, "The Effect of the Heavy Metal Subculture on Violence: An Analysis of Aggravated Assault," paper presented at the American Society of Criminology annual meetings, October 1993; Phoenix, AZ.

37. Shann Nix, "The Posties," *The San Francisco Chronicle* (9 March 1990), p. B-3.

APPENDIX A

▼

Methodology

After concluding my last book, *Children and Arson: America's Middle-Class Nightmare*, I continued to have an interest in studying middle-class, suburban juvenile crime and delinquents. Narrowing my focus to those youths that reside in the suburban areas thirty miles east of Los Angeles near where I live and teach, I wanted to know to what extent the youth styles of the trendier Los Angeles basin were filtering into the schools, neighborhoods, and shopping malls of these presumed "sleepy" bedroom communities, and reaching out to suburban youths.

California State Polytechnic University, Pomona, is one of the twenty campuses in the California State University system. For the past dozen years I have taught sociology and served as Coordinator of the Criminal Justice and Corrections program. Nestled into the rolling hills that once served as the summer home of the Kellogg family of Battle Creek, Michigan, the campus attracts some 18,000 students from the nearby high schools and community colleges. With a wide variety of polytechnic programs including Restaurant and Hospitality Management, Engineering, Environmental Design, and Agriculture, Cal Poly also offers a variety of liberal arts degrees in the College of Arts.

The Behavioral Sciences Department attracts both psychology and sociology students as well as those with an interest in criminal justice and/or social work. In rotation, each professor in the department teaches the senior seminar, and during spring quarter 1988 I selected the topic, "Youth Culture and Social Deviance."

On the first day of class I asked my assembled students what types of youths we should examine, and how we should go about conducting the study. Their feedback and suggestions led to the beginning of my research for this book. To my surprise, what several of these students wanted to explore were the youth styles that their younger brothers and sisters were embracing. Several spoke of the "sibling gap" that existed between themselves and others in their own families who were merely three or four years their junior.

227

Collectively the class developed and field tested the questionnaire of one hundred items that became known as the "Youth Survey" (see Appendix B). Early on I decided to interview teenagers at suburban shopping malls since this locale has become, apart from junior and senior high schools, *the* "hangout" for suburban youths (see Chapter 2). Armed with the questionnaires, my students fanned out to five such malls in the local area to administer the study.

Of particular interest was the desire to compare the responses of youths who self-identified as punk rockers and youths who self-identified as heavy metalers, as well as to compare the responses of these two groups to the rest of the youths we encountered in the malls (which became the comparative or control group). Why punk rockers and heavy metalers? Because these were the two youthful identities that my students' siblings had embraced, and that the students, and I, wished to know more about.

From that simple beginning, the study unfolded and took a variety of turns along the way. Originally, I thought that a study of "mall rats" would be sufficient, but I quickly realized that there were other issues involved. I needed to explore the broader focus of youth culture as well as try to delineate those factions within the rocker and metaler category that took their behaviors beyond mere youthful angst and into overt rebellion and delinquency. I also needed to understand whether or not such teenagers were highly valued by their fellow teens, and thus decided to look at clique structures in high schools. Also, I wondered whether such identities as a punker or rocker crossed regional and national boundaries, and thus decided to draw a comparative study as well.

In a sense, the sequence of chapters in *Renegade Kids, Suburban Outlaws* documents the path my study took. After examining punkers and rockers in the malls, I examined the hierarchy of youth cultures in suburban high schools by assigning students in my upper division sociology classes to analyze their senior yearbooks and delineate the various cliques that existed in their high schools. They were then to compare their findings with the studies of cliques conducted at other high schools. A synthesis of these case studies provided me with the material discussed in Chapter 3.

Further, I personally examined one middle-class school in the Inland Empire (an area in Southern California) in some detail, a school I refer to in the book as "Raging High." For several days I spent time on campus, interviewing the school psychologist who had been hired to work with troubled teenagers and coordinate programs that involved the local police department's gang-detail specialist as well as the counselors at the school. I also got to know the various cliques at the school as they staked out their turf or "corners" in the center of campus along one wall each lunch period. Further, I traveled to several other high schools and continuation schools to learn about the programs set up to make their educational environments more safe and productive.

In late 1988 I had the opportunity to travel to Christchurch, New Zealand, while on sabbatical. Bringing my youth surveys along, I administered the questionnaires, with the assistance of several sociology undergraduate students from the University of Canterbury, to a large group of teenagers, living "on the rough" (on the streets) in the center of the city, who embraced a punk rocker or heavy metaler identity. With the assistance of a colleague, Greg Newbold, from the University of Canterbury, I was also able to have the questionnaires administered to students in several high schools in the Christchurch suburban area. Christchurch, New Zealand, proved to be an enriching experience as my cross-cultural study supported my impression that youth cultures were universal, and that juveniles who embraced such identities shared similar backgrounds and problematic family situations.

Returning to Southern California, I thought of expanding my focus into a broader cross-cultural emphasis by administering questionnaires to youth in other parts of the English-speaking world, including Canada, Australia, and England. I even had visions of translating the questionnaire so that it could be completed by youths in Japan and Germany. But these lofty plans fell through. Even though I would collect news clippings of such youths in these other countries, and though I would travel to London in 1989 and interview punk rockers on Kings Road (where they charged tourists one pound [$1.80] to snap their picture), I decided to limit my focus—apart from the New Zealand sample—to youths in Southern California. Anyway, by 1989, the suburban punk scene was winding down, although it would reappear again with grunge and other variant forms in the early 1990s.

One day I called up a friend, Serena Dank, who, during the early to mid-1980s, had developed a program called "Parents of Punkers" to assist troubled youths and their families. She was one of the first persons that I had heard discuss the reasons so many teenagers were embracing these identities. I had known of her earlier work and program. In fact, Dank and several of the teenagers she counseled had been invited to Chicago and elsewhere across the country to appear on talk shows about the reasons children were drawn to punk.

Due to a lack of community funding and other reasons discussed in the text, Dank had to disband her successful program; but she offered to give me the boxload of letters the television shows received in response to her and her group's appearances. These unsolicited letters proved to be a gold mine of resources, like forgotten documents uncovered in an attic. I went to work reading them all, grouping them into some cohesive order. My findings were discussed in Chapter 4. I also spent some time with Serena Dank discussing the status of her young charges as she had kept in touch with them and/or their families over the intervening years. I wanted to know what had happened to these punk rockers who had embraced the movement so strongly earlier in the 1980s. Where had they ended up nearly a decade later? Did these rebellious youths outgrow punk? Had they reintegrated into society?

My study continued. As part of my research for my earlier book on juvenile firesetters, I had made contact with the Research Division of the California Youth Authority under the direction of Elaine Duxbury. For that earlier book, the CYA, located in Sacramento, had given me access to all 192 arsonists housed in one of the institutions' facilities at the time of my inquiry. For this new project on suburban youth cultures and delinquencies, I wanted to gain access to the files of all of the white juveniles who were self-labeled as punkers or metalers. In other words, I wanted to know what kinds of criminal offenses these youths had committed that got them institutionalized.

A decision to move my research in this direction meant that I was moving my focus from behaviors that were merely youth culture to ones that were more delinquent. And it was at this juncture in my study that I realized I needed to broaden the scope to encompass the more deviant end of the youth scale. Some such youths I had already encountered in the malls, nightclubs, and gigs or concerts. Some, primarily those who listened to heavy metal music, embraced more sinister identities as skinheads and satanists. Others, as I discussed in the book, were members of white stoner gangs.

I had, in the meantime, attended several community based workshops put on by representatives of the local police departments who were warning other law enforcement officials about the new types of white gangs that were engaged in anti-social behavior in the various Southern California suburban areas. News clippings in the local papers documented the arrests of juveniles for a variety of offenses ranging from attacks against individuals by racist teenage skinheads to vandalizing local cemeteries. Excerpts from these news accounts, as the reader has noted, begin each of the chapters in the book, setting the stage for the analysis that follows.

Once again the CYA was helpful in providing me with access to the case files of fifty-two white stoner gang members. Obtaining this material proved rather difficult as the CYA is quite sensitive about protecting the identities of all youths who affiliate with gangs to avoid further antagonization between gang members inside the institutions. But, after obtaining several different clearances, I was fortunate enough to obtain the list and access their files. Several chapters in the second half of the book documented my analysis of those files as I noted both the similarities of these stoner gang members in general, as well as distinguished between the subgroups of racist skinheads, stoners, and juvenile satanists.

As I continued on this project, several of my former students—now working in the various institutions of the CYA such as the different camps and the Youth Training School (YTS) located in nearby Chino, California—were invaluable in providing me with additional information and observations. At one point, because of these contacts, I was able to administer questionnaires to several incarcerated, racist teenage skinheads. Further, contacts in the local high schools led me to conduct interviews with teenagers who embraced a nonracist, but nevertheless skinhead identity. These were the juveniles who dressed the part but who referred to themselves as either SHARPs (Skinheads Against Racial Prejudice) or SARs (Skins Against Racism).

Field trips to YTS allowed me to observe several wards whose files I had access to, and who embraced one of these delinquent identities. No juvenile was more disturbing to me than one 17-year-old white male who looked like a young Charles Manson. On his forehead he had carved out the numbers 666, the devil's sign. At the time of my encounter with him, he had recently been placed in solitary confinement for trying to cut his wrists with a shard of broken glass from a mirror.

The last group I studied focused on the latest trend to hit the local area, teenage taggers. In spring 1993, at the urging of a local middle school that had problems with tagger crews on their campus, I conducted a study on one such suburban posse. One of my female university students introduced me to her younger brother who was a member of a tagger posse, a crew I dubbed the "KMTs" (Kids Making Trouble).

As I completed each segment of my research, I presented papers of my findings at the annual meetings of various academic conferences, including the American Society of Criminology, the Western Society of Criminology, and the American Sociological Association. The helpful suggestions and feedback I received from my colleagues were incorporated into this final revision.

▼

Youth Survey 1

Check the following:

1. With <u>whom</u> do you spend <u>most</u> of your leisure (free) time?
   _____ by myself
   _____ with a friend
   _____ with several friends
   _____ with a date
   _____ with members of my family
   _____ other _____

2. Where do you <u>most</u> often go when you are with your friends?
   _____ my home
   _____ friend's home
   _____ school area
   _____ movies
   _____ video arcades
   _____ beaches, parks, or mountains
   _____ mall (village or plaza)
   _____ fast food locations
   _____ other _____

3. How old were you on your last birthday? _____

4. What gender (sex) are you? _____ male _____ female

5. What is your race?
   _____ Caucasian (white)
   _____ Black
   _____ Hispanic
   _____ Asian
   _____ Other

6. What do you spend most of your money on? (Check three)
   _____ food (restaurant, fast food, snacks)
   _____ clothes
   _____ car (payments, insurance, repair)
   _____ video games
   _____ movies
   _____ dances/concerts/gigs
   _____ athletic events
   _____ dates
   _____ other _____

7. Religious affiliation
   _____ Protestant
   _____ Catholic
   _____ Jewish
   _____ Other
   _____ None

8. Father's job (describe)

_____

9.   Mother's job (describe)
_____

10.   How many brothers and sisters do you have? _____
        Ages: _____, _____, _____, _____, _____, _____
11.   What is your favorite musical group? (name it)
_____

12.   What type of group is this?   '
_____

13.   What do you like about this group? (describe)
_____

14.   Do you listen to messages in their songs? (If so,
        describe)
_____

15.   Do you feel that your music is violent? (If so,
        describe)
_____

16.   What kind of clothes do you wear? (describe)
_____

17.   Describe your hairstyle and dress:
_____

18.   How do you like school?
_____

19.   How do your teachers treat you at school?
_____

20.   How do the kids treat you at school?
_____

21.   Are you a punk rocker? _____ yes _____ no
22.   Which music do you like best?
        _____ country western
        _____ punk
        _____ pop or rock
        _____ heavy metal
        _____ soul
23.   Which one of the following do you identify with?
        _____ punk
        _____ heavy metal
        _____ none of the above
24.   Do you get along with your mother?
        _____ yes
        _____ no   Why not? _____
25.   Do you get along with your father?
        _____ yes
        _____ no   Why not? _____
26.   Do you plan on finishing high school?
        _____ yes
        _____ no
        _____ I have already graduated
27.   Do you plan on going to college?
        _____ yes
        _____ no
        _____ don't know

28. Do you currently have a job?
    _____ yes   What kind of job?

    _____

    _____ no

29. What kind of job would you like to have in the future?   (describe)

    _____

30. Who do you support politically?
    _____ Liberals
    _____ Conservatives
    _____ Undecided
    _____ neither

For the following statements, please answer: DY = Definitely Yes, Y = Yes, DK = Don't Know, N = No, DN = Definitely No

DY Y DK NO DN

1	2	3	4	5	31.	For me to like a musical group, it is important that they be political.
1	2	3	4	5	32.	Punk and punk music will become "establishment" just as Elvis Presley and all other forms of rebellious music have.
1	2	3	4	5	33.	Punk rockers are delinquents.
1	2	3	4	5	34.	Preppies are just as likely as punk rockers to be considered deviant from an adult's point-of-view.
1	2	3	4	5	35.	I am basically happy with my life.
1	2	3	4	5	36.	I identify myself as part of the punk lifestyle.
1	2	3	4	5	37.	Basically life is rather boring.
1	2	3	4	5	38.	Most kids involved in the punk movement tend to come from poorer backgrounds.
1	2	3	4	5	39.	One has to have a lot of money to afford to be a punk.
1	2	3	4	5	40.	Sometimes I feel like committing suicide.
1	2	3	4	5	41.	I am an above average student in terms of grades I receive in school.
1	2	3	4	5	42.	My parents approve of my life-style.
1	2	3	4	5	43.	I am not an aggressive person.
1	2	3	4	5	44.	I like my parents.
1	2	3	4	5	45.	Politically speaking, I tend to be a conservative.
1	2	3	4	5	46.	I will do more with my life than my parents have done with theirs.
1	2	3	4	5	47.	My parents disapprove of my friends.
1	2	3	4	5	48.	Other people my own age consider me to be a troublemaker.
1	2	3	4	5	49.	Punks are no different from the hippies of the 1960s.
1	2	3	4	5	50.	I consider myself to be religious.

1 2 3 4 5 51. My parents are happy with their life.

1 2 3 4 5 52. Kids who dress punk-style are popular
with the majority of students at
school.

1 2 3 4 5 53. Schools should have dress codes.

1 2 3 4 5 54. Kids who break the law should be punished like adults.

1 2 3 4 5 55. The kids I hang around with are
involved with drugs or alcohol.

1 2 3 4 5 56. I enjoy playing sports.

1 2 3 4 5 57. I have many close friends.

1 2 3 4 5 58. I am put down if I do not do drugs with
the group.

1 2 3 4 5 59. Right now my relationship with my parents is good.

1 2 3 4 5 60. In the past I have been in trouble with
the law/police.

1 2 3 4 5 61. New wave is my kind of music.

1 2 3 4 5 62. Most kids who are punk rockers will
eventually outgrow it.

1 2 3 4 5 63. I don't like heavy metal music and
heavy metal types.

1 2 3 4 5 64. I have a lot in common with my other
family members.

1 2 3 4 5 65. I spend a lot of time away from home.

1 2 3 4 5 66. Punk rockers represent individuality.

1 2 3 4 5 67. Parents don't have the right to tell
their kids how to dress.

1 2 3 4 5 68. Kids today are more streetwise than
their parents were at their age.

1 2 3 4 5 69. Voting in a presidential election makes
a difference.

1 2 3 4 5 70. Schools don't really educate kids; they just
prepare them for places in society.

1 2 3 4 5 71. There is going to be a nuclear war in
my lifetime.

1 2 3 4 5 72. Teenagers today pay too much attention to
their clothing and how they look.

1 2 3 4 5 73. Individuals can make a difference in
today's world.

1 2 3 4 5 74. The punk lifestyle is mostly for the
young.

1 2 3 4 5 75. Parents and grownups don't appreciate
today's music.

1 2 3 4 5 76. I dress to impress other people.

1 2 3 4 5 77. It is important to me that I fit in
with some group.

1 2 3 4 5 78. Music is a big part of my life.

1 2 3 4 5 79. The drinking age should be lowered.

1 2 3 4 5 80. I am a loner.

1 2 3 4 5 81. Preppies will become tomorrow's leaders.

1 2 3 4 5 82. The only people I get along with are
the ones in my group.

1 2 3 4 5 83. I don't want to get involved in what's
going on in today's world.

```
1  2  3   4   5    84.  Sex plays a role in the music I listen to.
1  2  3   4   5    85.  I am easily influenced by others.
1  2  3   4   5    86.  I would fight in a war to protect my
                        country.
1  2  3   4   5    87.  Marijuana should be legalized.
1  2  3   4   5    88.  The death penalty is a good way of
                        dealing with violent criminals.
1  2  3   4   5    89.  Punk rockers are a new form of gang.
1  2  3   4   5    90.  It is good for people to be rebellious.
1  2  3   4   5    91.  Punkers are intelligent.
1  2  3   4   5    92.  Females are equal to males.
1  2  3   4   5    93.  I prefer pop music to soul music.
1  2  3   4   5    94.  Preppies are just spoiled rich kids.
1  2  3   4   5    95.  Pop music represents conformity.
```

96.   A punk rocker is someone who

_____.

97.   People who like new wave music are

_____.

98.   The heavy metal scene is

_____.

99.   Three words that describe a punk rocker are
_____, _____, and _____.

100.   The major difference between a non-punk rocker and a
punk rocker is _____.

Thank you very much for completing this questionnaire. We
greatly appreciate your cooperation.

Youth Survey 2

1. How old were you on your last birthday? _____
2. What gender (sex) are you? _____ male _____ female
3. What is your race? _____
4. Religious affiliation
    _____ Protestant
    _____ Catholic
    _____ Jewish
    _____ Other
    _____ None
5. Are you a skinhead? _____ yes _____ no
6. Which one of the following do you identify with?
    _____ punk
    _____ skinhead
    _____ heavy metal
    _____ none of the above
7. Father's job (describe)
    _____
8. Mother's job (describe)
    _____
9. How many brothers and sisters do you have? _____
    Ages: _____, _____, _____, _____, _____
10. What is your favorite musical group. (name them)
    _____
11. What type of group is this?
    _____
12. What do you like about this group? (describe)
    _____
13. Do you listen to messages in their songs? (If so,
    describe) _____
14. Do you feel that your music is violent? (If so,
    describe) _____
15. What kind of clothes do you wear? (describe)
    _____
16. Describe your hairstyle and dress:
    _____
17. How do you like school?
    _____
18. How do your teachers treat you at school?
    _____
19. How do the kids treat you at school?
    _____
20. Do you get along with your mother? _____ yes _____ no
    Why not? _____
21. Do you get along with your father? _____ yes _____ no
    Why not? _____
22. A skinhead is someone who
    _____
23. People who like Top 40 music are
    _____
24. The heavy metal scene is
    _____
25. Three words that describe a skinhead are
    _____, _____, and_____

26.   Someonw who is <u>not</u> a skinhead is

_____

27.   Describe your tattoos, if any:

_____

For the following statements, please answer: DY = Definitely
Yes, Y = Yes, DK = Don't Know, N = No, DN = Definitely No

<u>DY</u> <u>Y</u> <u>DK</u> <u>NO</u> <u>DN</u>
1 2 3 4 5   28.   Skinheads are delinquents.
1 2 3 4 5   29.   I am basically happy with my life.
1 2 3 4 5   30.   I identify myself as part of the skin-
                        head lifestyle.
1 2 3 4 5   31.   In the past I've participated in gay-
                        or black-bashing.
1 2 3 4 5   32.   Basically life is rather boring.
1 2 3 4 5   33.   I spend a lot of money on drugs.
1 2 3 4 5   34.   I am part of a satanic cult.
1 2 3 4 5   35.   Most kids involved in the skinhead
                        scene tend to come from poorer back-
                        grounds.
1 2 3 4 5   36.   As a child I was abused by my parents.
1 2 3 4 5   37.   Sometimes I feel like committing sui-
                        cide.
1 2 3 4 5   38.   My parents approve of my lifestyle.
1 2 3 4 5   39.   I am a member of SHARP (Skinheads
                        Against Racial Prejudice).
1 2 3 4 5   40.   I am <u>not</u> an aggressive person.
1 2 3 4 5   41.   I like my parents.
1 2 3 4 5   42.   All skinheads are sexist.
1 2 3 4 5   43.   Blacks and Hispanics are equal to whites.
1 2 3 4 5   44.   Politically speaking, I tend to be a
                        conservative.
1 2 3 4 5   45.   I am against racism in any form.
1 2 3 4 5   46.   My parents disapprove of my friends.
1 2 3 4 5   47.   Other people my own age consider me to
                        be a troublemaker.
1 2 3 4 5   48.   We have too many immigrants and racial
                        minorities in our society today.
1 2 3 4 5   49.   I consider myself to be religious.
1 2 3 4 5   50.   My parents are happy with their life.
1 2 3 4 5   51.   Society should discriminate against
                        homosexuals/gays.
1 2 3 4 5   52.   When I'm <u>not</u> with my friends I act dif-
                        ferently.
1 2 3 4 5   53.   Kids who dress skinhead-style are popular
                        with the majority of students at school.
1 2 3 4 5   54.   Kids who break the law should be pun-
                        ished like adults.
1 2 3 4 5   55.   Kids I hang around with use drugs or
                        alcohol.
1 2 3 4 5   56.   I have many close friends.
1 2 3 4 5   57.   I am put down if I do <u>not</u> do drugs with
                        the group.

1 2 3 4 5   58. Minorities should <u>not</u> be allowed to
                      live in white neighborhoods.
1 2 3 4 5   59. In grammar school I was considered to
                      be a bully.
1 2 3 4 5   60. All of my family members agree with my
                      racial views.
1 2 3 4 5   61. Right now my relationship with my par-
                      ents is good.
1 2 3 4 5   62. In the past I have been in trouble with
                      the police.
1 2 3 4 5   63. Heavy metal is my kind of music.
1 2 3 4 5   64. I have a lot in common with my other
                      family members.
1 2 3 4 5   65. I spend a lot of time away from home.
1 2 3 4 5   66. There is going to be a nuclear war in
                      my lifetime.
1 2 3 4 5   67. It is important to me that I fit in
                      with some group.
1 2 3 4 5   68. The drinking age should be lowered.
1 2 3 4 5   69. I am a loner.
1 2 3 4 5   70. The only people I socialize with are
                      the ones in my own racial group.
1 2 3 4 5   71. I would fight in a war to protect my
                      country.
1 2 3 4 5   72. Skinheads are a new form of gang.
1 2 3 4 5   73. It is good for people to be rebellious.
1 2 3 4 5   74. The death penalty is a good way
                      dealing with violent crimnals.

Thank you for completing this questionnaire.

Table 1

Punk Rockers and Heavy Metalers in Cross-Cultural Perspective: Youths in Southern California and New Zealand

	CP	CHM	CC	NZP	NZM	NZC
Background Information						
I am a male.	67%	88%	48%[1]	82%	81%	59%[8]
I am a Caucasian.	86%	81%	66%[1]	81%	94%	75%[5]
I have no religious affiliation.	44%	30%	19%[1]	73%	66%	54%[5]
I am a Catholic.	23%	35%	38%[1]	20%	10%	10%
I am from a blue-collar background.	42%	35%	29%	71%	52%	33%[4]
Family Relations						
I spend a lot of time away from home.	79%	70%	62%	88%	55%	56%[5]
I have nothing in common with my family.	62%	40%	33%[1]	77%	30%	44%
I do not like my parents.	21%	11%	5%[1]	19%	10%	9%
I do not get along with my mother.	23%	14%	7%[1]	24%	16%	13%
I do not get along with my father.	33%	37%	14%[1]	38%	21%	17%
My parents do not approve of my lifestyle.	50%	28%	13%[1]	18%	17%	19%
My parents disapprove of my friends.	34%	33%	10%[1]	27%	17%	11%
Alienation and Isolation						
Sometimes I feel like committing suicide.	34%	14%	14%[1]	41%	20%	16%
Basically life is rather boring.	29%	26%	14%[2]	40%	32%	20%
I am not happy with my life.	15%	12%	8%	18%	7%	7%
I do not have many close friends.	29%	33%	27%	24%	17%	19%
I only get along with people in my own group.	25%	16%	17%	31%	13%	5%[6]
There will be a nuclear war in my lifetime.	36%	34%	27%[5]	24%	17%	19%

Code: CP = California Punk Rockers; CHM = California Heavy Metalers; CC = California Controls; NZP = New Zealand Punk Rockers; NZM = New Zealand Heavy Meta ers; NZC = New Zealand Controls

Punk Rockers and Heavy Metalers in Cross-Cultural Perspective: Youths in Southern California and New Zealand (continued)

Alienation and Isolation	CP	CHM	CC	NZP	NZM	NZC
I do not want to get involved in society.	18%	13%	14%[9]	24%	23%	16%
I would not fight in a war to protect my country.	48%	16%	26%[1]	47%	43%	25%
It is good for people to be rebellious.	55%	43%	54%	47%	43%	25%
Females are equal to males.	71%	55%	57%[8]	71%	80%	70%
It is not important to me that I fit in with some group	74%	56%	57%	53%	53%	32%
I am a loner.	20%	17%	17%[5]	6%	37%	27%

Juvenile Delinquency	CP	CHM	CC	NZP	NZM	NZC
I do not like school.	42%	44%	20%[1]	69%	62%	28%[1]
Teachers treat me poorly.	35%	15%	5%[1]	46%	33%	8%[1]
Schools should not have dress codes.	96%	74%	68%[1]	53%	66%	39%[7]
I am not easily influenced by others.	24%	26%	15%	12%	23%	17%
I am put down if I do not do drugs with the group.	12%	12%	4%[9]	10%	10%	5%
Other people my own age consider me to be a troublemaker.	34%	11%	5%[1]	35%	14%	9%[5]
In the past I have been in trouble with the law/police.	49%	37%	14%[1]	53%	36%	19%[7]
I am an aggressive person.	38%	46%	38%	44%	45%	38%
My friends are involved with drugs or alcohol.	71%	58%	35%[1]	80%	57%	44%
Kids today are more streetwise than their parents.	78%	68%	58%[3]	70%	71%	74%
Punk rockers are delinquents.	18%	44%	25%[1]	12%	29%	38%[8]
Punk rockers are a new form of gang.	37%	18%	22%[1]	20%	27%	28%
I listen to messages in my songs.	74%	48%	67%[5]	50%	52%	56%
Sex plays a role in the music I listen to.	54%	49%	40%[1]	47%	50%	29%[8]
My music is violent.	44%	23%	8%[1]	29%	45%	8%[1]

Punk Rockers and Heavy Metalers in Cross-Cultural Perspective: Youths in Southern California and New Zealand (continued)

Juvenile Delinquency	CP	CHM	CC	NZP	NZM	NZC
Kids who break the law should not be punished like adults.	47%	42%	29%[5]	53%	66%	39%
Marijuana should be legalized.	43%	54%	29%[1]	65%	60%	26%[1]
The drinking age should be lowered.	58%	55%	28%[1]	44%	50%	29%
Parents should not set dress codes for their children.	72%	54%	37%[1]	35%	42%	41%
The death penalty is not a good way to deal with criminals.	32%	27%	35%	38%	24%	47%

[1]sig. <.001
[2]sig. <.002
[3]sig. <.003
[4]sig. <.004
[5]sig. <.01

[6]sig. <.02
[7]sig. <.03
[8]sig. <.04
[9]sig. <.05

Table 2

Profile of Stoner Gang Members in the California Youth Authority (Number of Cases = 52)

	Information Gathered from Case Files		No Information Available
	% Yes (Number)	% No (Number)	Total Number
Demographic Background Information			
16 years old or under at admittance	42% (22)	58% (30)	(0)
Resided in Southern California	81% (39)	19% (9)	(4)
Resided in urban or suburban areas	73% (35)	27% (13)	(4)
Offense against property/drugs	74% (35)	26% (12)	(5)
Middle-class socioeconomic status	40% (11)	60% (16)	(25)
Caucasian racial background	96% (48)	4% (2)	(2)
Religious affiliation	37% (3)	63% (5)	(44)
Family Relationship			
Ward got along with father	7% (2)	93% (26)	(22)
Ward got along with mother	14% (3)	86% (18)	(31)
Presence of a stepparent	43% (20)	57% (27)	(5)
Parents abused drugs	89% (25)	11% (3)	(24)
Parents moved when ward was young	72% (38)	28% (14)	(0)
Ward was a middle sibling	47% (18)	53% (20)	(14)
Ward had been adopted	4% (2)	96% (46)	(0)
Parents were divorced	53% (25)	47% (22)	(5)
Ward had problems with parental authority	22% (11)	78% (38)	(3)
Ward reportedly sexually abused	25% (3)	75% (9)	(40)
Ward reportedly physically abused	47% (15)	53% (17)	(20)

Profile of Stoner Gang Members in the California Youth Authority (Number of Cases = 52) (continued)

	Information Gathered from Case Files		No Information Available
	% Yes (Number)	% No (Number)	Total Number
Peer Group Influences			
Ward influenced by peers	98% (44)	2% (1)	(7)
Peers used drugs	95% (18)	5% (1)	(33)
Ward abused drugs and/or alcohol	100% (52)	0% (0)	(0)
Ward was heavy or multiple-drug user	94% (46)	6% (3)	(3)
Ward was poor achiever in school	76% (28)	24% (9)	(15)
Ward affiliated with a gang	57% (25)	43% (19)	(8)
Ward involved with satanic activity	20% (9)	80% (36)	(7)
Ward into heavy metal music	67% (8)	33% (4)	(40)
Ward affiliated with white supremacist group	24% (10)	76% (31)	(11)
Psychological and Social Issues			
Ward had work history	88% (34)	12% (8)	(10)
Ward started taking drugs under age 13	69% (22)	31% (10)	(20)
Ward previously incarcerated	96% (44)	4% (2)	(6)
Ward in special education classes	65% (13)	35% (7)	(32)
Ward attempted suicide	12% (3)	88% (22)	(27)
Ward had dropped out of school	43% (13)	57% (17)	(22)
Ward had average or above average IQ	72% (18)	28% (7)	(27)
Ward had homosexual experiences	40% (6)	60% (9)	(37)
Ward had physically or sexually abused others	52% (11)	48% (10)	(31)
Ward had history of bedwetting	23% (3)	77% (10)	(39)
Ward was hyperactive as a child	19% (8)	81% (35)	(9)
Ward had some/many psychological problems	96% (47)	4% (2)	(3)
Ward had physical problems	32% (12)	68% (26)	(14)

Index